BANGALORE 1978

SHARIN IN ONE HOPE

REPORTS AND DOCUMENTS FROM THE MEETING OF THE FAITH AND ORDER COMMISSION

15-30 August, 1978
Ecumenical Christian Centre,
Bangalore, India

Faith and Order Paper No. 92

**Commission on Faith and Order
World Council of Churches, Geneva**

ISBN: 2-8254-0599-x

Cover design: John Taylor, WCC
Printed in Switzerland by Imprimerie La Concorde, Lausanne

Contents

REPORTS OF THE FOUR GROUPS ON SPECIFIC AREAS

Introduction

The Faith and Order Commission of the World Council of Churches occupied itself with two main themes when it met in Bangalore last year. Firstly, it wrestled with the problem of producing a contemporary *common account of hope*. Next, it tried to determine the steps which the churches need to take today if they are to *grow together into unity*.

In the present volume the results of the Bangalore meeting are made accessible to a wider audience. It is hoped that the following brief introductory remarks may make it easier for the reader to understand the texts reproduced here.

1

The most significant achievement of the Bangalore meeting was undoubtedly the document "A Common Account of Hope" (pp. 1-11). Everyone knew that the attempt to formulate an agreed description of the basis of Christian hope was a hazardous undertaking. Was it really possible for these 160 representatives of the various Christian traditions from more than 50 different countries to agree on a statement of this kind? The profound differences surfaced from the very beginning and became still more patent as speech followed speech. Nor was the common account itself composed at the first attempt but took shape only slowly in a laborious sequence of small steps. During the two weeks of the Bangalore meeting, four different drafts were presented to the Commission. Each time, new considerations and wishes were voiced which seemed to many participants to make further effort pointless. The version presented for discussion only two days before the meeting was due to end was still far from being even a passably satisfactory text. But on the final morning of the conference, when the revised version was read out, the Commission members rose to their feet and broke spontaneously into prolonged applause, so completely did they identify themselves with the new formulation.

In spite of everything, the common account of hope had been given, and all present felt this event was a liberating and significant advance, for one thing, simply because it showed that Christians from the most diverse traditions *were* able to give an agreed account of the wellsprings of their life as Christians. How often in recent years have we explained that agreed statements were no longer or not yet possible, that the faith could only be expressed in particular contexts! How often has this conviction inhibited ecumenical conferences from even attempting a common proclamation of the faith! It is easy to understand, then, why the final hours of the Bangalore meeting were felt to be an unexpected bonus. It was clear to us all that, though much in this statement could have been said differently and better, at least we had managed to speak together in words which carried conviction for us all. We suddenly realized how disappointed we would have been to have departed from the meeting without this common account of hope. We realized that to have done so would have been tantamount to an open invitation to the evil spirit of apathy towards the Gospel, to the deadly sin of *acedia*, arguably the most destructive of all sins. Amid the mists of controversy and confusion we had been privileged to catch a glimpse of our common Lord.

One difference in particular had seemed unsurmountable. On the one hand there were those who wanted to put the main emphasis on presenting the hope which is above all hopes, namely, Jesus Christ, the risen Lord, who has already overcome the world. On the other hand there were those who wanted to state as clearly as possible that hope finds expression in concrete hopes. Whereas the former feared that too much emphasis might be given to human desires and plans, the latter feared that the reference to the kingdom of God would blunt the urgency of necessary changes and conflicts. The abandonment of theology, charged the former: theology serving the narrow selfish interests of a purely theoretical fellowship, retorted the latter. But when the common account was read out, both sides felt they had been understood. This did not mean that the difference was settled for all time. It goes too deep to be settled merely by a statement. What had been made clear, however, was that the two tendencies could find a place within one and the same text.

2

How was this text arrived at? It has a long history behind it (see page 20). It is the fruit of the study initiated by the Faith and Order Commission at Louvain in 1971 on "giving account of the hope that is in us". From the very beginning, the intention was to produce a common statement. First of all, it was necessary to concentrate our attention on the variety of ways in which the Gospel is proclaimed. Testimonies were gathered from every tradition and from as many different situations as possible.

Six reports were sent to participants in the Bangalore meeting, setting out some specially typical examples, arranged according to continents (page 49). Another four preparatory documents dealt with particular aspects of the theme: accounting for hope in the light of the confrontation of faith and science; accounting for hope as witness to real partnership between man and woman; martyrdom as proclamation of hope; and, finally, a selection of testimonies of hope from the younger generation. The intention was that the Commission should take into consideration the whole diversity of this material. The common account of hope was not to be produced from scratch at Bangalore but to take shape in the light of existing testimonies.

To facilitate the Commission's task, a small group met twice to produce a first draft of a common account of hope. This draft was presented by Jan Milic Lochman at the beginning of the conference[1] and discussed thoroughly by the Commission.

The participants then divided up into ten groups, each taking one of the ten preparatory documents for closer examination. Two tasks were assigned to these groups: all of them were asked first of all to consider how the common account of hope could do justice to the diversity of the concrete testimonies; secondly, each group was asked to comment on the document assigned to it: What significance did the testimonies have for the churches throughout the world? What, on the other hand, should be said on behalf of the wider fellowship concerning a specific witness or problem? While the ten groups were at work trying to answer these questions, a special team set to work drafting the common account.[2]

3

How did we discover the way to this common account of hope at Bangalore? Some suspected that the Commission would impose a common account either by simply suppressing the diversity of views or by reducing it by judicious selection. The common account would prove possible only by winging away into abstraction. But even if anything of this kind had been attempted, such an account would never have been acceptable to the Commission. How could anyone forget even momentarily the conflicting testimonies, or possibly be content with a statement derived from general theological principles? The address of George Fernandes, the Indian Minister for Industries (pp. 40-48), was a fresh reminder of the diversity of the situations from which we came. "Someone's hope is somebody else's despair. The hope of the nations of the north is the despair of the nations of the south."

---

[1] Towards an Ecumenical Account of Hope. Published in *The Ecumenical Review*, Vol. 31, No. 1, January 1979.
[2] The comments of the groups on the six regional reports are printed in the minutes (p. 45). The texts which resulted from their examination of the four preparatory documents on aspects of the theme are included in this volume (p. 147).

It was essential, therefore, that the common account should reflect the diversity of the testimonies, and even their contradictory character. It had to grow out of the encounter between them. It had to indicate the common ground which unites the community of faith. It had to express our readiness within this fellowship to submit ourselves afresh to the message of Christ and to let ourselves be questioned by each other. It had to show clearly how churches in different parts of the world can act in such a way that the same hope is proclaimed even if in different ways. It had to be made quite clear that the Commission sees itself as a *communio viatorum,* a travelling fellowship, and, precisely as such, witnesses to the deepest ground of common hope.

The argument is clear from the structure of the account. The opening "Thanksgiving" reminds us of "God's 'yes'" which is the basis of faith and fellowship and the presupposition of all genuine human witness. The account goes on to speak of the diversity of hopes and the encounter between them. The distinction between real hope and mere wishes points to the need for self-examination and cleansing. The resurrection of Christ, faith in God − Father, Son and Spirit − can only be confessed anew when we are prepared for this encounter. The account goes on to emphasize the importance of the Church for hope. Membership of this fellowship in Christ and with Christ which supports, encourages, and makes fresh beginnings possible is an essential part of our ground for hope. It makes it possible for us to trust one another in our diverse situations. It enables us to regard still-unresolved tensions and differences as common tasks and to refuse even to entertain the notion that mutually agreed action is impossible.

4

There is an intimate connection between the two major themes of the Bangalore meeting. In attempting to speak together of our hope we are necessarily led to ask about the unity of the Church. "There is one body and one Spirit, as there is also one hope held out in God's call to you", we read in the letter to the Ephesians. The one Church called into being by the Holy Spirit is borne along by one and the same hope. The more successful the churches are in giving a common account of this hope in spite of their divisions, the more they will grow in unity.

But the converse is also true: the more successful the churches are in removing the barriers to visible fellowship, the more confidently and forcefully will they be able to give an account of their hope. The two themes are, so to say, part of one and the same circle. The common witness creates fellowship; the attempt to achieve visible fellowship releases energy for witness. When the Commission, in the second week of its Bangalore meeting, turned to the theme "growing together into unity", therefore, it was not really tackling a new question. This second theme was already implicit in the first.

A series of brief contributions (page 203) introduced the theme and a general discussion. The Commission then divided into five committees to discuss the following subjects: 1) The meaning of "conciliar fellowship"; 2) Towards communion in one faith; 3) Growing into one eucharistic fellowship; 4) The discipline of communion in a divided world; 5) New ecumenical experiences and existing ecumenical structures. The report produced on the basis of the work of these five committees can be found in this volume (page 233).

5

Attention very quickly came to focus on the question as to how the churches can achieve sufficient agreement between them for visible unity "in one faith and in one eucharistic fellowship". In recent years the question as to how "the unity we seek" is to be described has frequently been discussed. It was against this background that the concept of "conciliar fellowship" had been developed. The Nairobi Assembly of the World Council of Churches had adopted this term. The Bangalore meeting certainly carried the discussion of it further. In one of the committees an attempt was made to clear up certain misunderstandings which had cropped up frequently since the Nairobi Assembly. But the Commission soon came to the conclusion that further study of this subject could not be regarded as one of its priorities for the future. The need was rather to use the idea of conciliar fellowship as a framework and to concentrate on clarifying the conditions to be fulfilled if unity is to become a reality.

The committees next turned to the question as to how agreement could be achieved in the apostolic faith (page 243). It produced proposals for the continuation of work on the consensus on baptism, eucharist and ministry and tried to envisage more clearly ways in which the churches could gradually evolve structures for common teaching and decision-making (page 247).[3]

Work on these themes can obviously bear fruit only if done in close contact with the churches. This was understood from the very beginning (cf. Nissiotis, page 13). The task of the Commission is not only to throw light on specific problems by its theological studies but also to promote encounter between the churches. If they are to advance along the road to unity, the churches themselves must get involved in the discussion and take practical steps to make room for the consensus. It was clear to the Commission that its working patterns must in future increasingly be shaped with this object in view.

---

[3] Preliminary studies on this particular subject were available to the Commission. A special consultation had examined the question (Odessa, October 1977). Cf. *How does the Church teach authoritatively today?* Faith and Order Paper No. 91. Geneva: WCC, 1979. See also: *Ecumenical Review*. Vol. 31, No. 1, January 1979.

Although the Commission was deeply interested in the details of the required consensus, it did not lose sight of the fact that unity is a fellowship which is practised and which must be maintained in the midst of the tensions and conflicts of the contemporary world. At its meeting in Louvain (1971) the Commission had for its theme "Unity of the Church – Unity of Mankind". Although this theme itself was not on the agenda of the Bangalore meeting, the question about the Church as an experienced fellowship was implicit in the discussions from beginning to end. It had already arisen in connection with the theme "Account of Hope". But in the second half of the Bangalore meeting it was examined in the light of certain specific examples. What does the unity of the Church mean in the encounter with other religions? In what ways can the churches assist each other so that their fellowship with one another may be deepened and extended by such mutual assistance? What form should the fellowship of man and woman take in the Church today?

The Commission's reflections on the fellowship of man and woman in the Church will be especially important in the years ahead. The Nairobi Assembly decided to initiate a special study of this question. It provides an opportunity of carefully considering the theme "Unity of the Church – Unity of Humankind' in the context of a specific problem area.

"Consensus" and "Life in Fellowship" – these two catchwords also point to one of the deepest tensions characteristic of the whole Bangalore meeting. Certainly no one questioned the need to work towards a consensus or the need to examine the form and quality of a life in fellowship today. But the participants in the meeting differed considerably in their emphases and judgments. Some thought that the Commission's main business was to produce agreements. They frequently expressed apprehension that the Commission might waste its time on problems of merely secondary importance. Others, mainly from the Third World, asked sceptically, on the contrary, what could really and truly be achieved by theological agreements. Unity has to be a living reality within the historical movement of the contemporary world. It is with the conflicts which tear the churches apart today that theological reflection on church unity must therefore begin. Although this tension was not made into a theme of our meeting, we were constantly aware of its existence, and it will undoubtedly continue to accompany our work in the years ahead. It is to be hoped that in the future, too, we may successfully avoid capitulating one-sidedly to either option but rather bring them both into a fruitful interaction.

One final question remains to be mentioned. In growing numbers, Christians today are already experiencing fellowship outside the boundaries of the divided churches. What is the significance of this fact? Unity is in fact no longer merely a distant goal. However necessary it may be to stress that the churches still have a long way to go, the fact remains that a good stretch of the road is already behind them. The churches are not yet united, but neither are they any longer simply divided from each other. The dividing walls have been breached to such an extent that many Christians are beginning to share their life and to bear witness together. How is this fellowship to be assessed? As an impatient "jumping the gun"? Or as a foretaste of the future marked out for the churches? One of the committees of the Commission dealt with this question in detail. These new experiences of fellowship obviously deserve the closest attention. This is not to say that every fellowship across confessional barriers is necessarily an advance on the way to unity. "Just as every church needs the ability to distinguish true spirits from false, so too does the ecumenical movement." At the same time, it is also obvious that experience of fellowship is necessary "training" for unity. This new fellowship experienced by so many Christians today needs to be taken seriously, therefore, and encouraged and strengthened by carefully thought-out initiatives. The Commission with its theological reflections must be at the service not only of the churches but also of the growing fellowship between them. It has an increasing pastoral responsibility towards those who can press forward from the call to unity to new achievements of unity – a responsibility to accompany them and to address itself to the theological problems arising out of their experience, and to help towards the clarification of these problems.

LUKAS VISCHER

A Common Account of Hope
Bangalore 1978

I. THANKSGIVING

Blessed be God! The Father and the Son and the Holy Spirit.
Christ is our hope: the power of love stronger than the world.
He lived on the earth: God's Yes for the world's salvation. He
was crucified and is risen: the first fruit of the new humanity.

He is present in his Church; He is present in those who suffer;
   — He is with us.
He will appear again in glory : our judgment and our hope,
   — Unveiling this Yes of salvation.
We have this gift from the living God.
   — His Spirit poured into our hearts.
Let us give thanks with rejoicing!

II. VOICES OF HOPE

In many places all over the world people are participating in
this "yes". Even among the cries of despair we hear voices of
hope.

A Latin American song:

> Since He came into the world and into history ;
>   broke down silence and suffering;
>   filled the world with his glory ;
>   was the light in the coldness of our night ;
>   was born in a dark manger;
>   in His life sowed love and light ;
>   broke hardened hearts
>   but lifted up dejected souls ;

1

So today we have hope;
>   today we persevere in our struggle;
>   today we face our future with confidence,
> in this land which is ours.

Everywhere songs of hope and longing are being sung. We have
been able to listen to many of them in the accounts of hope
which we have studied. There is a bewildering variety: from
those who hunger for bread, justice and peace; those who long
for freedom from religious or political persecution; those who
hope for deliverance from infirmities of body and mind; those
seeking a new community of women and men; those who
search for cultural authenticity; those who hope for a responsible use of science and technology; those who evangelize and
work for the spread of the Gospel; those who labour for the
visible unity of the churches. We have even become aware of
intimations of hope from those who are silenced. In their
silence itself is a word for those who can hear it.

III. HOPES ENCOUNTER HOPES

We have been listening to these voices because we ourselves are
called to give an account of our hope (I Peter 3:15). We are a
group of 160 Christians gathered in India from many churches
in every continent as the Faith and Order Commission of the
World Council of Churches. Our mandate from the churches is
to further the cause of visible church unity. Central to that
task is the growth of an ability among the churches to bear
common witness to their faith.

As a preliminary step, the Commission has been working since
1971 to formulate a common account of hope. Today, we want
to speak of our common future to church members everywhere
and to any others who may be willing to listen. The problems
have been formidable: confessional and cultural diversity,
sharply divided political and social situations, the threat to
relevance in a rapidly changing world, the need to draw upon
new voices which have been marginal to the discussion of
theology thus far. Yet, the common attempt itself has become
a source of hope. We have discovered afresh the force of the
Gospel to inspire common witness. We have been drawn
together and new ways of communication have been established among those who hope.

The common account is based on the encounter among various accounts of hope. This encounter has proved significant.
It has helped us distinguish between one level where specific
things are hoped for, for example, to have enough to eat, and

another level where the question emerges: "Why do you hope at all for what you cannot see?" (Cf Rom. 8:25).

The encounter has been *humbling* because of the provocation to become more self-critical. It is necessary to distinguish hopes from desires or wishes. Some of our expectations are little more than unexamined desires and wishes, or expressions of fears and anxieties. And these often contradict one another. A desire for an expanding economy in one country can cause poverty in another. A necessary struggle for power in one country may appear to contradict the responsible use of power in another. Some even say: "One's hopes become another's despair."

But we refuse to believe that the hopes of humankind are ultimately contradictory: God-given hopes are many-faceted and complementary. But human hearts are sinful, and their desires can be false. They need to be judged and purified. Christ is the judge of human hopes. He weighs our desires.

The encounter of human hopes is also *encouraging* to us, for in it we become aware of the power and direction of the Holy Spirit. Through that Spirit the hopes of others speak to us, often unintentionally, sometimes unexpectedly. The encounter of hopes points to a wider communion of hope with each other and with God's Spirit. Beyond that it can point to a wider communion between those who believe in Christ and those who do not. "One's hope becomes another's hope!"

IV. OUR HOPE IN GOD

The Church is a fellowship of those who hope in God, and therefore a real encounter among our hopes is possible.

We are not the first to express such faith and hope. Many have gone before us. A cloud of witness surrounds us who gave their testimony even at the cost of their lives. The faithful witness of the human hope in God is Jesus Christ. And every time we celebrate the remembrance of him, we receive grace and power to give our testimony.

Jesus Christ is our hope. In his life He was completely obedient to God the Father. He identified himself with those who were despised by society. He preached a message of God's coming kingdom which sustains us with its vision of a tomorrow that cannot be denied. He was arrested, tortured and killed. In his cross and resurrection God dethroned the forces of sin, guilt, death and evil. God reconciled the world to himself. God defended his image in all — children, women and men — and

3

opened to them a new dignity as the children of God. That is why we hope that everything which threatens human dignity, including death itself, will ultimately be destroyed: ultimately, for in this world those threatening forces, though overcome, are not yet destroyed; our present hope is anchored in God's actions in history and in the eternal life of the age to come. But we know that we are accepted by God as forgiven sinners, and therefore we are certain that we can here and now be co-workers with God in pointing to his rule. In Christ as in a mirror we see the will of God. Christ will come as the revelation of truth and righteousness. The ultimate judgment of the world is his, our assurance that the murderer will never ultimately triumph over the victim. This ultimate hope in the lordship of Christ and the coming kingdom of God cannot be divorced from, or identified with, our historical hopes for freedom, justice, equality and peace. Our struggles for human well-being are judged and transfigured in a life with God marked by the free gifts of forgiveness, new life and salvation. In anticipation we dare to hope that human longings and struggles are justified and that their ultimate outcome is in God's hands.

In giving his Son not to condemn the world but that the world might be saved through him (John 3:17), *God the Father* affirmed the world as his creation and manifested his faithfulness to it. We too will be faithful to the world. He loved the work of his hands and called it good. Therefore we hope for a society which does not violate the goodness of nature. In trust that he has willed the creative powers of the human creature as well, we have hope that human reason can be used responsibly in shaping the future. The Creator is righteous; his law and his justice will restore the right of those who are oppressed. Therefore we have hope in our striving for justice and human rights. This world is full of suffering and injustice, but as God's world it is the place of our obedience in the confidence that He will not let it fall out of his hand. When, following Christ, we fight against evil, we do so not only in the hope for more human happiness; we do it also in the hope that oppressors will repent and be oppressors no longer, and that all will turn to God in faith and together receive the blessing that He wills for them.

The living God becomes accessible to us by the *Holy Spirit* who confirms God's presence in our lives and makes us members of Christ's body, the Church. By the Holy Spirit, we have hope that already our lives can show signs of the new creation. By the Spirit, God gives us his power and guidance. The Spirit sets us free from the powers of darkness, stirs up our spirits, rekindles our energies, gives us visions and dreams, presses us to work for real communion, overcoming the barriers which sin has erected. Through the Holy Spirit, God's love is poured into our hearts. There can be no real hope without love. Acting in hope is possible for all: for those who can work openly and visibly, and also for those whose love and action are expressed in suffering and prayer. Since God's promises concern the whole of humanity, we hope and pray that the Spirit will empower us to proclaim the good news of salvation and to strive for its realization in life. That is the one mission of the individual and of the Church as such.

V. THE CHURCH : A COMMUNION OF HOPE

"The Lord is risen!" He is present and powerful in the midst of his people, making them members of one another and of his Body, the Church. He is the Master; they are the disciples. He is the vine; they are the branches. To those who put their faith in him, He gives a communion of hope, and He sends them as a sign of hope for all humanity.

They share his own divine life, the communion of the Father, Son and Holy Spirit, one God whose own being is mirrored in all creaturely love. In the Christian community of faith, sharing in the confession of the apostles, gathered around God's Word and partaking of the sacraments, we are given the power to share with each other. We can rejoice with those who rejoice and weep with those who weep. We can bear one another's burdens. It is in this communion that we also learn to share one another's hopes. This encounter of hope in itself has been made by God to be a sign in every situation and place: Christ our hope, the power of love!

Because this is the spiritual reality of the Church, we are ashamed of how we in our churches actually look. The communion of hope is so obscured that it is almost unrecognizable. The common witness is wounded by divisions. Too often and too transparently, our churches reflect the sins of society, and are found on the side of the privileged and the powerful. Women are often denied their rightful places of leadership in church life. Members and ministers do not fully recognize each other. More scandalous still, our churches do not yet worship God together around the common table. Many of our contemporaries think it a travesty to call this people a sign of hope. Hope for the renewal and unity of our churches is often our most difficult spiritual task.

Nevertheless, we do hope for the Church of Christ to become more manifest in our churches. We hope for the recovery and fruitfulness of their mission. The communion, though obscured, is not lost; it is grounded not in its members, but in God. The Word has been given to it and the Word endures. The Spirit which has been at work throughout the ages is present in our times to re-establish a credible communion. Built on such foundations, this community will become a community of repentance!

Of this power among the churches we are witnesses. We do have hope for this communion. And we believe that this communion, incomplete as it is, can become a sign of hope for others. Communion in Christ provides the possibility of encounter across the human barriers. It reestablishes relations in mutual respect without sacrificing convictions. It can be a testing ground for the witness which each church bears. Without being pressed into conformity, churches can become accountable to each other. It is also a source of hope because as they live by God's forgiveness, they can extend forgiveness to other churches as well, and find in the witness and commitment of others an enrichment of their own. Finally, communion in Christ is a source of hope when it anticipates the reign of God and does not acquiesce in things as they are.

So the Church thanks God for a foretaste, here and now, of what it hopes for. Long since, it has anticipated its hope in its prayer: "Your kingdom come. Your will be done, on earth as in heaven. Give us our daily bread. Forgive us our sins. Deliver us from evil."

VI. SHARED HOPES IN THE FACE OF THE COMMON FUTURE

"Christ is risen!" What does it mean to have common hope in a world where we face common threats? There are common Christian commitments; concerted action is possible, although the emphases are different in different parts of the world.

Our common hope is threatened by *increasing and already excessive concentrations of power with their threats of exploitation and poverty*. They are responsible for the ever-widening gap between rich and poor, not only between nations but within individual nations. Political exploitation and dependency, hunger and malnutrition are the price paid by the poor for the superabundance of goods and power enjoyed by the rich. Concentration of power also leads to the preservation of the existing and the formation of new class distinctions.

Nevertheless, we share a common hope; for we believe that God has taken sides in this struggle (Ps. 103:6).

Our common future is dominated by our *increasing capacity to shape the physical world.* Science and technology have bettered the human lot. Wisely used, they can help to feed the hungry, heal the sick, develop communication, strengthen community. The refusal to use these powers responsibly on the part of all people everywhere, and especially the ability of the affluent to appropriate these benefits for themselves, threatens us with environmental collapse, biological catastrophies and nuclear destruction. Nevertheless, we hope in the continual action of the Creator Spirit who will not abandon his creatures and who can prompt us to act responsibly as stewards of creation.

The most alarming concentration of power in our time is the *seemingly uncontrollable growth of armaments.* The present arsenal of nuclear warheads held by the superpowers numbers well above 10,000 — more than a million times the annihilating power which devastated Hiroshima. Even the so-called Third World has increased its commitment to armament from eight billion dollars in 1957 to forty billion in 1977. It is important not to overstate our hopes, but God's Spirit opens doors beyond human expectations. Evil is not necessary. The Spirit can plant the leaven of peace in unexpected surroundings, and create hope that it is possible to establish justice without resorting to war.

There are pressures and forces everywhere which threaten to disintegrate the human community. Races, classes, sexes, even religions are set against each other. In all places inherited patterns of society are dissolving and weakening the sense of belonging which community provides. At the same time new forms of community are emerging which in their newness can also create anxieties. Nevertheless, the Spirit works with a surprising freedom, preserving that which sustains life and bringing to birth something genuinely new. Therefore, we can have courage to experiment with new forms of association, new structures and institutions, new forms of human relationships.

Our common hope is threatened by *assaults on human dignity.* Statistics for programmes, stereotypes for discrimination, slaves, victims, or simply the forgotten. Human persons and human possibilities are everywhere threatened today. Individual human rights are violated by arbitrary arrest and "disappearances". We are appalled at the growing numbers of "prisoners of conscience", and at the increasingly systematic use of torture as an ordinary method of exercising power. But social human rights are likewise violated by denial of food, housing, jobs, education and health care, compounded by racism and sexism. There is no part of the world where some of these violations are not present. Those who dehumanize others thereby dehumanize themselves. Nevertheless, we have hope because God affirms the dignity of "the very last".

Commitment to the common future and life itself are eroded by *meaninglessness and absurdity*. In situations of affluence, this may result from "playing by the rules of the game" in a success-oriented culture. In situations of rapid cultural or social change, it may arise in the confusion of being called to fill previously undefined roles. In situations of exploitation, dependency and "marginalization" it may be imposed by the sense of impotence and frustration which comes from the inability to act for oneself or one's class. Nevertheless, we share a common hope, for the Son of God himself withstood the threat of meaninglessness and absurdity. God's healing word will come with different accents: to the affluent it is the challenge to renounce false gods; to the confused it offers the light of Jesus' life to clarify perplexity; to the dispossessed it comes as a challenge and empowerment to take up the struggle. To all it promises that life makes sense.

The problems seem overwhelming. The cry for realism is deep in each one of us, and it expresses a kind of ultimate question about Christian hope. But we believe that each rightful action counts because God blesses it. With the five loaves and two fishes which the young man brought to him, Jesus fed the multitude. Hope lives with special power in small actions.

Above all, we dare to hope in the face of *death*, the ultimate threat to our aspirations and actions. As sinners under the judgment of God we are bound to die. Therefore death is the "last enemy" of our hopes. It penetrates life with paralyzing power, especially where it takes away people before they have had a chance to live. Yet hope in Christ focuses precisely on this enemy. The triumph of God's grace is the resurrection – Christ's victory over death and sin with all their allies. The Apostle says: "If in this life only we have hope in Christ, we are of all men most miserable" (I Cor. 15:19). We rejoice that his crucial *if* is answered unequivocally: *not only* in this life. It is this "not only" that gives life its hopeful horizon. Fate is broken. There is a tomorrow for us today – and in the day of our death.

The Christian hope is a resistance movement against fatalism.

VII. HOPE AS THE INVITATION TO RISK

"Christ is risen!" But the risen one is the crucified. This means that our life in hope is not a guarantee of safety, but an invitation to risk. To live in hope is never to have reached our goal, but always to be on a risk-laden journey.

To live in hope is to risk *struggle*. We are denied the privilege of being "neither hot nor cold", of adopting a pseudo-neutrality that covertly supports those in power. To struggle is to take sides openly, saying "yes" to some at the cost of saying "no" to others. If patient endurance is all that is possible, that too can be a form of protest. We can afford to fail, since God can use our failures in the fulfilment of his purposes. Hope embraces the risk of struggle.

To live in hope is to risk *the use of power*. Some have too much power to be trusted; most have too little to be effective. It is not right that a few should impose their decisions on the many. We must seek identification with the powerless and help them escape a life of dependency on others. But we must also minister to those in power, asking them to listen to "the wretched of the earth", to use power justly and share it with those who stand outside. Hope embraces the risk of the responsible use of power.

To live in hope is to risk *affirming the new and re-affirming the old*. To affirm the new is to acknowledge that Christ goes before us; to reaffirm the old is to acknowledge that He did not come to destroy, but to fulfil, for He is the same yesterday, today and forever. Hope sends us on untried ways and calls us to discover the new whether it is represented by the challenge of new cultural contexts, the call for new life-styles or previously unheeded cries for liberation. When we lock ourselves to the past we may become deaf to the groanings and pleadings of the Spirit. Yet, the Spirit will always reaffirm the truth of Christ. Therefore, hope embraces the risk both of new departures and of faithfulness to the past against the temptation of passing fashions.

To live in hope is to risk *self-criticism as the channel of renewal*. Within culture and within the Church, renewal comes through challenge to what is established, so that it can be revitalized or cast aside. But renewal in the true sense of the word is not within our power. It arises as we are judged by God and driven to repent and bear fruits worthy of repentance. This can also include, however, a certain light-heartedness, a willingness not to take ourselves too seriously. Only those who can smile at themselves can be ultimately serious about other selves. Hope embraces the risk of self-criticism as the way to renewal.

To live in hope is to risk *dialogue*. Genuine encounter with others can challenge us to vacate positions of special privilege and render ourselves vulnerable. To enter dialogue with people of other faiths and ideologies is to risk having one's own faith shaken and to discover that there are other ways to state the truth than we have yet learned ourselves. The dialogue with Jews holds special promise and difficulties; promise of enrichment, because with no other people are our common roots so deep; difficulties, because the theological and political questions which arise threaten to divide us from one another as well as from them. Because in dialogue we can receive a fuller understanding of our own faith and a deeper understanding of our neighbour, hope is not afraid of dialogue.

To live in hope is to risk *cooperation with those from whom we differ*. When we join with others in immediate human tasks we risk being used and absorbed. But when we find those who, not acknowledging the name of Christ, are serving humanity, we can side with them, both for the sake of all God's children and, if occasion permits, to give account of our own hope. Hope is willing to risk cooperation with those who are different.

To live in hope is to risk *new forms of community between women and men*. This calls for a grace and understanding that can take past structures, stereotypes and resentments and transmute them into new forms of living together, both inside and outside the Church. We are challenged to discover on the basis of scripture and tradition contemporary ways to express mutuality and equality, and especially to understand anew what it means to be created in the image of God.

To live in hope is to risk *scorn*. To most of our contemporaries our hope appears vain; it is at best irrelevant, at worst malevolent. To live in hope is nevertheless to continue to witness to the saving power of Jesus Christ, whether we are ignored or attacked. Because to spread the Gospel is not only our mission but also our privilege and joy, we can run the risk of ridicule.

To live in hope is to risk *death for the sake of that hope*. No Christian may decide that someone else should be a martyr. But each of us confronts the likelihood that faithful witness can be costly witness. The Christian hope is not that death can be avoided, but that death can be overcome. Those who truly live in hope have come to terms with death and can risk dying with Christ. For some that is rhetoric; for others it is the bedrock assurance from which they face each new day. To live in hope is to embrace the risk of death for the sake of that hope.

"The saying is sure
    if we have died with him, we shall also live with him;
    if we suffer, we shall also reign with him;
    if we deny him, he also will deny us;
    if we are faithless, he remains faithful;
for he cannot deny himself."

    (II Tim. 2:11-13)

The Importance of the Faith and Order Commission for Restoring Ecclesial Fellowship

NIKOS A. NISSIOTIS

Meeting in the name of Christ by the power of the Holy Spirit is always a real joy. The gatherings of the Commission on Faith and Order, within the framework of the ecumenical movement as it is represented by the World Council of Churches, remind us of this truth in a special way. Since 1920, at regular intervals, meetings on issues of faith and order have taken place to help the churches to come together through a process of regathering in one place with one accord.

As we come together again, we are called to experience the profound significance of this gathering which enables us to share in the fundamental truth of the Gospel. We are called into the synaxis of the Ecclesia. The experience will become more immediate and stronger if we succeed in grasping fully the reality which we represent as a Commission, the reality which has been created and shaped by the successive gatherings of the Faith and Order movement, each in its own way serving a process of consistent growth towards unity. This newly elected Commission, meeting now here in Bangalore, is one more link in the long chain of such gatherings. Actually, it is one gathering which has been in existence since the early days of the movement. Gathering at regular intervals gives to that one meeting its extension in time; regathering today in Bangalore acquires the value of unbroken continuity with the past. This gathering has its inspiration and quality in the past and is oriented towards the future. It is part of an organic and inseparable whole, which is continually growing into a new stage on the way to church unity.

Meetings on issues of faith and order began in 1920 as gatherings of church representatives who had decided to get to know one another, to be *informed* about their respective attitudes towards the Christian faith.

●Prof. Nissiotis, moderator of the Commission on Faith and Order, is Professor of Theology in the University of Athens.

They continued as meetings of *encounter* between these representatives sharing the same faith, and finally they have led to the present situation in which we are expected to articulate *consensus* on certain essential ecclesiological doctrines. Mutual information, encounter and consensus can, to a certain extent, express the process of growth towards church unity throughout the successive meetings of this Commission. These three approaches cannot be identified with three distinctive periods in the history of the Faith and Order movement because all three have been present right from the beginning, and all three still inspire the work of the Commission today. The emphasis has perhaps changed.

We have now come to speak explicitly of consensus. But the consensus which we now discover was already implicitly present at the first World Conference on Faith and Order in Lausanne (1927). It was conceived there as a future sure event.

In reality there is but one gathering, one growing organism throughout these past decades. Each gathering serves a dynamic process of the churches as they try to respond to their common calling by the Spirit to be regathered into one place and in one accord.

I. Hope and consensus

The Commission on Faith and Order is not simply an international meeting of representatives. It is not just a group of experts exchanging their views on unity in order to support their own theories or defend their own church traditions. A gathering of the Commission is rather a pentecostal event than a representative conference. It is more a kerygmatic, liturgical and eschatological gathering than a research group.

What keeps us together is the common calling to which we can respond only by the invocation of the Holy Spirit. Of course, the meeting has an external facade: it is set up, it has a function and structure, but there is a far deeper dimension to it as well. The fact of being together and the decision to stay together reveal the power of the Spirit. Invoking the Paraclete together means that we are all equally depending on God's guidance and grace, creating at the same time a new situation for the separated Christian confessions.

In the Old Testament the Spirit of God guides the people of God through chosen individuals, namely, the prophets. The act of invoking the Spirit as a part of the Body of Christ is different. The period of the Old Testament is the preparatory stage; with the coming of Christ the promise given by God to regather his people is fulfilled. The churches manifest this fulfilment by bringing together their members in regular eucharistic gatherings, catechetic and missionary activities. A church is a gathering realized by the invocation of the Spirit in virtue of the salvation given by Christ and the love of God the Father. Thus, every church gathering actually shares in the truth of the Gospel. Truth in Christ is never merely on the side of cognitive operation of the human intellect. It is rather in the act of sharing together in new life, through a "new event with the others". The epiclesis of the Spirit opens a new possibility to experience God's wisdom and truth within the community of believers making up the Body of Christ. The Spirit sends new life out of the Cross and Resurrection of Jesus Christ only through the gathered community which has invoked him from God the Father. The church gathering is as such the qualitative form of the Christian truth.

This newness of life is more evident and striking if the Spirit is invoked by a gathering of people belonging to separate traditions but grounded in the same faith in Christ, because the operation of the Spirit fills the gaps, unites the oppositions, bridges the distances, links the different gifts of grace. The Spirit always brings about unity out of the diversity within the one Body, transcending confessional boundaries and healing divisions. The Spirit is the advocate of the dynamic over the static, of the multiform over the uniform, of the exceptional over the regular, of the paradox over the normal.

The Spirit, invoked by a gathering of believers in Christ, reaffirms the past and opens up the future. Through the epiclesis, each church gathering is recreated as a community of faith and prepared for transformations and new attempts to become a more authentic Christian community in the world. Stability and change are both due to the same working of the Spirit. Stability refers to the permanence of being part of the one Body; change is necessary because of the constant danger of failure to be the authentic community of faith in the world. The dimension of the future opened by the Spirit has to be grasped by the churches through a continuous effort of recapturing faith in praxis, mission and diakonia in the world.

In other words, the dimension of the future is not the projection of the aspirations of the present moment. The Spirit does not open the future in this way. The Spirit gives the promise of fulfilment; He unites the community with the eschatological event of the second coming of Jesus Christ. The gathered church community does not simply look towards the realization of present wishes, plans and hopes, but represents the eschatological community itself receiving the exalted Christ. The dimension of the future is the eschatological reality which is not yet fully realized, but hoped for in the Spirit, that is, surely to be realized at the end of history. The anticipation of this realization orients the gathered community to the future. The new age is still to come. The individual experiences it through the tension between his failure in the present age and his hope for the fulfilment of his aspirations for salvation in the age to come. It is therefore the state of hope in penitence and the penitence in hope which is the main characteristic of Christian hope. We are constantly called by the Spirit towards a better future through a gathered community which has invoked him from God the Father in the name of Christ.

The tension between the charismata already received from the Spirit and the full communion not yet realized because of our failure leads us towards hope in penitence. This broken community requires consensus in faith and needs to regather for mutual edification and support. Both hope and consensus are the qualifications of the community of Christ regathered by the Spirit as an eschatological reality. There is no hope without penitence as much as there is no penitence without consensus nor *vice versa*.

II. An ecclesial and Church-bound movement

What is true for each individual Christian community is also true for the gatherings of our Commission. As we invoke the Spirit today we stand in the sequence of gatherings which have taken place in unbroken continuity since the beginning of the movement. The invocation opens the future of hope in penitence. It presses the members of this community to restore consensus as they gather anew to reaffirm their common origin and basis in the past and to seek to renew their calling by the Spirit as an eschatological community. In other words, the Commission meeting is not simply a conference of representative theologians, but a microcosm of the eschatological regathering of the people of God in penitent hope and communal consensus. Our present state of sin and failure is surpassed by the calling of the Spirit that we have invoked from God. Our gathering is the image of the perfected community which is to be realized at the end of time, but is already present now through the earnest and the promise of the Spirit we have invoked together.

We are not diluting our various positions on essential parts of the faith for the sake of reaching verbal or written theological agreements through new formulas and definitions. We can speak of consent in one faith because consensus is *synonymous* with the experience of truth through communion in love. Reaching consensus has nothing to do with tactics. It has to do with and reflects the ecclesial community which is represented and enacted in and by our gathering, although it is not yet fully realized as one community in full union and communion.

The nature of the Commission gathering cannot be adequately defined ecclesiologically either as a church or as a simple conference. It is a gathering resulting from the invocation of the Spirit. We are united by the same hope and directed towards a future opened to us by the same Spirit. Everything must take place in the light of the final fulfilment which liberates us from our isolation and transposes us into a relationship of love and communion where theological consensus becomes a necessary process for growing together in unity.

16

Only as we understand our gathering in this deeper eschatological and pneumatological sense can we do justice to the essence of the inheritance of the Faith and Order Commission meetings as they have progressed from mutual exchange of information through encounter to consensus. Only through this understanding can we avoid an illegitimate secularized interpretation of "hope" and "consensus" — the two main terms of this Commission meeting.

It is especially dangerous to neglect the eschatological aspect of our common invocation of the Spirit. If we do not commit ourselves together to the Spirit, we leave hope and consensus to the inspiration of individuals on the fringe of the Church and abandon the theme of eschatology to the preachers of the final judgment of God through apocalyptic catastrophes and unrealistic expectations.

The Faith and Order movement is an ecclesial and church-bound movement. The contrast, therefore, between the gift of community of the past already received and the community of the future yet to be fully realized is particularly intense. It is experienced with particular sharpness because the participants in the movement both wish to remain faithful to their past and know that they are called by the Spirit to live in consensus. This deeper ecclesial nature of our gathering as eschatological is of decisive importance especially in this stage of the movement; almost everything which can be said about the nature of the unity we seek and the ways of achieving the goal has been said in study conferences, papers and statements. We now face the essential issues. Using the theme of Christian hope as the point of departure, we are called to reinterpret the confessions of the past. The common attempt to articulate hope today renders these confessions more flexible and communicable.

At the same time we are called to proceed to a consensus on the most crucial issues which have been the stumbling blocks till now. We are confronted with the need to attempt these decisive steps; we experience, perhaps more than ever before, a situation without exit. But Christian hope is real, authentic and essential precisely in situations which, from the human point of view, are without hope, and eschatology has a more immediate meaning in situations where human inability is clearly manifest.

There is no longer a way back. The whole movement has reached the stage of decisions. The ecclesial gathering is distinguished by its faithfulness to the calling of the Spirit that we invoke. It is the living tradition which makes the Church continue its life against all kinds of obstacles and shortcomings. The Faith and Order movement has been created and is being sustained by the invocation of the Spirit; it is a movement of the churches; in a unique way it is therefore part of the tradition of the churches. Even if the present structure of the movement disappears, even if the persons are all replaced, the churches would have to work

17

further on the tracks of this movement, because it now belongs to their inner being as churches dependent upon the Spirit.

III. Unity of Church linked with unity of humankind

Gatherings between separated communities are no longer exclusively church events. As the Faith and Order movement has progressed from mutual exchange of information to consensus, another development has taken place. We have been led to a broader vision of unity, which includes the concern for the unity of humankind, with all the dividing factors of daily secular life: racism, sexism, exploitation of the materially weak, lack of human rights and social justice. If unity is experienced as a movement in an ecclesial gathering of church people coming from all parts of the world, it can never be understood as an end in itself. Christianity is no longer composed of the Christian East and West of Greek and Latin origin in Europe and North America. We have become an ecclesial community representing all parts of the world; and new cultural elements challenge the old patterns of a crippled and partial community.

The unity question, therefore, has been modified and its scope has been enlarged. Church unity is not possible any more without immediate reference to the disrupting elements in the unity of humankind. For some parts of the world this other aspect of unity has a priority over the former. Church unity is to be seen as a challenge to the world's disorder, splits, absolute ideologies, race and class mentality.

Certainly, in many respects, the more we progress in reuniting, the more we realize the enormous area that church unity has to cover. The unity we seek is the unity of the triune God; therefore, it is first the same unity that the Church had in the past. It is a process, in the sense of reunion or restoration of lost unity. But this unity is always received and manifested through the redemptive Cross of Jesus, which reveals the human predicament of sin and evil, by which this unity is threatened. Thus, we seek the same unity as in the past, but at the same time we always seek a broader unity in a new world. The Faith and Order movement must not neglect this aspect. It cannot leave the unity of humankind in the hands of secular powers and absolute ideologies raised and fed by economic factors and technocracy. It cannot remain inactive in face of the multiform injustice which continues to split peoples today. A church unity movement which does not immediately link with the world's endeavours and hopes for world unity and does not seek to defeat those forces which threaten it, cannot be an authentic search for church unity today.

As this Commission meeting is taking place in this vast and hospitable country of India, with such an ancient and rich cultural and religious inheritance, the challenge of conceiving church unity on broader terms is evident in a special way. If the world becomes increasingly convinced of its oneness, religions as living faiths today have to become more aware of the need to witness by their example to their common mandate to serve together this broad unity. Christian faith as well as other living faiths and those represented from ancient times in this country, understand unity in cosmic terms. The unity among Christians has to be in the service of mutual cooperation of all living faiths in furthering the reunion of all. There cannot be a broader concept and praxis of Christian unity, comprising the unity of humankind, without continuous dialogue and full cooperation with the other living faiths and religions.

It is thus evident that our meeting here is both crucial and difficult. We have to deal with a rich agenda during the coming two weeks. We feel our weakness as we face this heavy mandate. We must be prepared therefore for self-criticism and repentance. But whatever the difficulties are, it is one more meeting of the Faith and Order movement which takes place as an ecclesial gathering in virtue of the invocation of the Paraclete. It will therefore be a meeting of joy and thanksgiving to God who gives us again the chance to work together in the service of his one world through his one Church.

Above all we must be aware that we face a decisive moment for the future of the Faith and Order movement. For it is evident that new decisions are required to avoid stagnation and make a breakthrough. Determination and courage are needed. Action is called for to help the particular church communions out of their confessional isolation. Our main task is therefore to urge the churches to renew their ecumenical commitment through fresh decisions and through consistent application of dynamic and broader concepts of church unity in the service of all humankind.

Report of the Secretariat

LUKAS VISCHER

Why have we come together here from so many parts of the world? I suppose the simplest answer is the following: to further the unity for which Jesus prayed in his high priestly prayer. The purpose of our meeting together is that that unity may become visible today.

This answer obviously calls for further explanation. Two observations seem to me particularly important.

a) The unity for which Jesus prayed *already exists*. It is not merely a plan still to be put into operation. Jesus prayed the Father that his disciples might be one. The Father has granted this petition. It was not left an open question still awaiting an answer. In Christ, unity has irrevocably been given. If in faith we let ourselves be included in his petition, then everything necessary for the establishment of communion already exists. True, in the course of history this unity has been abused, betrayed and trampled on. Lack of understanding, blindness and obstinacy have distorted it beyond recognition. Above all, it has been eclipsed by the divisions which had lasting effects and resulted in separate confessional traditions. The unity for which Jesus prayed can only be dimly discerned through the anomalous division of the one Church into many churches. Nevertheless, it exists. The task of the ecumenical movement is simply to make it visible once more; to strip away the innumerable layers under which it has been buried and to create a new space for the irresistible power of the prayer of Jesus.

b) The second observation is no less important: the unity for which Jesus prayed must become visible *today*. It is not a case of retreating into the past. On the contrary, it is today that the unity already given in Christ is to be accepted and implemented. Just as in that prayer Jesus stood behind his disciples, so today he stands behind us: "It is not for

---

● Dr Lukas Vischer is director of the Commission on Faith and Order, World Council of Churches.

these alone that I pray but for those also who through their words put their faith in me..." He wants the fellowship which came into existence so unexpectedly at Pentecost to become a reality again in every generation. Unity has not always taken the same form throughout history. It must therefore find its appropriate contemporary form today, too. Fellowship in the Holy Spirit — what does that mean today? A fellowship which witnesses to the Gospel not just in words but also in its way and style of life? A fellowship of freedom, forgiveness and partnership which by its very existence contradicts the disabling effects of fear, which refuses to retreat behind the ramparts of self-interest and challenges the destructive inhumanity of exploitation, oppression and violence? There are no ready-made answers to these questions. They must be sought together and discovered together by the churches in the ecumenical movement.

But where do we stand in respect of this unity? Our present situation is a strangely paradoxical one. On the one hand new *communion between the churches* is undoubtedly growing. New breaches are constantly being made in the confessional walls. The apparently unrealistic dreams of fifty years ago when the Faith and Order movement was still in its infancy are today beginning to come true. The 1977 celebrations commemorating the First World Conference on Faith and Order at Lausanne in 1927 helped us to realize just how profoundly relations between the churches have changed in the course of a few decades.[1] New forms of common witness and new forms of common life continue their pioneering service. Occasionally unity seems already discernible at least in outline. On the other hand, it is also obvious that in many respects divisions persist intact; indeed, that *particularist currents* are again running more strongly today. There is a slackening of commitment to the universal fellowship and common witness of all Christians. In all areas of church life there is a tendency to focus attention increasingly on domestic matters and in many cases on immediate problems and concerns. It is as if, after years of strenuous endeavour on behalf of the common witness of all Christians, a certain fatigue had set in. The more immediate circle of unity is preferred to the wider fellowship. It is part of this general picture that, for a few years now, we can observe in certain quarters a renewed emphasis on the importance of the confessional heritage; terms such as "indispensable continuity" or "historical identity" have suddenly regained wide currency.

In this paradoxical situation, what can the Faith and Order Commission accomplish? The task is obvious. The Commission exists to recall again and again that fundamental unity in Christ and to promote it against all obstacles from whatever source they may come. It must encourage

---

[1] Cf. *Lausanne 77, Fifty Years of Faith and Order,* Faith and Order Paper No. 82, WCC Geneva, 1977.

the churches to build upon the fellowship already achieved and to consider against all doubts and hesitations the next steps to be taken. It must try to show that this unity in Christ is far stronger and deeper than all the lesser continuities and identities to which appeal is made today. It must help to ensure that the true tradition prevails again in the churches over against all human traditions. At the same time, however, it must also try to show the enormous liberating power available for the churches today in the vision of unity, in the vision of a universal fellowship in which all the members are bound together as mutually responsible partners in the service of the one Gospel. It must help to ensure that, in some measure at least, this vision can take concrete shape beyond the dividing barriers both old and new.

In the light of these introductory observations, let me now report on the work and the developments of the last four years.

I. Giving account of the hope that is in us

Firstly a word about the study "Giving Account of the Hope". This study will demand our special attention in this meeting and it could even be that it will reach at least a provisional conclusion at our conference. Basically, this study was also undertaken for the sake of unity. The Church is communion in *one* hope. Only when this *one* hope is able to shine through the witness and life of the divided churches will they have found their unity. But what is the present position of the churches? Can we really speak of *one* hope? From the very outset the study sought an answer to this question. How can the churches speak *together* of the ground – the *logos* – which impels them to hope?

It is now seven years since the Faith and Order Commission decided to launch this study (Louvain 1971).[2] The first step was to issue a general invitation to participate in the study.[3] Churches, groups in the churches, even individual Christians, and ecumenical groups especially, were encouraged to report on the ways in which they expressed the Christian hope in their particular context. The response was surprising. It was almost as if people had been waiting for such an invitation. At its next meeting in Accra (1974) the Commission was able to discuss the first replies and to arrive at a clearer picture of the significance and implications of the project. A first attempt was made to speak together about the ground of hope.[4] Since the Accra meeting the work has been continued. In a number of respects the basis of the study has been broad-

---

[2] Cf. *Faith and Order Louvain 1971*, Faith and Order Paper No. 59, WCC Geneva, 1971, p. 215 f.

[3] Minutes of the Meeting of the Faith and Order Working Committee, Utrecht 1972, Faith and Order Paper No. 65, Geneva 1972.

[4] *Uniting in Hope, Accra 1974*, Faith and Order Paper No. 72, p. 25 ff.

ened. Many more contributions have reached us during the past four years, some of them very substantial. But the Secretariat has also kept its eyes open for contemporary testimonies to hope which, while not formulated in response to the original invitation, were nevertheless important for our study. We tried to obtain as complete and as varied a survey as possible of the ways in which hope is now being confessed in the churches.[5]

Two consultations were organized, the first in spring 1977 and the second in spring 1978, at which we were able to examine in greater depth, in the light of the material collected, the possibility of a common account of hope. The fruits of all these efforts are to be found in the mimeographed volume which you received in preparation for this meeting.

Can we draw any conclusions from the work so far accomplished? Let me deal with some aspects in more detail.

Possible to confess hope together

1. Firstly, it is clear from the testimonies which have been collected that, in a great many cases, Christians from different traditions find it possible today to confess their hope *together,* in similar terms. To be sure, the differences which separate the churches from one another are still far from settled and it would be a mistake to underrate their weight and influence. In accounting for its hope, each church inevitably starts from the assumptions of its own tradition. Both the content and the form of its actual witness are decisively influenced by its view of the Bible, the authority of the Church, the confessions, the ministry and many other points. Indeed, even the decision of a church to speak out or to keep silent on a particular issue is to some extent rooted in the particular tradition in question. Nevertheless, where a deliberate effort is made to bear common witness, especially where some clear outward circumstance calls imperatively for a response from the Church, the traditional boundaries can often be crossed in astonishing ways. The common ground of hope seems sufficiently strong to be able again and again to outbid the still unresolved differences. Often the common ground is recognized *post factum.* There is more than one instance in recent years of a church's being able to adopt unreservedly, or almost so, the witness which another church has already borne to hope.

---

[5] The accounts have been published in four separate publications:
   a) *Study Encounter* Vol. XI, 2, 1975.
   b) *Study Encounter* Vol. XII, 1-2, 1976.
      1976.
   c) *Giving Account of the Hope Today,* Faith and Order Paper No. 81, Geneva, 1976.
   d) *Giving Account of the Hope Together,* Faith and Order Paper No. 86, 1978.

What are the implications of this amazing unanimity in actual contemporary confession? Must we not understand it as an invitation to the churches to use far more resolutely the possibility of giving together an account of their hope? Of course we must go on working to resolve our inherited differences. The broader the common basis, the easier it will be for the churches to speak and act in concert. But evidently, it is also possible to exaggerate the weight of the differences which still remain unresolved today. The attempt to bear common witness can be abandoned before it has really been tried. The impressive number of common testaments of hope demonstrates that the churches could show greater determination to cross the lines of division and commit themselves more confidently to the venture of giving a common account of their hope.

2. No less important, however, is the second observation which the material suggests. Even the most cursory examination of the collected testimonies reveals at once the *variety* of ways in which hope is spoken of today. The testimonies are widely divergent; indeed, they occasionally seem even to contradict one another. The differences are not based on the conflicting confessional traditions. They arise rather from the fact that Christians give different answers to the problems and challenges of our time. The differences are already noticeable at the local level. There is hardly any church which is not marked by a growing diversity of views and which has not had to face up afresh to the problem of the relation between unity and plurality. But the differences become even more obvious when we compare the accounts of hope from different parts of the world. What common ground is shared by the testimonies from Asia and Africa, from Latin America and North America, from Eastern Europe and Western Europe? They diverge so widely that one is tempted, at least at first glance, to ask whether they are really speaking of one and the same hope.

Study began from below

3. The study was deliberately planned in the first place to bring into the open the full extent of this diversity of views. Its method was governed by the conviction that the ground of hope is perceived and expressed most clearly where this ground has to be proclaimed. The study deliberately began, therefore, *from below* and not "from above". It would have been possible, theoretically, to have set to work at once working out a common declaration. The decision was made, however, first of all to collect concrete testimonies from as wide a variety of contexts as possible. This decision has occasionally been challenged and criticized. The fear was expressed that by concentrating in this way on the particular, the common basis in the Bible and the Creeds might be obscured and the Church imprisoned in isolated contexts instead of being led into new common perspectives of hope. It was essential to

hear this warning, of course, but there were also good reasons for not being too quick to heed it. How easily could a precipitate common declaration have led to the canonization of one particular understanding or theology of hope! How easily could it have neglected views and voices which are vitally important for the whole Church. Above all, how easily could it have diverted attention from each particular situation and the need to wrestle with its particular problems! If it is true that the ground of hope is perceived and expressed most clearly where it has to be proclaimed, then it is vitally important that Christians in each place should become involved in grappling with their own particular situation. Sometimes, the account they are called to give will not demand great efforts; their response will almost be dictated by the challenges and lines of conflict which they face in their situation. The task will be more difficult in other situations where the issues are less clearly contoured; the response will then be much less evident; it will require an initiative of discernment and choice from within ourselves. When Christians find themselves in such situations without outward pressure they are particularly exposed to the temptation to take refuge in general reflections on the meaning and possible implications of hope instead of proclaiming unreservedly its reason.

4. How then are we to give any *common account* at all? How are the churches to proclaim together the ground of hope which underlies all particular testimonies? Necessary as it is for it to be proclaimed in a special way in each context, it must also be possible for it to be expressed together. How are we to arrive at this common account of hope? Obviously, texts and declarations are not the only way of expressing the common ground. The fellowship in the one hope also finds expression in other ways, indeed is perhaps more effectively expressed in other ways. It is a reality where people invoke together the name of Christ. It is a reality where people listen together to the Bible, where they celebrate the eucharist together. The best medium for the expression of the common ground of hope is praise, worship, celebration. It is vitally important, therefore, that the churches in the ecumenical movement should find new forms of common celebration.[6]

But can the ground of hope also be expressed in a common verbal form? As you know, the Faith and Order Commission wrestled with this question at its meeting in Accra. It made a first attempt to compose a common statement. This was in three parts. The first part spoke in biblical terms of the basis, the power and the promised fulfilment of the hope. The second part dealt with a few carefully selected situations

---

[6] It is interesting to notice how much the importance of "celebration" has been stressed in recent years. Again and again we meet with the proposal that the unity achieved in the ecumenical movement should be expressed in the form of common celebration.

in some detail and in this way sought to illustrate how varied the confession of hope is today. The third part underlined the commitment of the churches, in spite of all their differences, to constitute one fellowship and to stand together in proclamation and service.[7] The underlying purpose of this threefold arrangement is clear enough. The statement should point to Jesus Christ as the ground of all hope; but it should do so in such a way that, at the same time, something of the variety of views in the contemporary world should be expressed. The Accra declaration was an extremely important step in the study. The importance of this double reference can hardly be exaggerated. The question arises, however, as to whether a new common account can go beyond this first attempt.

5.   Two questions seem to me especially important in this connection. Cannot the common account of hope deal more explicitly with *the major issues* confronting the world today than did the Accra statement? Can it not make a more conscious effort to relate the basis of hope to these issues? Instead of simply pointing to the ultimate ground of hope, could it not provide a common account showing why this ultimate ground justifies hope today, precisely in *this* contemporary world? The question, "What have you to say?" is addressed today to the Church as a whole. What have you to say in face of the advances in science and technology and the deadly dangers they also import? What have you to say in face of the flagrant injustices of our contemporary world: poverty, oppression, violence, tyranny and torture? What have you to say in face of the progressive disintegration of human community, in face of the deepening conflicts which endanger peace? What have you to say in face of the danger of destruction through the expansion of wars? If the Church is to be perceived as communion of hope, it must be able to offer common answers to these questions.

How to agree on all the answers?

6.   But how are we to reach agreement on the content of these answers? Where are we to find a language in which the Church can recognize its identity in all places? One thing is immediately clear: this common account will only carry conviction if it really *grows out of the diversity of testimonies.* In this respect, too, the Accra statement needs to be developed. While it brings out the diversity of views, it gives hardly any indication of how each individual testimony is to be assessed in the light of the proclamation of the Church as a whole. For accounts of hope are not simply opinions which can merely be juxtaposed. Each is an attempt to speak of the one hope which must ultimately be the basis of all the rest. In a certain sense, therefore, each account claims universality. However firmly anchored in a particular context, it is at the same time addressed to the Church as a whole. A Latin American theologian

---

[7] Cf. *Uniting in Hope,* pp. 25-80.

said to me some time ago: "What we are saying is not just the truth for Latin America: it is the truth for the Church throughout the world". What he meant was evident. In saying this he did not mean that his testimony had to be literally repeated by the whole Church. He meant that no common account could really be regarded as a common account of hope unless his testimony in its entirety could find its place in it. But if this is the case, how can there ever be any common answers? The only possible way is for the different testimonies to be brought together and confronted in encounter and debate,[8] the claims to universal validity must be thrashed out and the common language developed step by step through question and counter-question[9]. What is the significance of the accounts of hope which voice the rebellion of the oppressed? What is the meaning of the vision steadily gaining ground today, the vision of a new quality of community between man and woman? What are we to make of the views of those who remind us of the limits of human existence and who define hope primarily as a more obedient acceptance of these limits? The answer can only be arrived at through encounter and debate. Some of the differences will then prove to be simply variations of the same hope not requiring special attention. But others will be more difficult. It may turn out that Christians entertain hopes which are in fact at cross-purposes with the hopes of other Christians; indeed, testimonies which seem to some to be authentic proclamations of the basis of hope may seem to others to be on the contrary a ground for discouragement and despair. The fellowship of hope can then only be achieved by radical changes both in the proclamation and in the life of the churches. This discussion between the different accounts of hope has been launched in recent years. A series of meetings has been held with this objective.[10] The task is still far from completion; indeed it may well be one of those tasks which will never be completed. The issue will be with us no doubt also during the coming days. Given the diversity of our accounts of hope, how is the fellowship of hope to be deepened in exchange and confrontation?

7. One final observation. While it may be very difficult to formulate agreed answers and impossible to resolve our differences completely, is it not in itself a ground for hope that we belong to a fellowship in which everything revolves around hope? To a fellowship in which, throughout

---

[8] The report of the Accra meeting already includes an example of such discussion: cf. *Uniting in Hope*, pp. 33-35.

[9] On the question of mutual agreement, see especially the sensitive account by Choan-Seng Song "The Ecumenical Movement Inside Out", *International Review of Mission*, Vol. LXVII, No 266, April 1978.

[10] E. g. Conference in Detroit 1975, cf. Sergio Torres and John Eagleson (ed.), *Theology in the Americas*; Conference of European Churches, Geneva Conference 1976, cf. *European Theology Challenged by the Third World Church*, CEC Occasional Paper No. 82, Geneva 1976.

the centuries, hope has been a living reality from generation to generation; a fellowship in which, from Abraham and Sarah onwards, people have set out without knowing exactly whither they were being called; a fellowship in which even today people travel forwards into the future with the same faith? To a fellowship in which every member is compassed about and sustained by hope? There can be no common account of hope which does not also necessarily point to this *fellowship as source and spring of hope.* Not that this fellowship is perfect; indeed, measured against ideal pictures, it would rather have to be described as source of disappointment. But it is a source of hope because it always points beyond itself; because it proclaims pardon and thereby makes new beginnings possible; because it again and again breaches barriers which appear irremovable and does in fact bring people together in astonishing ways. It is essential that this fundamental fellowship be maintained and constantly renewed in face of all the forces of disintegration. Hope and unity are not two separate themes. Unity is part of the hope which the Church must proclaim. Every effort on behalf of unity is always at the same time, therefore, an effort to ensure that hope may become more visible and more vital.

II. Visible unity in one faith and in one eucharistic fellowship

But what has been done in recent years to make the unity of the churches more visible? Attention has been focussed on describing the goal of unity more clearly and reflecting on how this unity can gradually be achieved.

For the churches to be able to agree on a description of the unity they are seeking in the ecumenical movement is far from being a matter of course. In its encounter with other churches every church starts from its own ecclesiological presuppositions. A common understanding of unity can only be achieved, therefore, in the dialogue itself. The World Council of Churches itself has to face up to this problem. Although brought into existence to promote the unity of the churches, it cannot commit itself to any particular view of unity. Certainly an important step forward was taken at the Nairobi Assembly when, as you know, a *new Constitution* was adopted which states the tasks of the Council in greater detail and more precisely than before. In respect of unity, the Council's function was defined as follows: "To call the churches to the goal of visible unity in one faith and in one eucharistic fellowship expressed in worship and in common life in Christ and to advance towards that unity in order that the world may believe."[11] This decision is obviously of great

---

[11] The formulation goes back to the Louvain Conference of the Faith and Order Commission 1971. It had been drafted by the Commission at the request of the Executive Committee of the World Council of Churches.

importance. Both for the World Council of Churches and for the member churches it amounts to a new commitment to the cause of unity.

Even more important, perhaps, is a second decision: the proposal to describe the unity of the Church as "conciliar fellowship". It is impossible here to trace in detail the course which led to this description.[12] All of you are familiar with the brief statement which was drafted at the Salamanca conference (1973), discussed in detail at the Accra meeting of the Faith and Order Commission (1974) and finally incorporated into the report on unity adopted by the Nairobi Assembly. Like the earlier statement on unity by the New Delhi Assembly (1961), it was an attempt at an agreed description of the goal of the ecumenical movement. Basing itself on that earlier text, it sought to offer a still more inclusive picture of unity. The Nairobi report led to a wide range of discussions. On the whole the response was very encouraging. The description was felt to be especially helpful because it succeeded in showing how unity at the universal level is related to unity at the local level. There were criticisms, too, of course, and this from opposite angles. Some questioned whether the description allowed sufficient room for diversity within the Church.[13] Others, on the contrary, wondered whether it went sufficiently far in its demands. They expressed the anxiety that the need for organic church unity in each locality was no longer taken seriously enough.[14] To protect it against such misunderstandings, the concepts of "conciliar fellowship" will therefore need to be further clarified and explained.[15]

But the Nairobi report has in any case already achieved one important result. It has compelled *a wide variety of partners* – churches, confes-

---

[12] The important texts can all be found in: Choan-Seng Song (ed.), *Growing Together into Unity,* Texts of the Faith and Order Commission on Conciliar Fellowship. Madras: CLS, 1978.

[13] The question can be asked for a variety of reasons, of course. It has been raised with particular emphasis by certain Lutheran theologians concerned that the confessional heritage should continue to live even in the one Church as an identifiable reality, though of course transformed by the dialogue with other churches. For this reason they prefer to talk of unity as "reconciled diversity". This concept has been chiefly expounded by Harding Meyer in numerous articles. In the form in which the concept is interpreted in his latest article, it is distinguished only in a few points from the concept of "conciliar fellowship" and even from that of "organic unity". Cf. Harding Meyer, Einheit in versöhnter Verschiedenheit, konziliare Gemeinschaft, organische Union, in *Ökumenische Rundschau,* Vol. 27, 1978, 3, pp. 377-400. It cannot be overlooked, however, that the term is used by many in the sense of the old idea of "federal union".

[14] Cf. Lesslie Newbigin: "What is 'a local church truly united'?" *In Each Place: Towards a Fellowship of Local Churches Truly United.* Geneva: WCC, 1977.

[15] The Faith and Order Secretariat took a first step when in 1976 it combined with the WCC's Sub-unit on the Renewal of Congregational Life to organize a consultation on the meaning of the term "local church". Cf. *In Each Place,* WCC Geneva 1977.

sional families, bilateral conversations, national Christian councils, ecumenical groups – to reopen the discussion of the goal of unity. It has introduced into the debate a term which stimulates them to deepen *their* understanding of unity and to face the question as to how an agreed description of the goal can be achieved. It has thus strengthened the common consciousness that unity can only be achieved by mutually concerted efforts.

There is another question which has been raised insistently in recent years: What conditions must be met if unity is to be achieved? It is not only for the achievement of greater clarity as to the common goal that this question is of key importance but also for the planning of the work to be undertaken by the Faith and Order Commission itself in the immediate future. In the light of the new Constitution of the World Council of Churches and the Nairobi Assembly report, what can we say on this score? It would seem to me that in the light of these two texts, there are at least three conditions to be fulfilled: agreement in the apostolic faith; mutual recognition of baptism, eucharist and ministry; structures which make joint consultation and decision possible.

Let me briefly discuss each of these three conditions:

1. *Consensus in the apostolic faith:*

Unity is primarily unity in faith. If they are to be able to live in unity, the churches must be able to convince one another that they share the same faith. This lends all the greater urgency to the question: in what form must and can this required agreement in faith be expressed? There was considerable discussion of this question in the early days of the Faith and Order movement. It played an important part, for example, at the First World Conference on Faith and Order in Lausanne in 1927. To the great disappointment of many who came to Lausanne with great expectations, however, it proved impossible then to offer any convincing answer to the question.[16] The attempt has not been repeated since then. Instead, attention was focussed on specific questions of faith and doctrine in dispute between the churches. But is it not time to try again to offer a more comprehensive answer? What would this involve? A new creed to replace the old confessions? Hardly! What is needed is that the churches should be able to agree on how to make use of the tradition of the Church, the Bible and the confessions, as they seek to confess the faith today. Let me try to define this task with the aid of the term "conciliar fellowship". When one day a universal council should assemble, what must the participants be able to agree in confessing on the very first day, even before they have got down to the specific tasks of that council? It seems to me conceivable that fresh attention may

---

[16] Cf. *Faith and Order Lausanne 1927,* ed. H.N. Bate, SCM London 1927, p. 160ff.

have to be given to this question in the coming years. The earlier studies conducted by the Faith and Order Commission on tradition and the traditions, on the authority of the Bible, on the importance of the church fathers, will afford precious help in this task.[17]

2. *Mutual recognition of baptism, eucharist and ministry:*

The clarification of this second condition of unity has been one of the main focusses of our work in recent years. You are all familiar with the three agreed statements on baptism, eucharist and ministry.[18] The decision of the Faith and Order Commission in Accra to submit these texts to the Central Committee of the World Council of Churches and through the Central Committee to the member churches was more far-reaching in importance than was realized at the time. In taking this decision it initiated a process which was in many respects new for it. The Nairobi Assembly asked the churches to transmit their comments on the three statements to the Faith and Order Commission by 31 December 1976. A large number of churches, more than a hundred all told, responded to this request. The total number of responses which reached the Commission was, of course, much higher.

But how is this work to be continued? Certain immediate steps have already been taken. The responses of the churches have been carefully examined and summarized.[19] At a special consultation (Crêt Bérard, Switzerland, June 1977), a "Reply to the Replies of the Churches" was drafted, then revised by the Standing Commission of the Faith and Order Commission and sent to the churches by the Central Committee of the World Council of Churches (August 1977).[20] In addition to this, about thirty responses in which particularly important questions were raised received individual replies. But the main question has not yet been answered: How is a new text to be drafted on the basis of the responses of the churches? These responses certainly contain a great many suggestions. But before detailed work can begin we have still to decide on the best form for such a new text on baptism, eucharist and ministry if it is really to help the churches to advance on the road to unity. What is consensus? How far must agreement extend? Some of

---

[17] Cf. Montreal 1963 (Section II "Scripture, Tradition and Traditions", p. 50ff), Bristol 1967 (The Significance of the Hermeneutical Problem for the Ecumenical Movement, p. 32ff), Louvain 1971 (The Authority of the Bible, p. 9ff). A study of the authority of the Old Testament has been conducted in recent years in the framework of the Faith and Order Commission.

[18] *One Baptism, One Eucharist and a Mutually Recognized Ministry,* Faith and Order Paper No. 73, Geneva, 1975.

[19] This was carried out by Professor Bert Hoedemaker, Holland. The survey was published in duplicated form in a limited edition.

[20] *Towards an Ecumenical Consensus: Baptism, Eucharist and Ministry,* Faith and Order Paper No. 84, Geneva, 1977.

the responses of the churches seem to assume that any future text must provide an agreed account of an even greater number of questions. Others think that the Accra text has tackled too many questions already. What form then is the consensus to take? A small group recently proposed that the agreement should be presented in the form of a catechetical text and this certainly deserves consideration. But whatever answer we give to these questions, it is important that in these coming days you should produce guidelines for further work on the three themes. The "Reply to the Replies of the Churches" suggested — somewhat rashly perhaps — that a new text might possibly be presented to the churches even before the next Assembly of the World Council of Churches. If that is to be possible, the work must be taken in hand immediately.

3. *Structures making possible common deliberation and decision:*

For unity to be possible, the churches must also be able to teach, speak and act in concert. The third condition for church unity, therefore, is structures which permit common debate and decision at every level of the Church's life. But what does this involve? The concept of "conciliar fellowship" points the direction in which an answer is to be found. Synodal assemblies are the primary instrument of consultation and decision-making. The churches must, therefore, rediscover together the potentialities of synodal assemblies at every level, universal, regional and, above all, local. Countless questions still require to be answered, however. What are synodal assemblies? How are they rooted in worship and the eucharist? What authority can they claim? In what way can they be truly representative of the whole people of God? What is the role of the ministry in such assemblies? What attitude is to be taken to a special "ministry of unity" embodied in one person? Can agreement be reached on that "ministry of Peter" of which there is so much talk today? Above all, how are the churches, all of which now have their own structures of consultation and decision-making, to find these common structures and gradually grow into them? At its meeting in Accra, the Commission recognized the urgency of these issues and therefore recommended the study on "How does the Church teach authoritatively today?" This has since been set up. At a small consultation (Geneva, February 1976) a study document was prepared.[21] A number of study groups have taken up the theme[22] and the initial findings were summarized at a larger

---

[21] "How Does the Church Teach Authoritatively Today?" A study document prepared by the Faith and Order Secretariat, cf. *One in Christ,* 1976, 3-4.

[22] There were study groups in Italy, the Federal Republic of Germany, the German Democratic Republic, and in Greece. The studies of the Italian group appeared in *Il Regno,* No. 365, 15/12/1977. Those of the German Ecumenical Study Committee (Federal Republic) have been published in a supplement of the *Ökumenische Rundschau,* No. 33, Verlag Otto Lembeck, 1978.

consultation last year (Odessa, October 1977). But the study is not yet completed and we shall have to decide here how it can be advanced in the coming years.

III. Church as lived communion

But are these three conditions an exhaustive description of our task? I spoke in my introduction of the need for the unity for which Jesus prayed in his high priestly prayer to become visible *today*. When these three conditions are fulfilled, has that unity really already become visible? Surely unity becomes visible primarily by demonstrating its unifying power in life. It becomes visible when it breaches the walls which divide human beings from each other today. It becomes visible when Paul's affirmation: "There is no such thing as Jew and Greek, slave and freeman, male and female" ceases to be mere rhetoric and becomes actual life. To work at the achievement of the three conditions without *at the same time* paying attention to unity as lived communion would be unrealistic.

As you know, this is the underlying conviction of the study on "Unity of the Church − Unity of Humankind" to which the Faith and Order Commission first turned its full attention at its meeting in Louvain (1971) and which has remained an integral part of its programme ever since. What has been attempted in this area in recent years? At its Accra meeting, the Commission decided no longer to concentrate on the general clarification of this theme but to turn rather to actual life situations and problems. The more general discussion has not been suspended, of course. A survey of the course of the discussion within the ecumenical movement as a whole has been produced and a number of leading figures from a wide variety of backgrounds were asked to comment on this survey from their particular standpoints. This survey was recently concluded and has now been published.[23]

But work in recent years has concentrated primarily on a number of concrete problems. Let me give five examples.

1. *Church Unity and Racism:* How can the churches deal effectively with the divisions which racism produces in their own ranks? How can they create communion in a human society torn by racism? As a result of the discussions provoked by the Programme to Combat Racism, these already urgent questions became even more pressing. The call to unity can easily be exploited to weaken the struggle against racism, in fact any struggle which disturbs complacent peace. Was it not necessary therefore to re-examine the imperative of unity in the light of this experience? Shortly before the Nairobi Assembly, a joint consultation was organized

---

[23] Geiko Müller-Fahrenholz: *Unity in Today's World,* Faith and Order Paper No. 88, Geneva, 1978.

by the Faith and Order Commission and the Programme to Combat Racism to go into this and similar questions.[24] Since then reflection has been continued at the regional level.

2. *The Place of the Disabled in the Church:* One of the ways in which the unity in Christ must demonstrate its effectiveness is by enabling handicapped and disabled people to feel themselves accepted as full members of the fellowship. *De facto,* however, they are often excluded from fellowship. This aspect of the unity of the Church was first discussed at the Louvain conference. After being overshadowed for a time by other activities, it returned to the forefront once again at the Nairobi Assembly, not least because of the personal testimony of a disabled woman who had made the effort of attending the Assembly. Since then there has been intensive reflection on the theme. A book will shortly be published containing a series of contributions and testimonies.[25] A recent European consultation in the organization of which the Faith and Order Secretariat had considerable part formulated a set of recommendations intended to stimulate discussion of the theme in the churches (Bad Saarow, GDR, April 1978). The decision of the United Nations to declare 1981 the "Year of the Handicapped" lends additional importance to this study; it may assist the churches in preparing significant contributions to the celebration of that year in their respective countries.

3. *Dialogue with Other Faiths:* The dialogue with people of other faiths also introduces new perspectives into the efforts for church unity. Dialogue is at once a unifying and a divisive factor. On the one hand, by setting inherited differences in a completely new light, the encounter with other faiths brings the churches closer to one another. On the other hand, by raising fresh questions, it leads to new divisions. We have only to think, for example, of such questions as the election of the Jewish people, the presence and work of God in the other faiths, and the authority of the Old Testament. What form must church unity take so that there can be genuine dialogue? The question has been taken up on several occasions by the Dialogue Sub-unit of the World Council of Churches in recent years. It played an important part, above all, at the Chiang Mai Conference (April 1977) in which various members of the Faith and Order Commission also participated. [26]

4. *Community of Women and Men in the Church:* This theme was already on the agenda at the Faith and Order Commission's Accra meeting. Since then it has assumed a still greater importance in its programme. As a result of discussions between the Faith and Order Secretariat and

---

[24] *Theology in Racism and Racism Against Theology,* WCC Geneva 1975.

[25] Geiko Müller-Fahrenholz: *Partners in Weakness,* Geneva 1978.

[26] Chiang Mai report, Dialogue in Community, in *Faith in the Midst of Faiths,* ed. S.J. Samartha, WCC Geneva 1977, pp. 134ff.

the WCC Sub-unit on the Role of Women in Church and Society, it was decided to launch a special study on the theme with its own study secretary. The green light for this new venture was given at the Nairobi Assembly but it took some time to implement the plan, mainly due to the need first of all to secure the necessary financial resources. The study has now begun. Dr Constance Parvey took up her work in Geneva at the beginning of 1978. The study is jointly sponsored by the Faith and Order Commission and the Sub-unit on the Role of Women in Church and Society. It is expected to take from three to four years. The purpose of the study is to throw light on a number of theological questions. What has the Church to say on the community of men and women in the Church? What does genuine partnership mean today? Men and women are one in Christ; on that the churches are all agreed. But they are not in accord as to the implications of this affirmation. How are we to view the evidence of the Bible? What weight must be given to tradition? How are the churches to achieve an agreed witness in this area, not in words but a witness expressed in lived communion? The study is planned on a wide scale. It is hoped to secure the cooperation of as large a number of study groups as possible. An "invitation" with relevant questions has now been drawn up and will shortly be distributed. To give greater depth to the discussion, a series of publications on more general theological questions is planned. In about two years' time a major international consultation will take place, the findings of which will be submitted to the World Council of Churches and through it to all churches. The theme will therefore certainly occupy your attention again at the next session of the Commission.

5. *Church and State:* At its Accra meeting, the Commission encouraged the initiation of the study on Church law. So far not much progress has been made on this proposal and, given the limited resources available to the Commission, the study will probably never get very far. But at least a way was found of examining closely one question in this area, namely, the relation between Church and state. The importance of this issue for the unity of the Church is so obvious as hardly to require explanation. If the unity of the churches in proclamation and service is to be made visible not only within each country, but also across national boundaries, what form must their relationship to the state take? How are they, on the one hand, to achieve greater freedom from the powers and authorities which seek to restrain them and, on the other hand, to serve with greater solidarity the society in which they live? A consultation on this theme was jointly organized by the Faith and Order Secretariat and the Bossey Ecumenical Institute (August 1976). The report of this consultation has just been published.[27]

---

[27] *Church and State, Opening a New Ecumenical Discussion,* Faith and Order Paper No. 85, Geneva 1978.

IV. The road to unity

We have spoken of the goal of the ecumenical movement. But how is this goal to be reached? What can we say about the road to unity? The fellowship which binds the churches together today is still not that "conciliar fellowship" in which they are to be united. At most it can be referred to as "pre-conciliar" fellowship. How then are they to advance step by step beyond this present situation? Theological discussion of the unity of the Church often suffers from a failure to pay sufficient attention to the intermediate stages between division and unity. Unity is spoken of as if it could one day be reached in one bound. But that final leap will only become possible when it has been preceded by a number of individual steps. We must therefore consider the road to unity.

1) First of all, a word about the style which must characterize the Commission's work. If this work is to lead us forward on the road to unity, it is essential that it be done in close contact with the churches. The Faith and Order Commission is not simply a platform for theological debate. It is an *instrument of the churches*. The debate takes place to help the churches in their efforts to achieve unity. In recent years the style of the Commission's work has already begun to turn in this direction. The decision to submit the three texts on baptism, the eucharist and the ministry to the churches and to invite their comments on them is a good example of this change in style. The response to this decision shows the need to move still more consistently in this direction.

2) Secondly, if we are to advance along the road to unity, it is essential that the various efforts to achieve unity should be *more effectively concerted*. There is a bewildering variety of efforts towards unity today: official and unofficial meetings with a wide range of objectives; bilateral and multilateral conversations at every conceivable level; union negotiations, and so on. An optimistic view would be that, in one way or another, *all* these efforts will ultimately contribute to the attainment of the one goal. But the Nairobi Assembly was surely closer to the truth when it declared that these "diverse activities do not always assist and enrich one another".[28] Can the Faith and Order Commission offer help in this matter? Can it help the partners in the ecumenical movement to enter into a more fruitful relationship with one another?

In recent years the Secretariat has tried in various ways to promote this concertation of efforts. Let me mention the two most important examples. On the one hand, it has cultivated contacts with the world confessional families and with the bilateral conversations. It has published a

---

[28] *Breaking Barriers*, Nairobi 1975. Ann Arbor: Wm. Eerdmans and London: SPCK, 1976, p. 65.

detailed survey of the course of these bilateral conversations.[29] At the request of the world confessional families it agreed to be responsible for organizing a series of three meetings giving representatives of world confessional families the opportunity for an exchange of information and views on the development of the bilateral conversations. The first of these meetings took place this spring (Bossey, April 1978). On the other hand, the secretariat made its services available to united churches. At their request, it arranged a conference at which representatives of united churches met for the first time and were able to articulate some of their common convictions and hopes (Toronto, June 1975). Since then the secretariat has continued to work in close contact with united churches.[30]

In these as well as in all other relationships and contacts, the Commission has an obvious role to perform. It exists to point as consistently as it can to the *common* goal of unity and to keep it before all partners in the ecumenical movement as they seek to achieve unity in their own ways and from their own perspectives.

3) At this point I should like to mention a particular project whose purpose is to deepen this common commitment of the churches: the *Prayer Calendar,* the manuscript of which has now been completed and will appear in print in a few months time.[31] The proposal is a very simple one: namely, that the churches should regularly pray for each other throughout the year. Each week they should remember especially the churches of one particular country or group of countries, and in this way "visit" all the other churches at least once each year. In a sense, the plan is simply the extension of the Week of Prayer for Christian Unity to the whole year. It is an attempt to anticipate, at least in prayer, the unity for which the ecumenical movement exists. Above all, it is an attempt to view the churches in each place as a fellowship, as the people called by God in this particular place in order that His Name may be glorified in it. The proposal for such a Calendar goes back to the Accra meeting of the Commission and to the Nairobi Assembly. I hope that the Commission will commend it to the churches in some

---

[29] Nils Ehrenström and Günther Gassmann, *Confessions in Dialogue,* 3rd revised and enlarged edition, Geneva, 1975, Faith and Order Paper No. 74.

[30] The report of the Toronto conference was published in *What Unity Requires,* Faith and Order Paper No. 77, pp. 18-29. A Continuation Committee was appointed in Toronto to implement the recommendations of the conference. Its first action was to contact the world confessional families and the Vatican Secretariat for Promoting Christian Unity to discuss the influence of bilateral conversations on union negotiations (June 1976). It met a year later in Geneva (August 1977) in order to evaluate the responses of the united churches to the Toronto report. It summarized its conclusions and proposals for the future in an open letter to the united churches. The Faith and Order Secretariat was involved in all these measures.

[31] *For All God's People.* Geneva: WCC, 1978.

appropriate way, for its success depends largely on the extent to which it is adopted by the churches.

4) One final observation. The most effective service which the Faith and Order Commission could perhaps render the churches on the road to unity would be to give much more attention in future to the question of how *unity* is to become visible *in each place.* This was already discussed at our meeting in Accra. In its report on unity it had pointed out the almost fatal tendency of the discussion of unity to rest content with abstractions and generalities. While it is certainly true that the basis of unity is ultimately the same for all situations, the task of uniting presents itself in a different form in each situation.[32] The devil of division lurks in the details! An attempt should perhaps be made, therefore, to develop a number of models and with the help of these to show how the churches in each place can arrive at a more exact picture not only of the obstacles dividing them but also and above all of the possible next steps. Do the grounds for division still have the same cogency? Has fellowship increased? Have new tensions arisen which need to be examined together? Are the existing ecumenical structures still adequate or have they become a monument to an already outdated stage of the ecumenical movement? How can they be made into an instrument to prepare for the next step? All these questions need to be asked again and again, since to contemplate, in intercession only, the churches in each place as one fellowship cannot possibly be the last word. Their unity must become visible and as their unity becomes visible in each place so too will that universal conciliar fellowship gradually become visible in which the churches of all places are bound to one another.

Summarizing the work of four years is not easy. It is hard to convey the fundamental drive which underlies it all. The emphasis falls almost inevitably on all that needs doing and is still undone. Problems, programmes and plans occupy the front of the stage. Can the problems ever be solved and the programmes and plans ever be completed? Is it even worthwhile devoting so much effort to them? Merely to describe the activities undertaken does not answer the question.

A few years ago my daughter asked me what exactly my work was. I tried to explain to her. A few days later she placed on my desk a cartoon she had come across in a newspaper. It consisted of four scenes. The first picture showed a little man using a watering-can. "I'm getting fed up", he sighs. On the second drawing he is still using the watering-can. "I'm really getting fed up with this", he repeats. Then he asks: "... and, anyway, what good does it do!?" But finally we see him gazing in astonishment at a little flower which has sprung up before his very eyes.

---

[32] *Uniting in Hope,* p. 110

In conclusion, therefore, let me express the hope that, both here and during the days of conference which we spend together and beyond them in the years to come, many unexpected flowers may spring up before our very eyes.

Hope and Despair in India

GEORGE FERNANDES

All of you are aware of contemporary Indian history. The World Council of Churches (WCC) was to play a notable part in that history. I must mention Dr M. M. Thomas (former moderator of the Central Committee of the WCC) here. It was in this city of Bangalore that in August/September 1975 I was to meet him, always under cover of darkness, to exchange notes with him, to be briefed by him, and to interact with him in a common struggle to restore democracy in this country.

The Nairobi Assembly was then a few months away, and I was aware of the work the WCC was doing from Switzerland, the work that helped us in our movement. Some of the letters which the WCC sent to the authorities in India were a source of great strength to all of us who were fighting underground. When Rev. M. A. Thomas (director of the Ecumenical Christian Centre in Whitefield) mentioned to me some months ago about this meeting, perhaps the most compelling reason which prompted me to agree to spend this afternoon here with all of you was the role that the WCC played in the struggle we went through to restore freedom and democracy in India.

In March 1977, after 20 months of struggle, the people of India achieved what was till then considered impossible. In fact, I was one of those who believed that it was impossible, because never before in history had a people voted out an autocratic or authoritarian regime. It happened for the first time. Some of us were committed to overthrowing the authoritarian regime by any means. A few days ago in Parliament we were discussing *khadi,* the hand spun and hand-woven cloth we wear in this country, and Mahatma Gandhi's philosophy. Someone from the opposition, which 16 months ago was the ruling party, said that a man who operated with dynamite during 12 months of the Emergency when he

•Mr Fernandes is Minister for Industries in the Government of India. This is his address to the Faith an Order Commission at its meeting in Whitefield, Bangalore, India, on 18 August, 1978, transcribed from a tape recording and edited.

40

was underground had no right to speak about Gandhi who was the apostle of non-violence. My only reply was that, in order to overthrow any fascist regime, all means were justified. Gandhi himself said: "I shall risk violence a thousand times, rather than risk the emasculation of any race." But we went through this exercise, violent on the part of some, non-violent on the part of many others.

Some 250,000 people were imprisoned during those 20 months — more than the population of quite a few countries in the world. But every year we produce a nation of the size of Australia or Canada, about 30 million. And finally in March last year, through the ballot, the people succeeded in restoring democracy and the values for which another generation of my countrymen and women had fought under Gandhi's leadership — the democratic values, and along with it certain spiritual values. As a government, I believe that our task is not only to govern in the sense of looking after the economy, managing the politics of the country and generally administering the country; we also have the task of protecting and preserving the democratic values and freedoms. And it is my belief today that if anything should happen to the party which the people of this country returned to power, it would be disastrous for the people. Therefore, even when one tries to reconcile, one has also to fight. There is a struggle even in the effort of reconciliation. This is the point we have just been discussing before my speech — the whole concept of hope which is the theme of your meeting.

The depth of poverty in India

I am not qualified nor competent to speak on subjects of philosophy or theology. I left the seminary 30 years ago when I was studying for the priesthood. I was born in a Roman Catholic family in Mangalore, about 250 miles west of Bangalore. I studied in this city from 1946 to 1948 at St Peter's Seminary. I was disillusioned, because there was a lot of difference between precept and practice where the Church was concerned. The Church said: "The priest is an *alter Christus.*" But somehow the life of the priest was nowhere near the life of a *Christus.* And this created a problem for me, a personal one which no one could help me resolve at that time. The only course open to me then was to leave the seminary voluntarily. So I am not competent to discuss or to speak on the philosophical or theological aspects of the question that you are discussing here. I know you are all distinguished people, and I know the learning and the experience which you are applying to this subject. But we were discussing hope in another sense, in the sense that someone's hope is somebody else's despair. The hope of the nations of the north is the despair of the nations of the south. For the last five years, the North-South dialogue has been going on, and someone's hope is someone else's despair.

I do not want to discuss wide economic questions. I don't think you would have the taste for that kind of discussion either. But I would certainly like to present some of the problems we face today, what our hopes and aspirations are. What is it that we are trying to do in this country, and why is it that we need today to try to reconcile and not divide?

We have been a free country for 31 years now, for India became free in 1947. We inherited a devastated economy. We inherited a nation which had a political unity of sorts, but which had been robbed of most of its economic strength over 150 years. In the last 31 years, we pursued a certain pattern or system of reconstructing our country. People like me were not reconciled to that pattern or system. We opposed it. We believe that the pattern which was followed was not solving the problems, but in fact was creating them. For instance, on 15 August 1947, India had 350 million people. In 1977, 30 years later, India had 420 million illiterates living below the poverty line. And what is the poverty line in India?

I remember one of those — I would not call it a debate, because the then Prime Minister never debated these issues, but I certainly remember entering into an argument in 1974 (I was in prison at that time also), when the then Prime Minister got on to a discussion on poverty and said that there was poverty in the United States of America also, and so no one should complain about poverty in India. I was to tell her that the poverty in the USA was at a certain level: whether one should have one car or two, or whether one should have a holiday or not. But of course, there is poverty in the United States of America. The people are deprived socially and economically; there are slums and there are problems. But equating the poverty in the USA with the poverty in my country is not merely a demonstration of ignorance, but also a vulgar exercise, because poverty in my country means, with the present value of the rupee being what it is, not having even Rs 2.50 to spend per day. Now, Rs 2.50 means two bottles of soft drink, as the carbonated drinks cost Rs 1.25 or 1.30. In an ordinary roadside café, it would also mean three cups of tea. Or at best four cups. In a posh restaurant it would not fetch even half a cup of tea. That is the size of poverty in my country. I am not trying to frighten you. But I want people to understand the problems and what our hopes are in regard to the resolution of these problems.

That is perhaps the size of our problems — that we have 420 million who live below the poverty line. In the abstract, from a distance, it does not make much sense, but when you get down to the personal level where you start interacting with the people, where you start dealing with their problems, the size and magnitude of this problem overwhelms you sometimes.

I have been returned, for instance, to the Indian Parliament from a constituency north of Bihar called Muzzafarpur. Half of it has been under water for a fortnight. My constituency has 1,200,000 people, and there are 650,000 voters, of whom 396,000 voted for me while I was still in prison. I was released from prison and 48 hours later I was elected. Muzzafarpur has 650 villages. Of the 650 villages, 350 have no linking roads of any sort, not even a bullock-cart track, no drinking water facilities, no wells. Now this is just to concretize this poverty of 420 million people not affording Rs 2.50 per day.

Unemployment despite planning

At another level, the problem is unemployment. We have at the moment 40 million able-bodied people who want to work, but have none. We have gone through five five-year plans and three one-year plans in 28 years of highly centralized planning, during which we spent 100,000 crores of rupees (1 crore = 10 million) in developmental activities. And at the end of it all, you have 40 million unemployed. This year, another six million will be joining the queue for employment. We fought against this. Well, we have a planning commission of which the Prime Minister is invariably the chairperson. Ever since the planning commission was set up in 1947, it has been located in what is known as *Yojana Bhavan. Yojana* in Hindu means planning; so it is the planning house, with able, intelligent, patriotic men and women. But we still do not have a woman member in our commission. This commission has worked over the years and at the end of every five years it has successfully created more unemployment. This is not to say that factories did not go up. Of course they did. Bangalore, where industry is concerned, is the fastest growing city in our country. More industry has come up here in the last 20 years than perhaps to any other city in the country. Bombay was saturated long ago. We have in Bangalore a factory which produces modern aircraft. We have a telephone industry here which produces all the telephone equipment the country needs and some for export. We have the Hindustan Machine Tools which is one of the ten largest machine tool companies in the world, and exports machine tools to such countries as Switzerland and the USA. We have a great number of other large and small industries here.

So we did set up factories. There was investment in the rural and urban areas. But somewhere along the line, the thinking was that investment is for the sake of investment. People never mattered. If the whole concept of planning is to solve the problem of unemployment and other problems of the people, then the individual becomes the centre of attention. When people are not the centre of developmental activities, you set up the factories and in the process you create more unemployment.

Any solution not related to the problem of poverty or of unemployment was no solution. In fact, if anything, the problem was aggravated. That is why I said that compared with 350 million people in 1947, we now have 420 million below the poverty line, who are utterly, totally illiterate. They are educated, but they are illiterate. There are large numbers of

43

literates, but they are totally uneducated. It is these illiterates who restored democracy in this country, while the educated sang songs in favour of the dictatorship and justified it inside and outside. And that is why I was to tell people in Europe a month after I came out of prison, at a meeting of the leaders of the socialist parties of the world at Amsterdam, that a lot of people were led to believe in Europe and elsewhere that freedom and bread do not go together. That is what even the erstwhile rulers of my country tried to propagate inside and outside the country, that freedom and bread do not go together. But it is those people who had neither freedom nor bread who finally demonstrated that freedom and bread are equally important and that they must go together.

The point is that, over the years, first they denied bread, then they denied freedom also. Today, we are concerned with these problems. I do not want to go into the further micro levels of these problems. It is not important. But the mere fact that there is this colossal poverty, that there is this colossal unemployment, and that these are the problems any government of this country must deal with, is where our hopes are centred.

More jobs needed in rural areas

I would like to mention one or two wider issues. We need to create jobs very fast. In fact, my party before it was returned to power, told the people that we shall create jobs for 100 million people in the next 10 years, that is 10 million jobs a year. We know that these jobs need to be created where the people are, not with a conventional concept of industrialization. We need to create these jobs in agriculture, in small industries, in cottage industries in rural industries.

The new thrust is to move away from the cities, away from the machines and into the rural areas. One of the positive decisions we took among many others was to freeze the capacity of our organized textile industry. We have 280 composite mills which produce cloth in India. There are some right here in Bangalore. We have about 690 textile mills, of which 280 are composite and the rest are spinning mills. But where the loomage is concerned, we have frozen the capacity and have decided, as a matter of policy, that from now on there shall be no additional loomage in the textile sector. What we have in the way of mills and power looms, we operate to optimum capacity and efficiency, but no more looms. We need much more cloth than we are now using; our per capita use for last year was 12.5 metres per annum, which is what most of us have on our body at any given moment. Twelve years ago it was 16.5 metres, a steady decline year by year. Our plans are to increase it to 14.5 metres in five years, and increase it still further. The looms will be in the rural areas, and they will be hand looms, not power looms, not in the automatic mill sector, not machine-spun cloth, but hand-woven.

44

We have at the present time also hand-spun and hand-woven cloth. But it is not much really. I refer to this because ultimately in this world we have to depend on trade. In the last 12 months, we have been trying to persuade the countries of the European Economic Community and the USA to buy some of our hand-loom cloth. There is so much protectionism; they are so much concerned primarily with their industry and also with their investments in industry in Singapore and Hong Kong that their hope has become our despair.

We have 10 million people employed in the hand-loom sector in our country; that means 50 million mouths. We need to expand this, because 80% of our unemployment is in the rural areas, since 80% of India lives there. So we intend to create jobs in the rural regions. We do not want to create any more in cities. They are a social liability, among other things. When I say this, I am not talking only of pollution or crime. When I was at school, I used to take pride in that Bombay was the fourth or fifth largest city in the world. I would now like to dismantle Bombay as soon as possible, and send people out there where the green is, where life is, and not one maddening race.

We need a market outside

So in the villages where the traditional weavers lost their jobs — for generations they have been denied their bread and butter — we want to recreate these jobs out there. But we need a market; the domestic market is there, but we need also a foreign market. We are running into trouble, because someone's hope is someone else's despair. We tried to persuade the president of the USA when he was here. We tried to persuade the EEC, and almost every Prime Minister in Europe. I went to Luxembourg, visited all the capitals of Europe and said: "Please, we have only 4% of the European market. Only 4%..." Out of a total import of cloth and garments into Europe, India, which has 10 million weavers and spinners in the rural areas, has only 4% of the market. Hong Kong, with a population of three million, has 40% of the European market for cloth and garments. India has 10 million weavers — the people who live on weaving and looming number 50 million, and we have only 4% of the European market. Singapore has 30%, South Korea has the rest.

The reason is European money is invested in these areas. European capital is free of all the tax problems, all the tariff problems of the home countries. It goes out, produces cloth and brings it back to Europe. The money, of course, can be spent anywhere. And here we are: 630 million people this year and 643 next year, with 50 million mouths depending only on hand looms, wanting a slightly larger share in the European market, wanting to live on our own. I am not talking of aid, assistance or grants. I am talking of a fair chance, just a fair chance, for India which produces the most beautiful garments and cloth. I would

45

in fact suggest that you visit some of our textile centres in the city or elsewhere in the country if you have an opportunity.

This is the problem and this is how our hope is related to our problems. This is where I thought some of you could help us, by relating our hopes to the hopes of people elsewhere and perhaps trying to reconcile them – reconcile, not in terms of the abstract contradictions, but in terms of the concrete problems that we have at all levels. I believe that these are problems whose solutions are not merely related to what we are going to do in terms of our trade and our relations with other countries. I also believe that these are problems whose solution will have to be found in creating a more just and equitable society in our own country. This is a much bigger battle. It might be difficult to get into the European market, but it is more difficult to deal with the large houses which control not merely the wealth, but also the media. This is an uphill task, and I should know it as Minister of Industries of this country. Not that those who control the wealth own it themselves; they just control the wealth. Wealth is ultimately of the people. No industrialist of this country owns more than 2% of his assets. Ninety-eight per cent of the assets are public funds, most of them from the financial institutions, which are, again, publicly owned. But there is a concentration that has partly been responsible for this social and economic injustice one sees here; for the imbalance one sees in urban and rural areas; for the wide gulf between the rich and the poor; for the development of a culture which, for want of a better definition, I have been calling the "five-star culture", which has been trying to coexist with the vast slums in my country.

How one's hope is another's despair

There are little islands, little islets of affluence in this huge ocean called India, an ocean of poverty. The other day, I was engaged in a debate with a great man of my country called Baba Amte. He runs a leper asylum. He lives near Nagpur. He is a great man, a lawyer by discipline who defended the Hatch Timour victims at the time of Mahatma Gandhi; and then, I do not know what reasons motivated him, he went to work among the lepers and has spent a lifetime among them.

He was honoured recently by my country. He told me: "Poverty is vulgar." I disputed that in my country riches were vulgar, not just vulgar but obscene, because you have a five-star hotel where the standard tariff is Rs 490 for bed and breakfast only. The per capita income of my country last year was Rs 1,000 per annum. In other words, for one night's bed, breakfast and a meal, and perhaps the cocktails that precede it, the cost would equal the per capita income of my country per annum. If that is not obscene, what is?

Our problem, then, is not only rooted in our relations within the context of the rest of the world, the North and South, the rich and the poor,

46

but must also be seen in terms of the need to reconcile these contradictions within my own country. And this is a big fight, much bigger than taking on the trade and the tariff and the protectionist policies of others. It is easier there; it is more difficult here. But that is a part of the struggle and that is again where hope and despair are constantly at war. On both sides there is hope, except that one's hope is the other person's despair.

I hope, and I really want to hope, that all of us together in this country and outside who are concerned with social values (call them Christian values if you wish; we are at the Ecumenical Christian Centre where we discuss not only in terms of Christian values, but also human values) will put our heads together, not at the abstract, but at the concrete level, to realize those values.

A problem of contradictions

This is not a battle of "isms"; not a battle of the East and the West. But there are contradictions, the primary contradiction being between the rich and the poor, between the haves and have-nots, between the five-star hotel and the slum. This is the fundamental and primary contradiction where one man's hope of making a fast buck is the other man's despair of being forever condemned to a life of poverty. This is the fight in which I am involved today as a member of the government. If we run into political crises sometimes, and try to keep things still going, and still cling to hope, it is because of the size of this problem. We have been through this experiment in development for 30 long years, and that experiment has brought us to where we are. I do not want to see a situation where bread has to be denied again, which will lead to freedom being denied. For once, it is not a fight *against* something. It is a fight *for* something. That is where I hope the world will also try to understand what we are going through.

In the plane on my way to Bangalore, I was reading a talk by Dr Bruno Kreisky, my very dear friend, who is partly responsible for keeping me alive today. The day they arrested me, 10 June 1976, in Calcutta in my hideout, someone in the police thought it proper to let the world know. So even before my country knew that I had been arrested — we had a censorship of the kind which was never witnessed in the world, at least in the so-called free world — the rest of the world knew. Three men sent a cable to the lady who was then in power: one was Willy Brandt, then Olaf Palme, who was then Prime Minister of Sweden, and the third was Bruno Kreisky. That cable which said in so many words: "If anything should happen to George Fernandes' life, we shall never forgive", that saved my life. I was reading Bruno Kreisky's speech on *détente,* which was sent to me last week and which he delivered in London last month. In it, he speaks of the 400 billion US dollars being spent in the current year alone on armaments. That is more than one billion dollars a day, or 1,000 crores of rupees a day.

My country's gross national product last year was only 850 billion dollars. Some of us have been telling the leaders of the world that we do not want to be whistling in the dark; we do not want to be idealists to a point where we look ridiculous. But we have been telling everyone in the world, particularly the countries that have the resources: "Why do you not earmark 2% of your gross national product for the development efforts in those countries where there is great poverty? Why not use your technology, your know-how, for developmental activities? Why not look at the world as a place where at least on certain fundamental issues there can be no division? It is not enough to say that freedom is indivisible. If we believe that, then there can be no division in tackling the problems of poverty, unemployment, ignorance which have been accumulating for decades, if not for centuries."

Our hopes and outside happenings intertwined

But somehow these words make no sense. The United Nations is one of those places where I suppose everyone acts in a certain ritualistic manner, where you have your say and set your sights perhaps in the smoking rooms. But in terms of coming to grips with those problems, in terms of creating a better world where someone's hope does not become someone else's despair, one does not really see anything substantial happening. If I am making this comment and this observation, it is because I am in a hurry. We are in a hurry because we also know what it can mean to the world if some of us *lose*. If we lose this fight against poverty, against the colossal problems that plague us here in this country and elsewhere in the world, in the countries of Africa, in the other countries of South East Asia, in parts of Latin America, then I do not know who is going to survive. I do not want to sound hopeless; I am full of hope; I am an optimist. I am only trying to present and to put into focus some of the problems that we face, to say what our hopes are and how the solution to our problems and the attainment of our hopes are invariably intertwined with what happens elsewhere in the world. I refuse to accept that Christianity is only concerned with piety and the life after death. I refused to accept it 30 years ago in 1948, when I grappled with these problems alone, without anyone to help me. Finally, I decided to leave.

I therefore want to hope and to believe that the World Council of Churches and the entire Christian world, interacting with all those who are concerned with humankind and with its future, will be able to relate the fundamental values of Christian belief to the resolution of the problems and be concrete at the grass-roots.

Giving Account of Hope

Preparatory Statements
from Six Regions

1. Giving Account of the Hope in Africa

JOHN MBITI

Introduction

The spread of the Christian faith in Africa during the present century has become explosive. It is estimated that in 1900 there were about nine million Christians in Africa; and now in 1978 there are about 190 million Christians. Within this short span of time a great deal has happened to the total life and history of the continent. The southern two-thirds of Africa and Madagascar have become predominantly Christian, while the northern one-third remains predominantly Muslim. Many political, social, economic and technological changes have taken place and are continuing to shape the total life of the people.

In this complex situation, the "Giving Account of Christian Hope" in Africa is also complex. Many "case studies" could be used to illustrate what is happening. However, for our purposes, we shall take two concrete examples. They show the diversity of accounts, the determination of African Christians to give account of their hope, and even the readiness of the faithful to die for the sake of the Gospel. The first illustration comes from Zaire, a vast country at the centre of the continent. Since missionaries began to preach the Gospel – Roman Catholics in 1865 and Protestants in 1878 – 88% of the population has become Christian. The second illustration is a more continental expression of giving hope. It comes from the All Africa Conference of Churches. Titled "The Confession of Alexandria" it was issued in February 1976. Both accounts are very contemporary; they arise out of living concerns and experiences of Christians and churches in Africa today.

● The Rev. Dr John Mbiti is a professor in the Ecumenical Institute, Bossey, near Geneva.

I. "Our Faith in Jesus Christ: Declaration of the Episcopate of Zaire, 15 January 1975"

a) *The Background*

The Roman Catholic Bishops of Zaire held their 12th Plenary Assembly in Kinshasa, January 6-19, 1975. They produced two declarations, respectively on January 15 and January 16, 1975. The first declaration,[1] *Notre foi en Jésus-Christ* (Our Faith in Jesus Christ), is theological, while the second, *Déclaration de l'épiscopat face à la situation présente* (Declaration of the Episcopate regarding the present situation), concerns practical issues. Both documents are closely interrelated, and even overlap in words in some parts. Our concern here refers to the first Declaration which was signed by 47 bishops (of whom 39 were Zaireans and 8 expatriates).

The Declaration was prompted by a series of events brought about by political powers in Zaire. It was in response to a serious challenge of the Church by the state. Some examples will illustrate concretely the background which called for the bishops' declaration at that time. In October 1971, President Mobutu launched his campaign for "authenticity", which was then taken up by the political party in the country, Mouvement Populaire de la Révolution (MPR). "Authenticity" was now to become the political-cultural ideology in the country. Subsequent actions of the state were taken in reference to and support of this new ideology.

The Zaire government took the following measures, among many others: it nationalized the Catholic University, Louvanium (1971); suspended the church paper, *Afrique chrétienne* (January 1972); closed down John XXIII Major Seminary (January 1972); forced Christians to change their names which were not Zairean or African (February 1972); suppressed all religious youth organizations (November 1972); suppressed 31 confessional newspapers and periodicals and Roman Catholic Church radio and television services (February 1973); prohibited all meetings outside the political party (MPR) and its youth wing (April 1973); dissolved the Episcopal Assembly of Zaire (February 1973); suppressed the public holiday for the celebration of Christmas (June 1974); removed crucifixes from public places (1974), and so on. Some of these measures were later modified or revoked. (See further details in *Pro Mundi Vita Special Note 39*, 1975, pp. 2-16).

All these and other measures inevitably precipitated a major tension between the Roman Catholic Church in particular and the state. Matters reached a serious point when in December 1974 it was announced that

---

[1] For the full text see *Giving Account of the Hope Together*, Faith and Order Paper No. 86, Geneva: WCC, 1978, pp. 13-22.

52

religious education in all primary and secondary schools would be abolished and replaced by courses on civics, political education and traditional Zaire morals. At the end of the year, radicalization measures were taken, criticizing Zairean society as a whole and proposing practical steps to deal with the total life of the nation.

Furthermore, in December 1974 a prominent leader of the Protestant Church of Christ in Zaire made a statement that President Mobutu was a messiah. The Roman Catholic bishops felt it necessary to contradict that statement. In February 1975, President Mobutu himself publicly announced that he was not a messiah.

Briefly, this is the background against which the bishops had to make their declarations, in order to give some guidance to the Roman Catholic Church in particular and the Christians in general. They had no choice but to do it, and to do so in a theological style. The government measure had affected the Roman Catholic Church more seriously than they had other (Protestant) churches, and there had already arisen a personal conflict between President Mobutu and Cardinal Malula since 1967, leading to the temporary expulsion of the cardinal from his residence in 1972 and his being attacked in the press. The government considered the Roman Catholic Church to be a "state within the state", and as having a strongly colonial mentality. The church was not against authenticity as such. It only reacted against measures that threatened to injure its work and jeopardize its teachings.

"Authenticity" aims at recovering the values of Zairean traditional heritage, using them today, and adopting certain new ideas and modern techniques that are necessary in the world of today. It is an attempt to "decolonize" Zairean mentality; to instil "pride" in Zairean values; and to educate Zaireans on how to be genuinely (authentically) African (Zairean) in all spheres of life: religious, cultural, political, economic, and so on. In this understanding of the meaning, content and aims of "authenticity", the Church in Zaire felt able to go along with and support "authenticity". The clash came when the government began to enforce authenticity at all costs, and to encroach upon areas that the Church had considered to be its rights. Furthermore, in their zeal to propagate authenticity some of the government officials became rather excessive in their enthusiasm. For example, the State Commission of Political Affairs and Coordination of Party Activities said in a speech to directors of national education in December 1974: "... Our religion is based on the belief in God the creator and the cult of ancestors ... God has sent us a great prophet, our wondrous guide Mobutu Sese Seko ... He has delivered us from our mental alienation. He is teaching us how to love each other. This prophet is our liberator, our messiah, the one who has come to make all things new in Zaire. Jesus is the prophet of the Hebrews. He is dead. Christ is not alive. He called himself

53

God. Mobutu is not a god and he does not call himself God ... Our church is the Popular Movement of the Revolution. Its head is Mobutu, whom we respect as the Pope is respected. Authenticity is our law... Our gospel is Mobutism..." (*Pro Mundi Vita,* op. cit., p. 11).

At this point, the Church felt that propagators of authenticity were encroaching upon the person of Jesus Christ, and attacking a central belief of the Church. The bishops had to say something about this encroachment and attack ... hence the need arose for them to give account of their faith in Jesus Christ, in a particular situation and in respect of particular tendencies and fears.

b) *General Content of the Declaration*

The declaration is based strongly on the biblical foundation of the Christian faith. After a short preamble, it gives in 40 paragraphs the basis of the Christian faith in response to the actual situation in Zaire at that time. It also alludes to the Zaire Constitution, thus adding support to its appeal and legality. In the preamble, the bishops affirm that it is their pastoral duty to exhort the people of God to "persevere in their faith", and to affirm their position of the Church of Zaire concerning its fundamental faith and its character within the universal Church. They do not wish to pose as a rival power to the State, but simply to serve those who believe in Jesus Christ.

They go on to make reference to the "lay character" (laïcité) of the state as proclaimed in the Constitution which, thus, does not impose any religion upon the citizens. On the one hand, the state has declared its intention to work on the principle of authenticity. Nevertheless these two principles have appeared to be working against religion, and particularly the Christian religion against which various measures have been taken. The Church, on the other hand, is not against authenticity; nor does authenticity exclude the universal salvationary action of Christ. Indeed, the Church itself has already been engaged in the process of research and revaluation of traditional Zairean culture.

In eight paragraphs devoted to faith in Jesus Christ, the bishops affirm that He is "God made man". The New Testament declares his divinity, and his pre-eminence in the history of salvation. "Christ is Lord, Head, Principle and Fullness"; in the divine wisdom Christ occupies a unique place, sitting at the right hand of God, and exalted above all creatures. The Lord Jesus is head of all things, before all things, and head of the Church. He is the Principle of creation, the revelation and the resurrection. Being the Principle of all things, He is also the end, the completion, and fullness of life and salvation. *"By reason of these prerogatives, we confess that the person and salvation act of Jesus concern all men. He is the unique Mediator between God and men (Heb. 9 : 15). He is also for us the ultimate reference. He is the Alpha and the Omega (Rev. 1 : 8).*

54

This is the most central part of the Declaration. It then goes on to reiterate in summary the Christian creeds, especially the "Apostles Creed", ending with the statement that "He is also the new Adam who has conquered sin and death in our world marked by universal deprivation".

The Declaration goes on to speak about faith in Jesus Christ and the ecclesiastical communion. Those who believe in Jesus form or constitute the new people of God, and they are not constituted by power parallel to temporal power. "Their raison d'être is their faith in Jesus Christ". There are, however, certain demands on the Christian life. "The African upon conversion to the Gospel, does not disown his authenticity. Among other things, this conversion to the Gospel is a completely free act". "Man is free before God to say yes or no". Faith in Christ demands sacrificing all for the kingdom of God, detachment from material things, entry through the narrow gate, vigilance, etc. "Christ's appeal is always real: 'Repent, for the kingdom of God is near' (Mt. 4:17). The Christian experience is an experience of suffering and of glory. It is a paschal experience (Phil. 3:10)".

The Christian finds in the faith in Christ a new approach to the world. "The intimate union with the Crucified, who is at the same time the glorified Lord, having conquered the world (John 16:33), permits us an openness to the world which is not nourished from ideologies or illusions, but which equally desregards resignation and despair". "Christian ethic is, above all, an imitation of Christ, and therefore, in the last account, an acceptance of the Cross ... This cross guides the Christian to glory (Phil. 3:10-21)".

The Declaration makes the following conclusions. "If the laicity is a strict right of the state, religious liberty is likewise a strict right of individuals and communities". The principle of authenticity "is an important factor and a positive broadening in view of enriching the Church". The bishops reiterate their recognition of Jesus Christ as head of the universe, the unique Mediator and his lordship as being over all and without end. "The Church, the community of those who believe in Jesus Christ, is not a state within the state, it is not a rival power, it is not a pressure group, but it exists only by its faith and it is organized only to serve God and the nation." Faith is God's gift; and this faith in Christ "is not the negation of the identity of the believer; it is its promotion". This faith is personal and freely accepted but also "faith in Jesus Christ is equally a communal engagement. Nobody is saved alone. We are in solidarity and have responsibility of one to the others before God". The bishops caution against "confounding faith with doctrinal formulation, faith with culture, that is to say, the modes of life, of thought and behaviour in which a civilization has been able to incarnate its faith." They end with an appeal, in the words of St Paul, for the Christians (both priest, members of religious orders and lay persons), to take heed to themselves and their teaching (I Tim. 4:16).

c) *Concluding Comments*

This Declaration is extremely specific in terms of time, place and content. It is addressed to the situation in Zaire, in view of a series of events that were still very much fresh in the minds of the Christians, and genuine fears about what lay ahead of them. We have given the long background and content of the document because most readers will not be fully informed about these events.

The Declaration is specifically concerned with affirming a particular christology and a particular ecclesiology in answer to the situation that existed in Zaire at that time. In a classical and biblical style, the Declaration reaffirms faith in Jesus Christ and his supremacy over all things and all powers. Jesus Christ is supreme, Chief, Lord, principle of creation, raised from the dead and seated on the right hand of God. A lot of New Testament passages are quoted or mentioned in support of the nature and position of Jesus Christ. A lot of theological terminology is used for the same purpose. Christians will understand some of this language, but opponents of the Church are unlikely to understand it so as to challenge the affirmation of the Declaration. The bishops rightly use the Scriptures not only to support and justify their claims, but as an unchallengeable weapon of protection for what they say and what the Church believes. It is, in effect, the New Testament speaking to the situation (and not the bishops as such, who could be prosecuted or persecuted.

This appeal to the Scriptures will no doubt encourage greater use of the Bible in Christian circles, and hence a more biblically directed process of "giving account" of the Christian hope and faith. It is remarkable that this Roman Catholic declaration is so strongly biblical (New Testament) and so much less an appeal to the authority or tradition of the Church as such. This makes the Declaration the more ecumenical in its basis and appeal.

While acknowledging Jesus Christ as Lord and supreme, the Declaration does not imply to deny the authority and reality of the state. But Jesus Christ is supreme over state powers and leadership. It could be argued that in challenging the Church so seriously, the state in fact shook up the Church to take more seriously its local setting and to reexamine the fundamentals of its beliefs. The state forced the Church to "give account" of its hope and faith before a joint cultural revolution and political ideology.

The Declaration reaffirms the reality and nature of the Church, particularly in view of the political statement which had asserted "the Popular Movement of the Revolution" to be the "church" of the nation. The true Church is made up of those who have faith in Jesus Christ, it is both local and universal, and its head is Jesus Christ. The bishops appeal or reaffirm the faith of the Church as proclaimed by Christians through the creeds, since this is a catholic (universal) faith. Nevertheless, these members of the Church are not alienated from their roots, or nation; on the contrary, they are reaffirmed and participate fully in the life of the nation. Christian faith puts its own demands on its adherents. Authenticity is not the problem for Christians. Therefore the Church is not opposed to authenticity.

In stating that the Church is "not a pressure group" nor a "state within the state", perhaps the bishops may have given the wrong impression of yielding too readily the power of the institutional Church. As long as the Church, which is the community of those who have faith in Christ, takes particular views and stands on private or national issues, it is acting as pressure group". This reality belongs to its prophetic ministry and should not be denied for the sake of appeasing the secular powers. The Declaration avoids confronting political matters by saying that the Church is not a rival power to the state. In reality the Church is a power — whether rival, parallel, conforming or complementary, to the power of the state. Therefore, the Declaration could, or should, have articulated more clearly the nature, limitations and exercise of the power of the Church. In particular it should have spelled out clearly that the state has no power to regulate in the deep religious or spiritual dimension of man, and that this realm is the domain of the Church (or other religious powers). The state has no power to legislate what people may or may not believe in matters spiritual.

The Declaration resolves, perhaps too readily, the question of "authenticity", without giving clearer indications as to how Christians may judge what is "authentic" from what is false, the value of authenticity, and the methods employed to attain it, if it is attainable. Authenticity is a "catchword", a popular ideology that can easily divert attention from serious issues in the life of the nation. The Declaration cautions Christians to be open to the world but not to be nourished by "ideologies or illusions", but it does not indicate how one is to make a judgment about this danger. As such, while the Church is ready to embrace authenticity, that authenticity is defined and dished out by the State. The Church should define the nature and content of the authenticity which it opts to follow, and indicate the theological basis for its approach.

The closing paragraphs are important, though too brief if not elusive. They draw a distinction between faith and doctrinal formulation, faith and culture, faith and modes of life in which that faith is incarnated. This is the crux of the matter with regard to the authenticity campaign and the Church. The issue is not resolved by the Declaration, but the need to draw the distinction is felt and, hopefully, the distinction will be worked out in the life of the Church in Zaire.

The bishops' confession of "Our Faith in Jesus Christ" illustrates very clearly how the Church in one African country has responded to a cultural-political ideology which had begun to restrict the beliefs, teachings and activities of the Church. There is a universal pattern and applicability of this declaration, since it is a response to a situation that has been, and will continue to be, duplicated in the history of the Church. It is very significant that the Declaration is very strongly grounded in the Scriptures, that it reaffirms the centrality and supremacy of Jesus Christ, and reiterates the multi-dimensional nature of the Church as being both universal and local. The second Declaration from the same meeting of the Zaire bishops dealt with the service dimensions of the Church in Zaire, while this first statement was much more of a doctrinal confession of faith. The statement was very timely, and its effects will no doubt be felt for many years to come. Since then, a process of reconciliation between the Roman Catholic Church and the state has begun to develop, prompted no doubt by these declarations of the bishops among other acts of courage and wisdom by both Church and state leaders.

II. "The Confession of Alexandria", All Africa Conference of Churches, February 1976

a) *Introduction*

Having taken one example from a specific local situation, Zaire, we take now another example from a more continental expression of "Giving Account of the Hope in Africa". "The Confession of Alexandria" is concerned with major Christian values: justice, peace, liberation and human rights. It speaks for the Church in the whole continent, highlighting issues which have been of great concern for the All Africa Conference of Churches (AACC) in the last five years.

"The Confession of Alexandria" is a statement issued by the General Committee of the AACC at its meeting in Alexandria, Egypt, in February 1976.[2] The AACC represents 114 member churches in more than 30 African countries. It was inaugurated in 1963, and has held three General Assemblies. Its headquarters is in Nairobi, Kenya. This "Confession" was first read at St Mark's cathedral in Alexandria, during the course of the meeting, and then published in the *AACC Bulletin*, Vol. 9, No. 1, 1976, Nairobi.

The Confession is to be understood in the light of the third Assembly of the AACC in Lusaka, May 1974. The assembly engaged itself with, inter alia, the question of liberation, and appealed in its message to "the churches in Africa to allow Christ to set them free" from "theological

[2] For the full text see *Giving Account of the Hope Today*, Faith and Order Paper No. 86, Geneva: WCC, 1976, pp. 24-26.

conservatism ... denominationalism ... fear ... hypocrisy ... selfishness [and] easy dependence upon foreign money and men". The "Confession of Alexandria" came nearly two years later, and captured the mood of the times as well as the geographical region where the meeting took place. On the one hand the General Committee met on the layers of deep Christian history that went back to St Mark's evangelism in Egypt where he established the Church in 43 A.D. On the other hand the majority of the AACC member churches are largely young, with a brief history of less than one hundred years in Africa. The meeting of the General Committee made a significant link between this ancient Church in Egypt, with its rich traditions and liturgy, and the very young churches in other parts of Africa with all their contemporary problems and vitality. Thus, history and geography met at Alexandria, and the Confession is both a historical and geographical confession of faith.

b) *AACC as Africa's Ecumenical Voice*

The All Africa Conference of Churches is the main ecumenical fellowship or organization in Africa. Its present 114 members include the major families of the Church except the Roman Catholic Church. As an organization, the AACC is very representative of the Church in Africa. But obviously, it is difficult to draw the line between the views of the AACC as an organization, speaking through its officers and committee members, and the voice of the masses of the Christians in its member churches. In any international and interconfessional organization of this nature, the gap between the top echelon and the people in the parishes, can be both real and wide. To what extent such a gap might exist between the formulators of the Confession of Alexandria and the people in the parishes, is an open question which I cannot attempt to answer.

The Confession is made by "African Christians gathered from all parts of the continent". They have every reason to "praise God for having brought us together in Alexandria". The occasion helped to make the Church in Africa conscious of both its rich heritage and deep roots as witnessed by the long tradition and continuity of the Coptic Church in Egypt. Praise is a common element of Christian appreciation of the Gospel and the doings of God among his people. One hears African Christians praising and thanking God frequently in prayer, song and conversation.

The Confession continues, and reiterates four important elements of the Gospel: repentance, forgiveness, confession of faith and fellowship (koinonia) with the saints. In these elements the Confession speaks very universally, since they are essential contents of the Gospel, experienced throughout the world and at all times.

c) *Liberation*

Then the Confession turns to particular issues that relate to the contemporary problems in Africa, namely, "our current concern with issues
related to:

economic justice,
the total liberation of men and women from every form of oppression
and exploitation, and
peace in Africa".

Here lies the main weight of the Confession. Again these are universal
concerns, but they are put into the African context.

Liberation features strongly in the remaining half of the Confession.
This is very much in line with the Third Assembly of the AACC held in
1974. The Confession does not distinguish between "liberation" and
"freedom" and uses the two concepts synonymously. Theologically
there should be some distinction, even though the terms are related.
"Our commitment to the struggle for human liberation is one of the
ways we confess our faith in an Incarnate God", says the Confession.
This commitment is related to the passion of Jesus Christ: "through the
continuing work of Christ, God is charting his highway of freedom
(Isaiah 40: 3-5) from Alexandria to the Cape of Good Hope". The Confession says that Christians in Africa are "co-workers with all those
who are called by God to participate in his work".

A list of "our" sins is drawn up in the Confession — a list which is sometimes marred by rhetoric and self-chastisement, ending with "we are
sorry and ask God to forgive us". These African sins in the Confession
are very much related to "liberation", because they arise from the
assumption that "We have been too willing to rush off this highway
into dead-end paths" — the "highway of freedom from Alexandria to
the Cape". Forgiveness in this context is seen in terms of having "no
choice but to continue the struggle for the full liberation of all men and
women, and of their societies ... Liberation is therefore a CONTINU-
ING STRUGGLE" (*Lusaka 1974*).

The Confession of Alexandria is clearly an attempt to give account of
the Christian hope, within the political framework in Africa. It can
rightly be argued that the political issues of contemporary Africa are
so pressing that the Church cannot act as though it were deaf or blind
to them. But "liberation" is not the final word in giving account of the
Church's hope in Christ.

d) *Right Thing at the Right Time*

Giving account of the Christian hope in Africa is being carried out in a
complexity of situations and emphases. The Confession of Alexandria
has highlighted one or two of these emphases. PACLA made a wider

listing of issues, according to its own style. These emphases are not exclusive of others, and in local situations the Church finds itself drawn to highlight those issues which have an immediate urgency out of a wider agenda. As an illustration of this, we have already presented the case of Zaire and the question of "authenticity", being an attempt to respond to local and immediate agenda of the Church in Zaire. This illustration links up with the Confession of Alexandria.

The Confession of Alexandria has said one thing emphatically and at the right moment. This is the question of "liberation" in Africa, which is a burning issue today. But the question needs to be taken further by the local churches within their immediate contexts, since the Confession treated it "continentally". When it comes to other aspects of Christian presence in Africa, the Confession is either silent or not so emphatic. Those other aspects are also important, and they are venues through which an account of the Christian hope is given, often in practical terms. The Confession was an "official" proclamation of an organization of churches in Africa. Therefore it carries the weight of officialdom and formalization. The General Committee did not give directives for the Confession to be adopted or incorporated as part and parcel of the "confessions" of local congregations or member churches of the AACC. I do not know how the local and/or member churches of AACC reacted to the Confession, and what effect it has had on them. The Confession may not be a product of theological genius, but it is definitely one of political necessity. The Confession is definitely a product of political necessity. It is a clear declaration of the stand taken by the All Africa Conference of Churches in matters to do with "liberation" in Africa today: between Alexandria in the north and the Cape of Good Hope in the south, and between the Horn of Africa in the east and Cape Verde Islands in the west. But between these four points, there are also many other items on the agenda of churches in giving account of their Christian hope in Africa.

2. Reflections on Confessing the Faith in Asia

CHOAN-SENG SONG

How does a Christian church confess its faith in a society largely shaped and conditioned by other religions? What are the basic convictions underlying its witness to the Gospel? What should be the contents of its message to those who suffer from poverty, hunger and other forms of social and political malaise? What should its role be within a society and culture alien to the ethos, values, or belief-patterns taken for granted by Christians living in a society under centuries of Christian influence? For churches and Christians in Asian countries these are not new questions. They have had to wrestle with them in fact ever since the Gospel was introduced to Asian countries at different stages of their history. It is true to say, however, that in recent years these and similar questions are being raised with particular urgency and relevance. One of the basic reasons is to be found in the radical change of structures, conditions and contents of relationships which govern nations and peoples of the world. Caught in this radical change, churches and Christians in Asia have had to reassess their relations with the churches in the West as well as their role in their own society. Inevitably this results in their understanding of the Christian faith and hope in ways quite different from what they were used to.

Many examples can be cited to illustrate this. Efforts towards "living" theology is one of the most obvious examples. The Christian Conference of Asia must be commended for its various programmes to engage churches and Christians in Asia in reflection and action which bear a direct relation to the life situations of Asia today. Its General Assembly in 1977 with the theme "Suffering and Hope in Asia" dealt in depth with this central concern. The Assembly did not produce a statement as such. Instead there were lively witnesses of those involved in struggles for hope in the midst of unfavourable situations. There were also testimonies of those engaged in testifying to the truth of the Gospel

---

• Dr Song in on the staff of Faith and Order, WCC, Geneva.

under pain of suffering. In short, churches and Christians in Asia have entered an era in which they must give their own accounts of faith and hope in faithfulness to the Gospel and in relation to the issues and problems which arise in their own nations and societies.

Obviously, the changed and changing situations and responses to the Gospel in these situations provide a common background for churches and Christians in Asia in their mission and witness. Against this common background, responses and witnesses may vary in different situations and under different circumstances. For our discussion and study, the following four examples are selected not because they are representative, typical or exhaustive of church situations in Asia in general, but rather because they illustrate how churches and Christians in Asia seek to be faithful witnesses to the Christian faith and hope in a given time and in a given context.

1. Confessing the Faith in Asia Today (1966)
2. The Confession of Faith of the Batak Church, Indonesia (1951)
3. Confession on the Responsibility of the United Church of Christ in Japan during World War II (1967)
4. Theological Declaration by Christian Ministers in the Republic of Korea (1973)

In analyzing and studying these documents, one may gain a better understanding of the continuing task of the churches in Asia today and also discover some implications for the Faith and Order Commission in its effort to arrive at a common account of the hope that is in us.

I. Confessing the Faith in Asia Today

In 1966 the East Asia Christian Conference (EACC) — now called the Christian Conference of Asia (CCA) — convened a Faith and Order Consultation in Hong Kong on the theme: Confessing the Faith in Asia Today.[1] Its chief purpose was to try to understand and articulate the Christian faith in contemporary Asia. "Asia Today" was the main setting for confessing the faith. The focus of the Consultation therefore was set on the Gospel become flesh in Asian time and in Asian space. This did not mean that the consultation considered the Asian setting to be more important than the Gospel itself. Far from it! It became clear in the course of the consultation that a confession of faith which does not address itself to specific issues and concerns is bound to be abstract, out of focus and thus lacking in convincing power.

This was a conviction which the consultation tried to articulate. Its report says in part: "To confess Jesus Christ is to acknowledge him in

---

[1] See *Giving Account of the Hope Together,* Faith and Order Paper No. 86, Geneva: WCC, 1978, pp. 25-34.

his Lordship as well as to point to the ways in which his Lordship is being exercised in the specific situations in which we confess him. What God has done, through Jesus Christ and in the Holy Spirit, has to be declared in relation to the work of the Holy Spirit in the hearts and minds of men as He seeks to bring them as persons and as communities into Christ's obedience. This means, for the churches in Asia, such an experience of their self-hood in Christ as will make them true messengers of the Gospel, and give them such a discernment of God's purpose and power in the world as will make their message contemporary."

What is stressed here is that the incarnation, the Word become flesh, must be the centre of the act of confessing the faith. Conformity to the traditions of the Church, adherence to creeds and confessions, sensitivity to doctrinal orthodoxy, and preservation of inherited patterns of the life and worship of the Church in the West become definitely secondary in comparison with this central importance of incarnating the Gospel in today's Asia. In addressing itself to this basic concern, the EACC Faith and Order Consultation in Hong Kong can be regarded as an important landmark in the history of the churches in Asia.

The report of the consultation is long. It is a far cry from being a succinct and systematic statement of faith. It is rather descriptive and discursive. Even when an affirmation of faith is made, the implications of the affirm-ation for "today's" situations are not forgotten. Since the entire report is too long for our discussion here, two of the most relevant sections are selected for our consideration: "Jesus Christ, the Confessor" and "The Criteria of Confession".

1. JESUS CHRIST, THE CONFESSOR

In "Jesus Christ, the Confessor", Jesus Christ is confessed as the New Person making it possible for a new community to come into being. The close relation between faith and community deserves our attention. Jesus Christ as the New Person creates new men and women not as isolated individuals but as members of a new community. This emphasis on the community character of the Christian faith and hope is an important one, especially in view of the fact that community has been the strongest basis of most Asian societies. It is in the life of community that new men and women in Christ must demonstrate the signs and fruits of their relationship with God and with their neighbours. Thus, the report refers to "all divisions of race and class, nation and culture, caste and language" as challenges to a new community made possible by Jesus Christ. On account of this, reconciliation is felt to be most important. Reconciliation ceases to be a nice theological idea and acquires a real and practical meaning, for true community is not possible without reconciliation.

It is at this point that confessing the faith turns into repenting of sin. The churches in Asia, states the report, "failed in such large measure to be the reconciling community in the world, failed so woefully even to demonstrate with any adequacy the power of the Gospel to unite us". A divided church is a counter-witness to the God of reconciliation and an obstacle to the formation of a new community. Confessing the faith is therefore not merely a matter of confessing it in right words and formulas, but more importantly, of bearing the fruits of unity in the service of a new community constituted both by Christians and those outside the Church.

Another striking thing about "Jesus Christ, the Confessor" is the recognition of hopelessness in Asian society on the one hand and affirmation of Jesus Christ as our hope sharing in this hopelessness on the other. There is no assumption that our hope in Jesus Christ can easily change hopelessness into hope. The dire situations of suffering which a large number of people in Asia have to face daily do not allow an easy escape from hopelessness. That is why the sharing of Jesus Christ as the hope in the hopelessness of people becomes extremely important. Hope without such sharing in hopelessness is a deceptive hope. There were times in the past in which such hope seemed to have worked. It was the hope preached by other-worldly Christianity. People in agony and suffering were diverted from their hard life to a hope in an abundant and glorious life in heaven. In contrast the report says: "We confess Jesus Christ sharing in the agony of this predicament in which men are, announcing to them the sure and certain hope that is in him who bore our humanity, lived our life and died our death..." Identification with suffering people through Jesus Christ — this is what makes confessing the faith credible and convincing. Thus, in a true sense, the 1966 consultation already anticipated the 1977 General Assembly of the CCA which focused on the problem of suffering and hope in Asia.

2. THE CRITERIA OF CONFESSION

Since the consultation emphasized the relationship between the Gospel to be confessed and the Asian situations in which the confession is to be made, the problem of criteria of confession becomes important. For this reason, the consultation dealt with it, not as a general hermeneutical issue, but as a problem raised within the concrete situations in Asia.

The criteria of confession, as the consultation saw it, has to take into account two pressures, namely, "a pressure to conform to the world" and "a pressure to transform the world". Thus, criteria concerned has to do with both the biblical and theological foundations of the Christian faith, and the ways in which the Gospel is to be related to and practised in a certain situation.

First of all, Scripture is affirmed as the ground of the confession of the Christian faith, that is, the Scriptures of the Old and New Testaments. This at once relates the churches in Asia to the traditions of the churches outside Asia. This basic affirmation is however immediately qualified, or expanded rather, for its concrete application. Thus, the consultation went on to raise four questions to test, as it were, the validity of the faith derived from Scripture when applied to the Asian context: (a) Does our confession present the Gospel as the proclamation of events, of the deeds of God in history? (b) Does our confession make clear the relevance of the Gospel for people in Asia today? (c) Does our confession lead others to commitment to Christ? (d) Is our confession made in such a way as to establish others in the household of God?

Secondly, the criteria of confession has to do with the self-examination of the Church. Confession of faith must be an expression of the Church conscious of its own shortcomings and willing to listen to the voices that may not be familiar to it. This is the acknowledgment of the fact that the Bible is not a closed book which has ceased to speak afresh in Asia today. Confession of faith in this sense is something like a conversation which develops, takes new turns, reaches new heights or new depths as Christians seek to give witness to God's message in the contemporary world.

This leads to the third criteria which the consultation states as follows: the Faith we confess must be relevant to the people of Asia today. The word "relevance" is often misunderstood when it is used to describe the relationship between the Gospel and the world. It does not have to mean accommodation or compromise. It means primarily "related to", or "directed to". The faith is not confessed in a vacuum. It has to be confessed in a concrete life situation. What then could be more natural than to say that confession of faith must be "related to" or "directed to" that particular situation or particular people? Situations are of necessity many and varied and in the report of the consultation three areas are mentioned: nature, society and religions. It is the issues related to religions that engaged most the thought and effort of the consultation. It is clear that the way in which the Christian Gospel is to be related to other religions in Asia is one of the most difficult and yet most urgent issues facing Asian Christians today. "... the confession of faith in Asia", says the report, "is also a confession made to people ["men" in the report] who live by the many Asian faiths." What does this entail? The answer given by the consultation is: "Just as we emphasize that the individual Christian is a part of the total heritage and fellowship of the Church, we must recognize that people ["men" in the report] of other faiths share a similar solidarity. Therefore, an understanding of their systems of life and thought is essential for a relevant confession of the Gospel." This is an important statement. It not only urges Christians to have a better understanding of other systems of beliefs and ways of life, but requires them to apprehend the Gospel in a new light and communicate it in a new way.

A consideration such as this inevitably leads to the question of change or conversion. This is the fourth criteria mentioned in the report. "The faith we confess", says the report, "must have converting power." Where is this converting power to be manifested? It is to be manifested not so much in the people converted to Christianity as in the life of Christians who live the faith in "an act arising from and embodied in a life lived". The source of this converting power is Jesus Christ, but the power of this source must be expressed through Christians in the community they share with people of other faiths. Confessing the faith therefore is not just a verbal expression of some eternal and unchangeable truth. It is an act of life which shares in the despairs and hopes of the community and makes real the saving love of God in the midst of suffering.

II. The Confession of Faith of the Batak Church, Indonesia

The beginning of the Batak Protestant Christian Church in North Sumatra, Indonesia, can be traced to the work of the Rheinish Missionary Society in 1862. Progress was inevitably slow in the beginning, but a strong mass movement into Christianity began in 1883, and for twenty years the evangelization of the Toba Bataks proceeded rapidly. As a result, the Church became one of the most prominent institutions in Batak society and Toba Batak came to be identified with Christianity. In 1971, the Batak Protestant Christian Church claimed a membership of 916,000, the largest Christian community in Indonesia. Naturally the Batak Church has played an important role in Indonesia, not only in the life of the Church, but also in society as a whole.

The Confession of Faith of the Batak Church[2] was formulated by a commission of its own theologians and declared by the Synod of the Batak Church in 1951. Historically, the Confession was formulated in preparation for the Batak Church to join the Lutheran World Federation. The Church eventually became a member in 1953. This immediate purpose affected considerably the language, style and content of the Confession. But, on the other hand, it gave the Batak Church an occasion to reflect on its faith as it took a serious look at the challenges raised by other Christian bodies, by other religions such as Islam and animism, and by the nation as it was undergoing reconstruction in the aftermath of the Second World War. Here was a church which laboured very hard to articulate its faith in the midst of conflicting forces at work in its own nation and society.

The Confession begins with the acceptance of the three ecumenical creeds — the Apostles' Creed, the Nicene Creed and the Athanasian Creed — as the basis of its faith. In this way, the Confession establishes a historical continuity with the traditions of the Christian Church. Then in eighteen articles the Confession covers the main contents of the Christian faith —

---

[2] Op. cit., pp. 35-44.

the triune God, sin, salvation, church, sacraments, government, the last judgment, and so on. References to biblical passages are abundant. And after the statement of faith in each article "damnamus" follows on the one hand to reinforce the faith confessed and on the other to make the Christian stance clear in relation to specific issues. In the following, the Confession is summarized under the four headings: God, Salvation, the Church and other issues.

1. *The Triune God (articles 1-4)*

The trinitarian understanding of God forms the basis of this Confession. "Our God is one, and also triune", says the Confession, "namely, God the Father, God the Son, and God the Holy Spirit" (article 2). Creation redemption and sanctification are the work of this triune God. Thus, the belief that forces other than those of this God are also doing work of healing and redeeming in the world must be rejected. Especially, Jesus Christ as the sole mediator between God and man is affirmed very strongly. Implied in this rather formal statement of faith in God is the acceptance of the world as God's creation and recognition of the hand of God at work through medicine, improvement of human conditions, and redress of human sufferings.

2. *Sin and Salvation (articles 5-7)*

The strong affirmation of original sin in its classical form ("Since Adam and Eve fell into sin, sin has passed on to all their descendants" — article 6) was regarded as necessary due perhaps to the fact that outside the Christian church sin tended to be seen merely as moral failures and legal offences. In fact, these moral and legal offences come from the root of sin, namely, disobedience to God. Salvation has to do with this root of sin and can be achieved only through Jesus Christ (article 7). The Confession does not go into the problems such as freedom of will, relationship between God's saving grace and human responsibility, and other issues.

3. *The Church (articles 8-11)*

The understanding of the Church in the Confession is also very trinitarian in nature. The Church is said to be "the gathering of those who believe in Jesus Christ, who are called, gathered, sanctified, and preserved by God through the Holy Spirit" (article 8). Under this trinitarian rubric, stress is laid on Jesus Christ as the one who commands supreme authority in the Church. Thus, instead of "democracy", the Confession advocates "Christocracy" (article 8, 2). It also rejects the concept of a state church (article 8, 3) and substitution of ecclesiastical institution or organization for the Church itself (article 8, 4). In this way, the Confession seeks to stress the spiritual nature of the Church with Jesus Christ as its only head.

This concept of the Church is the basis for the understanding of the sacraments of baptism (including infant baptism) and Holy Communion (article 10), the threefold ministry of prophet, priest and king (article 9), and church order as "an instrument which regulates the life of the Church and gives it peace" (article 11). It is of interest to note that under church order (article 11), church festivals are mentioned with some restraint: "...the church festivals are to be celebrated, namely, the festivals of the birth, death, resurrection, and ascension of the Lord Jesus, and the feast of Pentecost. But it must be distinctly remembered that the faithful observance of all these cannot bring us the benefit of the forgiveness of sin." Perhaps this refers to the tendency in the Batak Church, and for that matter in most churches in Asia, to celebrate these festivals as if they were an end in themselves, chiefly as occasions for festivity, thus giving an impression to those outside the Church that Christians are not different from them.

4. *Others (articles 12-18)*

In the remaining articles (12-18) the Confession deals with certain issues which arise out of the practical life of Christians in the Church and in society. In article 12, the Confession states how the Church should view government. It recognizes government as having authority derived from God (Romans 13). But having rejected the notion of a state church earlier (article 8), the Confession urges Christians to make a right decision when conflict of authorities occurs. It quotes Acts 5:29 which says: "We ought to obey God rather than man." The implication here is that the relation between Church and state must be viewed in the tension between Romans 13 and Acts 5. It is important to note at this point that in Asia today Christians are being forced more and more to take Acts 5 as the basis of their confessing the faith in a politically repressive situation.

The other issues to which the Confession addresses itself are those of Sunday observance (article 13), food (article 14), remembrance of the dead (article 16). This reminds us of the fact that Paul had to deal with such issues in his letters. Concerning food, the Confession sees no need for Christians to observe prohibitions prescribed in Muslim laws or other traditions. In relation to the dead, both animistic teaching of the soul of the dead communicating with the living and the Roman Catholic teaching with regard to purgatory are regarded as not in keeping with the faith. The Confession asserts that in life and in death our hope comes from fellowship with God through Jesus Christ.

The Confession concludes with the article on the Last Judgment through which "the believers will go into everlasting life, but the unbelievers will go into everlasting torment".

This in brief is how the Batak Church confessed its faith in 1951. As has been pointed out already, the Confession is a strong affirmation of the Christian faith. At the same time it directed itself to the social and religious situations prevailing at the time when it was made. It served to strengthen the faith of Christians in the Batak Church; it drew a line between what the Batak Church considered to be in line with biblical teaching and what it regarded as misrepresenting or even contradicting the Christian faith. Further, the Confession was not without missionary concern. By making clear where the Church stands in relation to both theological and practical issues, it bore witness to God as judge and saviour.

Having said this, one needs to point out that there are a few things which require further reflection and thought. In the first place, in using highly compressed language to express the faith of the Batak Church, the language which needs to be contemporized, the Confession has left unsaid much that needs to be said. The question of freedom of will in relation to original sin, as has already been mentioned, is just one example.

This leads to a second observation that the strong language in which the Confession stated its disagreement with other theological and religious views will perhaps have to be modified if the Batak Church undertakes reformulation of its confession today. During the past two or three decades the climate of the religious situation in Asia has definitely shifted from that of confrontation to that of appreciation of mutual relatedness in community. In this changed situation, the Christian Church is called upon as never before to be an instrument of God's reconciling love. This does not mean that the question of truth is now to occupy a secondary place. But it does mean that the centre of the Christian truth is the love of God which is greater than the truth apprehended by human beings, even by Christians. Therefore a confession of faith should be an act of faith and love through which God's truth may manifest itself. As the Confession of the Batak Church stresses the centrality of Christ in its understanding of the Church, a confession of faith should be an expression of faith in Christ as one who is the ultimate judge of truths, even truths confessed by Christians.

Thirdly, one area which requires much probing is that of the relation of the Christian faith to other faiths. Most churches in Asia form a small minority in the midst of the huge community of Asian humanity under the influence of Buddhism, Hinduism, Confucianism or other traditional beliefs. Take Indonesia, for example. The Muslim population there is 100,120,000, 84% of the total population, while Christians, both Protestant and Roman Catholic, number 10,642,000, only 8.9%. In India, according to the 1971 statistics, the Hindu population is 453,292,086, 82.72% of the total, whereas Christians number 14,223,382, a mere 2.6%. In Japan, the country which has been most receptive to western influence, the Christian population consists of barely 1% of the total population of 111 million, while a new religion such as Soka Gakkai alone claimed 15 million adherents in 1972. These are just some examples. This does not mean, of course, that truth is on the side of numerical majority. It does mean, however, that the churches in Asia cannot go on confessing the faith and giving account of the hope as if these other faiths mattered little in the life of the people. Any reformulation of the Christian faith must therefore take this problem into serious consideration.

Fourthly and finally, the Confession of the Batak Church did not touch on the problem of suffering. No one can deny that suffering is a fact of life for millions of people in Asia. And suffering is going to be with them always. The Christian symbol of the cross points to the reality of suffering which God shares with humankind. It is well known that in Buddhism suffering occupies the central place. It is all the more important for the churches in Asia to confess God as the suffering God who identifies himself with the suffering humanity. Christian faith and hope must be rooted in this suffering God. Can one not say then that suffering must form an important part of a confession of the Christian faith? Is it not in suffering that all people seek to find salvation in communion with God and in fellowship with one another?

It has been said that "in a variety of ways the Batak Church has developed a life and style of its own. It is an ethnic church in which the Batak language, Batak *adat* (custom and law) and Batak identity play a strong role".[3] This implies that the Batak Church is in an excellent position to gain new insights into the Christian faith and into the world of cultures and religions surrounding it. Thus one may pose a question: What kind of confession of faith would the Batak Church formulate now, after 15 years, if it sought to express afresh its faith and hope in response to the ways of God's working in Indonesia today?

III. Confession on the Responsibility of the United Church of Christ in Japan during World War II

On Easter Sunday, 25 March, 1967, the United Church of Christ in Japan (the Kyodan) published a statement confessing its responsibility in Japan's involvement in the Second World War.[4] It is significant that the Kyodan chose Easter Sunday to make this particular public confession. Jesus Christ rose from the dead on Easter Sunday. It is the day when death is overcome by life. God's light begins to shine again in the

---

[3] Frank L. Cooley: *Indonesia: Church and Society*. New York: Friendship Press, 1968, p. 68.
[4] For the full text see *Giving Account of Hope in these Testing Times, Study Encounter*, Vol. XII, No. 1-2, Geneva: WCC, 1976, pp. 48-49.

darkness of the world. The Confession of the Kyodan was a confession of sin, failure and death. The fact that this confession took place on Easter Sunday must have meant that for the Kyodan the Confession was at the same time a confession of the forgiveness and life given by the risen Lord. The Confession was therefore one of the most important events in the life of the Kyodan in post-war Japan.

Historically, the Kyodan does not owe its existence to a response to the call for the unity of the Church. It was formed under the pressure of the war-government in 1941 just before the outbreak of the Pacific War. A full-scale war of aggression against China had begun in 1937. And the Japanese military government was about to carry its war plans into the Pacific. No less than a total mobilization of the whole nation was demanded for the execution of this cruel and monstrous war. The Christian churches were not exempted of course from this national mobilization. As has been pointed out, "the government's concept of the role of every religious organization was to serve unreservedly as an instrument to further the war effort. The organizations, their members and physical facilities were to be at the disposal of every local enterprise which might serve this purpose. The government's understanding of the role of religious teaching was primarily that it should strengthen popular conviction of military victory, affirm the moral rightness of the war".[5] Thus, a united church came into being as part of the government's mobilization effort. The course was then set for the Kyodan as the official Christian institution to cooperate with the government in the latter's policy and practice of war. This was the surrender of the Church to the power of Caesar. The burden of prophecy was laid on the shoulders of some individual Christians, notably those belonging to the non-Church movement. The Kyodan lost its sense of prophetic mission. The churches in Japan during this period could be aptly described as "churches in the valley of darkness".

When the terrible nightmare of the war ended in Japan's total defeat, the time of repentance for Christians, and particularly for the Kyodan, began. As one writer puts it: "Japanese Christians of middle age and older carry a heavy burden of memory. It could be called the memory of retreat from prophecy, and it is a part of the history of World War II. All Japanese Christians occasionally join in a confession of having failed to speak out against the military state when it was coming into being. Some Christians, notably among the holiness groups, did challenge the militarist sect, at the great cost of imprisonment and torture. Many Christians today, however, confess having a part in responsibility for suffering, terror and death in Asia".[6]

---

[5] Richard H. Drummond: *A History of Christianity in Japan.* Grand Rapids: William B. Eerdmans Publishing Company, 1971, p. 264.
[6] Charles H. Germany: *The Response of the Church in Changing Japan.* New York: Friendship Press, 1967, p. 163.

The Kyodan's Confession on Responsibility during World War II is a collective admission by Japanese Christians of the part of accomplices they played during the war. This in fact is the confession of sin. Sin for the Kyodan is no longer an abstract theological concept that needs to be analyzed and defined. The church's acquiescence in the act of war, its support for the military regime, its failure to speak out for peace, and its prayers for the victory of the war of aggression — all these are sins. All that the Kyodan can do is to repent these sins and ask for forgiveness. That is why the Confession is a prayer for forgiveness. In the words of the Confession:

> Indeed, as our nation committed errors we, as a Church, sinned with her. We neglected to perform our mission as a "watchman". Now, with deep pain in our heart, we confess this sin, seeking the forgiveness of our Lord, and from the churches and our brothers and sisters of the world, and in particular of Asian countries, and from the people of our own country.

This paragraph forms the centre of the short Confession. It was as if Lazarus had come back to life from death. With genuine repentance and forgiveness of sin the Kyodan seemed to have embarked on a new course of life. The Easter Sunday on which this Confession was issued will remain an entirely new Easter Sunday for the Kyodan and its member churches.

In actual fact, the Confession was not mere words. The Japanese Christians did demonstrate the fruits of repentance and forgiveness. A hostel was built in Tokyo for students from Indonesia. At the Assembly of the World Council of Churches in New Delhi in 1961, a Japanese colleague refused to be transferred from an extremely inadequate room because his next-door neighbour was a Filipino delegate. The churches in Japan have been making efforts to establish relationships of brotherhood and sisterhood in Christ with the churches in other parts of Asia.

At the same time, however, there has been a deep concern for the fact that in recent years the Kyodan has been involved in internal conflicts. It has come to be beset with disagreements. The causes of these conflicts and disagreements are many and complicated. Somehow the Kyodan has allowed itself to become enmeshed in doctrinal, political and social disputes and is unable to come to a common mind about them. In the meantime, Japan has grown into an economic super-power, making its impact felt all over the world. But this spectacular economic feat has not been achieved without great cost to the quality of life, traditional value systems, or human relationships. Surely all this must be a challenge to the Kyodan to become a sign of hope in present-day Japan, to utter a voice of hope for the Japanese people, and to be an instrument of meaning and purpose in a changing and confused society. It is beyond doubt that only a truly united church can undertake such mission, a mission which is perhaps more difficult than that which the Kyodan failed to fulfil during the war.

The Confession on Responsibility of the Kyodan during World War II concludes with the following paragraph:

> More than 20 years have passed since the war, and we are filled with anxiety, for our motherland seems unable to decide the course that we should follow; we are concerned lest she move in an undesirable direction due to the many pressures of today's turbulent problems. At this moment, so that the Kyodan can correctly accomplish its mission in Japan and the world, we seek God's help and guidance. In this way we look forward to tomorrow with humble determination.

The situation in Japan today definitely calls for an implementation of this determination. Perhaps the members of the Kyodan will be inspired to give account of their hope and faith in Japan today in the spirit of repentance and forgiveness expressed in the Confession in 1967. If such an account is to come into being and serve the Kyodan as a new rallying point for its mission, it will perhaps not be a confession of faith in a form of theological theses and doctrinal propositions. Rather, it might be an expression of the Kyodan's readiness to respond to the challenge to be a sign of hope in the society in Japan and in Asia today.

IV. Theological Declaration by Christian Ministers in the Republic of Korea

During the past few years the world's attention has been very much focused on internal political upheavals in South Korea. In October 1972, President Park Chung-hee consolidated his power by the institution of martial law. In this way, he was able to amass enormous power of government on his own person and installed himself above law, Constitution and the will of the people. Opposition is suppressed and political opponents are imprisoned. Some Christian leaders, both Protestant and Catholic, have struggled to become the voice of the silenced people. They speak out for justice and human rights, and above all, they declare that the absolute power in the hands of President Park is a power against God. Consequently, police and security agents have invaded the churches and those Christian leaders who had spoken out have been tried before the military court. Undaunted, Korean Christians continue their struggle for democracy and human rights.

The "Theological Declaration by Christian Ministers in the Republic of Korea"[7] is one of many confessions and expressions of faith and hope made in response to the critical situation in South Korea. Issued on 20 May 1973, the Declaration stresses the Christian faith as the basis for

---

[7] Op. cit., pp. 50-53.

the struggle for democracy, points out the evil effects of dictatorship for the life of the people and the nation, and calls for the solidarity and support of churches throughout the world.

The Declaration is not just an expression of conviction on the part of a few Christians. At the outset it boldly states that those making the Declaration do so "in the name of the Korean Christian community". The Declaration is therefore a corporate manifestation of faith and hope cherished deeply in the hearts of many Korean Christians.

Having made this basic stance clear, the Declaration immediately goes on to challenge President Park's consolidation of power as having "certain demonic consequences for the life of the Korean nation and people". The most demonic element, according to the Declaration, is found in betraying the people in their aspiration and longing for "a new humane community". How important the emergence of such a community to all Korean people is, is shown by recalling the hardships they had to go through during World War II and the tragic Korean War.

Of course, the repressive social and political situation caused by President Park's absolutization of power concerns *all* people in Korea. Then why should Christians feel compelled to speak out? What are the specific reasons that make them break their silence? Do they have reasons other than those which are more or less political? The Declaration gives the answer by listing the following reasons. Korean Christians feel compelled to speak out because (1) they should be faithful to the Word which commands them to speak the truth; (2) they hear the people in Korea calling upon God to deliver them from evil days; (3) they hear their fellow Christians who struggled against powers of evil in World War II and the Korean War calling them to resist evils today.

Surrounded by the Word of God, by clouds of witnesses in the history of the churches in Korea, and by the people with whom they live and suffer, Christians feel there is no alternative but to become the "mouthpiece" of the people. The situation is critical and the burden is heavy. They are thrust back on their faith for assurance, courage and help. In this way the Declaration becomes a strong and clear affirmation of the basic elements of the Christian faith, the faith which believes "in God as the Lord of history, in Jesus as the proclaimer of the Messianic Kingdom, and in the Spirit as one who moves vigorously among the people". This trinitarian God who acted in the past and is acting now in Korea is the centre of the faith expressed in the Declaration. This God is also the God of the future. Therefore the Declaration is not totally conditioned by the present situation, however critical it may be. This God who now vindicates the poor and the oppressed will be the God who is "working for the new creation of history and cosmos". The present and the future are thus brought together as Christians in Korea try to bear witness to the freedom and justice of God over against the absolutization of power by a human ruler.

If this is the God in whom they trust, what can hold them back from what needs to be said about the present situations of suffering and evil? In what it feels constrained to say, the Declaration is not general but specific, not implicit but explicit. It points out that the present dictatorship in Korea practises "rule by force and threat", destroys "freedom of conscience", controls people by "using systematic deception, manipulation and indoctrination", uses "sinister, inhuman and ruthlessly efficient means to destroy political opponents, intellectual critics and innocent people", creates conditions in which "the people, poor urban workers and rural peasants, are exploited". These are severe indictments against the Park regime. The Declaration thus uncovers the root-evils of the politics practised by a repressive government. It must have pricked the conscience of those in power. The result, however, was not repentance but retaliation. As mentioned already, a number of Christian leaders were arrested and sentenced to prison terms of varied length.

The conclusion of the Declaration is a moving statement on Jesus the Messiah who set people free by his own suffering. It is also an expression of a firm resolution to follow this Jesus. "We resolve", says the Declaration, "that we will follow the footsteps of our Lord, living among our oppressed and poor people, standing against political oppression, and participating in the transformation of history, for this is the only way to the Messianic Kingdom." What we see here is the Church struggling to be the Church of Christ, confessing its faith in words and in action.

SOME CONCLUSIONS

Discussion of these four documents from Asia leads to a few observations. It can be pointed out first of all that a confession of faith, even though often made in a highly formal and theological language such as the Confession of the Faith of the Batak Church, grows out of a specific context in which Christians are challenged to give account of their faith. Faith and context are therefore inseparable. Of course, faith is not a by-product of a context. But for the faith to have meaning in the life of the people, a contextual grasp and understanding of faith is a pressing necessity. Various efforts towards the so-called "living" theology in the Third World today testify to the importance of this necessity for doing theology. This will inevitably affect the language, manner of expression, and form of Christian discourse. The language and contents of the faith will become more "popularized", that is, there will be ongoing attempts for the churches and Christians to speak about and bear witness to the faith in the language, thought forms or culture patterns of the people.

Secondly, insofar as Asia is concerned, there are two outstanding issues which will increasingly engage churches and Christians in their life and work. These are the issues related to suffering and religions. This is not to minimize the importance of more ecclesiastically oriented issues such as unity, liturgy, systematic formulations of doctrines, and so on. But the growing tendency is for these ecclesiastically oriented issues to be considered in the light of human and religious problems which Christians have to share with their fellow Asians. On account of this, suffering and religions can be the two important points of entry for Christians and churches in their fresh reflection on the meaning of Christian faith and the mission of the Church in Asia. As has already been pointed out above, "Confessing the Faith in Asia Today" in 1966 set the course for the churches in Asia to rethink the life and work of the Church in relation to issues and challenges posed by suffering and plurality of religions. In fact, the Christian Conference of Asia has set its programmes and planned its course of action in this direction. It is thus to be expected that expressions of faith and hope in Asia will come to reflect more and more these two overriding concerns.

Thirdly, the "Confession on Responsibility of the Kyodan during World War II" shows how the churches in Asia, especially as a minority within a nation, are in a socially and politically vulnerable position. Confrontation of the "powerless" church and the "powerful" state in recent years in countries such as Korea, Taiwan or the Philippines, is evidence of this. But many signs and events strongly indicate that churches in Asia have gained strength despite their vulnerability. This is the case in Korea, for instance, where Christian leaders are arrested and imprisoned for speaking out against the absolutization of the ruling power. The "Theological Declaration by Christian Ministers" is an eloquent expression of this. In many ways, these churches have become suffering churches. Consequently, it is a matter of course therefore that accounts of the Christian faith and hope in Asia will of necessity be directed more and more to the issues of Church and state and demonstrate the social and political stance of the Church in repressive political situations.

Fourthly, Asia is far from being a homogeneous entity. In many ways it is very heterogeneous — culturally, socially and in religions. It is thus to be taken for granted that churches, their forms of life, their organizations and structures, their expressions of the faith, and so on, will reflect national and local differences and characteristics. But this does not mean that they will grow and develop away one from another. In fact, the opposite seems to be the case. In the midst of heterogeneity, they increasingly recognize that there are common concerns and problems for which they need each other's understanding and support. There is thus the possibility of a common language being developed to convey Christian convictions, to foster unity among churches and Christians, and to make visible their solidarity with their fellow Asians.

It would seem that a new ecumenical era in word and in action has arrived in Asia. One may foresee in this an emergence of a dynamic unity, bringing churches and Christians together in common witness to the vision of hope given in Jesus Christ.

3. Giving Account of the Hope That is in Us

A Contribution by the East European Members of the Faith and Order Commission

Introduction

At two conferences held in Geneva (10-14 December 1977 and 2-5 March 1978) we East European members of the Faith and Order Commission tried to consider precisely what the Christian message of hope consists of, in the context of the socialist countries of Eastern Europe today. The following pages are intended as a contribution to the "Giving Account of Hope" study which is to be dealt with again at the Faith and Order Commission meeting in Bangalore.

East European churches have contributed statements previously to this study. Two documents played an important role, for example, in the preparatory work for and the discussion at the Faith and Order Commission meeting in Accra in 1974 (both published in Accra preparatory paper No. 6). Firstly, the statement on "The Mission of the Church of Today", approved as a basis for discussion by the Synod of the Church of the (Czech) Brethren (CSSR) in 1973. This dealt, among other things, with the prophetic task of the Church, its presence in the world through prayer and service, and the Church as sign of the new creation, these themes being considered with specific reference to the context of socialist society. The second document was the 1974 contribution of a research group of the Ecumenical Committee of the Federation of the Evangelical Churches in the German Democratic Republic (GDR), dealing directly with the "Giving Account of Hope" theme. This document linked up with the "doctrinal discussions" between Lutheran and United churches in the GDR and considered three problem areas which are of special urgency in the context of socialist society: the question of God; society and the individual; and the congregation as brotherhood and community of service.

Following the Commission meeting in Accra, further contributions to the study have been produced in our churches in preparation for the Bangalore meeting. In addition, there is a whole series of documents in which fundamental statements have been made in our churches in recent years concerning the faith, hope and service of Christendom. All these texts formed part of the background material for our reflections.

In the rest of this paper we try to present a common account of the Christian hope in socialist society. General affirmations of this sort can obviously be made only with considerable caution and in quite a provisional way, since the situations in which the churches in Eastern Europe are challenged to witness and service differ in important respects. Not only are there marked differences in the actual form of socialist society in the different countries but the attitude of the churches also differs according to their origins and size.

Confessional differences are very important since they mean that concrete situations and Christian witness within them are tackled from a variety of standpoints. The fact that the confessional landscape of Eastern Europe is dominated by Orthodoxy makes the contribution of its churches of prime importance. Besides Orthodoxy, the views of the evangelical churches played a large part in our consultations. At certain points the following reflections reveal very clearly the resultant patterns of discussion. The Roman Catholic Church, the third partner in confessional discussions in Eastern Europe, was unfortunately not represented in our discussions, since there is no Roman Catholic from Eastern Europe among the members of the Faith and Order Commission.

In spite of the differences mentioned, we regard the common features of the social situation in our respective countries as substantial enough to justify common reflection and a joint statement within the context of an ecumenical "accounting for hope". Certainly our attempt is no more than a contribution to the continuing discussion. In many respects it is tentative and incomplete, an invitation to further discussion in our churches and with representatives of churches in non-socialist countries.

Our reflections fall into three parts. In the first part: "Our Christian Hope in Concrete Situations in Socialist Society", we try to show where the witness of Christian hope is especially required of us in socialist society. In the second part: "Particular Theological Emphases in our Account of Hope", we try to specify which particular fundamental theological problems are presented to us by the challenge described in the first part. The final part, "Our Contribution to an Ecumenical Account of Hope", will try to deal with questions which are put to us by Christians and churches of other countries and to emphasize our hope for the unity of Christianity.

1. Our Christian Hope in Concrete Situations in Socialist Society

1.1 Experience of God's Faithfulness

We give account of the hope that is in us as Christians in a socialist society. It is God himself in his faithfulness who enables us to offer this account of our hope. We feel the force of his promises at a time when hardly anyone would venture to hope on the basis of human prospects. Throughout a long period of radical and religious change, God has acknowledged his Church, opening up to it new freedom and offering it new opportunities to an extent which far exceeds our expectations. It is this faithfulness of God which is the basis of our hope. It is this that gives us confidence that in the future, too, despite all human prognostics, He will uphold his Church, secure for it the room it needs in order to live, send it forth to witness and serve, and awaken it to praise the name of the Lord. And it also leads us to ask ourselves whether we have yet seen clearly enough or dealt faithfully enough with the opportunities God has already created for us.

1.2 The Altered Situation of the Church

The situation in which we are called to give an account of the hope that is in us differs in many respects from that in which the Church existed before the socialist revolution and outside the socialist world.

(a) One consequence of the social and political revolution in the East European countries was the separation of Church and state and the placing of all churches on an equal footing. The churches lost their power and their privileges, together with the possibilities of influencing public life they once had in virtue of this privileged position. For some churches (for example, the Orthodox churches in Czechoslovakia and Poland, and the free churches) this revolution has meant the achievement of full and equal rights for the first time. Churches and Christians now live in a radically and systematically secularized society, sometimes referred to as a "post-Christian" society.

(b) This revolution challenged the churches in Eastern Europe to reflection and repentance. They learned and are learning to accept this challenge in the light of the Gospel of the crucified and risen Christ. Had the official representatives of our churches, had all Christians, been sufficiently engaged in the struggle for social and political justice? Had they not been far too deeply identified with the various rulers and consequently often unfaithful to their calling? Probing deeper, had they lived by the Gospel? Had they been credible witnesses of the love of Christ and of faith in Christ? Had Christians made a sufficiently positive and humane contribution to social institutions and relationships? Had they been bold enough in tackling problems and deficiencies in the life of society? Like the churches in the Third World, the churches and individual Christians in the socialist countries know that the Gospel has to a large extent been identified with the bourgeois, liberal view of society and with the bourgeois style of life. In part, therefore, the alienation of people from the Christian faith has certainly been caused by the failures of Christendom itself. Moreover, one important factor leading to the present shape of Eastern Europe was the Second World War, and this inevitably poses the question, in Germany for example, even for the churches, of their share in the responsibility for this calamity and all its consequences (in particular also for Germany itself). Such questions and thoughts continue to accompany the faith and life of our churches. We are continually faced with the question as to how far we practised then, and practise now, genuine *metanoia*.

(c) At the same time the churches have been and are still challenged to accept the altered situation as an opportunity for genuine renewal. They have been given the opportunity for new and intensive religious experiences; above all, for new forms and experiences of supportive religious fellowship. What was required was not a retreat within but new obedience to the task of missionary witness and service to man and society entrusted to the churches by their Lord. The challenge to Church and theology was to discover the essence of their proclamation in the Gospel and to interpret the Gospel in a new way. In many cases, churches and Christians found themselves being met with a new trust and confidence. The way, the attitude and the practice of love secured for them a new credibility. Churches and Christians learned not to let their lives be controlled by resentment or anxiety but to prove their Christian hope by putting their whole confidence in the Word of God, by practising love to all, and by engaging in the ministry of intercession. Even controversies over difficult questions had to be tackled in the spirit of love. We were required to learn all over again that God's promises hold good for the "little flock", that his strength is made perfect in weakness (II Cor. 19:9f), that God achieves his own victory by the way of the cross. The new equality of the churches also produced a new ecumenical situation rich in possibilities.

(d) It was not always easy for Christians and even for churches to accept this new situation. It sometimes produced despondency and fear and led people to ask: "Lord, where are you leading your Church?" Mistaken alliances and hopes of a former time made it necessary for us to undergo a process of education in which, in experiencing the cross, we were taught to comprehend the power of God, the God who raised Christ from the dead. We were taught to see the new situation more and more clearly as one full of hope, as an opportunity held out to us by God. So the churches in Eastern Europe learned the lesson that God grants us new life. This is the ground for our hope which constrains us again and again to pray: May God maintain his Christendom in this experience and in this hope!

1.3 The Challenge of Socialist Society

We have been challenged to give an account for our hope by the actual form of socialist society. For we do not live apart from, but are a part of this society. In other words, we share in everything which concerns it and we bear our share of the responsibility for its development. What are the possibilities of Christian witness in this situation? We shall try to answer this question by considering a few of the main characteristics of our society.

(a) In socialist society, people are furnished with the vital necessities, and sometimes a fair measure of prosperity, by human labour and organization. We recognize in this, even through the instrumentality of this society, the hand of the Creator who ensures life and blessings. But in this society people are also faced with problems which are sometimes very distressing. We are all agreed that the Christian hope opens our eyes to this, so as not to ignore deficiencies and problems in our society but to be prepared to overcome them to the best of our ability. Part of the programme of socialist society is the participation of all its citizens in the decision-making processes. We are resolved to cooperate in ensuring that this principle is implemented to the full at all levels, since we are convinced that this is vital for the development of our society. We are also resolved to fulfil our joint responsibility for the welfare of society by the ministry of intercession. We do this in the knowledge that our Christian hope is focused on a divine promise which far and away transcends even the best conceivable society and prevents us from looking for the fulfilment of our ultimate hopes in any social development within history.

(b) In socialist society, labour, achievement and consumption occupy an important place in the general consciousness and even in the official scale of values (although in different degrees in different countries). We as Christians know of the divine command to cultivate the world by our labour (Gen. 1:28), the dignity of labour, the satisfaction derived from real achievement, and the joy of reward. To us, people are co-workers with God and we therefore feel responsible for the well-being of our society. For us, too, labour is a way to self-fulfilment and we know that the fruits of the earth are accessible to us only through human labour. We, too, appreciate the importance of the right to work, therefore, which socialist society sets alongside the right to leisure and recreation as basic human rights. On the other hand, the Bible also teaches us that human labour is inseparable from effort and limitations (Gen. 3:19) and we know the pain caused by the fruitlessness of many struggles.

But we also attach great importance to the fact that human beings are more than they achieve or consume. We encounter this insight even among Marxists. We consider it very important that socialist society should seek to assimilate the positive cultural heritage of history, which also includes the Christian traditions. It is our hope that this will ultimately lead to the creation of new qualities of social life. As Christians we are convinced it is God's graciousness towards humans, apprehended in faith, which gives them their deepest value. The real attestation of their personhood, therefore, is something which they do not need to produce for themselves. We also discover this love of God in the love and friendship of other human beings who understand and accept us. This exonerates us and sets us free for self-fulfilment. We rediscover the value of thanksgiving, celebration, play and fellowship. These become for us signs of that which we cannot provide for ourselves and they substantiate our hope in a world which is not contructed by our own labours.

(c) As it understands itself, socialist society promotes peace in the international field, and this necessarily includes the deliberate adoption of political positions and, therefore, too, material and political opposition. This effort for peace and this hope of peace correspond to an ancient and fundamental Christian hope. We are reminded of the biblical promise addressed to the peacemakers (Matt. 5:9). The peace of which the Bible speaks is, of course, rooted ultimately in God's reconciliation with humanity and the reconciliation of human beings with one another which also includes respect for those whose opinions differ from our own and victory over hatred of others. The ending of all social and political injustice is also part and parcel of this peace.

Directed by our hope in the peace promised by God, we Christians will unite with all persons of goodwill and work tirelessly with them in all genuine efforts to maintain and establish earthly peace. This also has implications for the intercessions of the Church for the peace of the whole world and for the divine blessing on the world. Of special importance in this context is the fact that Marxist insights have opened our eyes to the part played by economic factors in the genesis of wars and international conflicts.

Inescapable as material and political controversies may be, we take care not to cast the political and ideological opponent in the devil's role. We strive to ensure that political controversy is conducted without enmity, in a spirit of mutual openness and attentiveness. We do our best to see that the political education of the young is conducted in a spirit of genuine understanding and reconciliation.

In all this, we are aware of the fact that all our efforts are provisional, all our insights imperfect, because we have the promise of a peace and we live by a reconciliation which will far transcend anything that can be initiated by human endeavour and which keeps alive in us a hope in the future of God beyond all our plans and dreams.

(d) Although religious freedom is guaranteed in the constitutions of socialist states, we are also challenged to account for the hope that is in us by the view, widely held in our society, that religion is a pernicious survival from a past age. Many Christians are often distressed and feel themselves threatened by this widespread attitude and by the kind of arguments about belief in God produced in the name of science, of human autonomy and in connection with the world's suffering and injustice. This challenges us in our families and in our congregations to reformulate the grounds for our hope and to interpret them anew in secular society.

On the other hand, even in the socialist world we discover signs of a new religious wave which has its counterparts in other parts of the world. It would certainly be overhasty and mistaken to invest our hopes in these new religious phenomena, which often also appear in distorted forms, especially since they frequently lead people away from the Christian faith. But it is surely impossible to avoid asking ourselves whether such phenomena may not indicate that there is no such thing as unadulterated secularism. In thoughtful people we also find a new and deeper probing of the dimension of mystery and profundity of the world and human life. Surely all this is an invitation to hope and trust that the truth of God revealed in Jesus Christ is finding its way once more into human hearts today and that it will there be discovered not as tutelage or illusion but as an enrichment.

2. Particular Theological Emphases in our Account of Hope

2.1 God's Mercy as the Basis and Substance of our Hope

(a) The character of society, of the system, the favour or the hostility of the government towards the Church — it is not by these things that our hope can be determined. This hope towers above the plains of history and is rooted in the resurrection of Jesus Christ, in the justifying mercy of God and in the divine promises. We have discovered this, and it is our constantly renewed experience, in the presence of the risen Lord in our congregations. It has not been and is not at all easy for us to put our whole trust in God's promises and to abandon all other established data, to devote ourselves to the service which looks for no reward or recognition. It often demands of us a readiness for suffering and sacrifice. But as we accept this road in penitence, we discover the liberating power of the cross as God's victory. In the light of the cross, we learn to live as the apostle Paul lived: "as sorrowful, yet always rejoicing; as poor, yet making many rich; as having nothing and yet possessing all things" (II Cor. 6:10).

(b) This hope and this life are the gift of the Holy Spirit which we receive anew again and again as we listen to God's word, as we pray, and, above all, as we partake of the eucharist. For us, life in the congregation is the place where our temptations are overcome and new horizons opened up to us. Our Orthodox brothers and sisters remind us that the operation of the Holy Spirit is universal; in its worship, therefore, the Church blesses and sanctifies all aspects of human life and the whole of creation.

The importance we attach to worship has often been seen as a necessity forced upon us by outward circumstances in the socialist countries. But we see that this emphasis on worship is rooted in the new understanding of the grounds of our hope. We rejoice that Christians in other parts of the world, who have also ventured with various "ecclesiological" experiments, have reached the same conclusion, namely, that the congregation and its life of worship are of central importance for the confession of our hope.

(c) God is the creator of human persons and has made them in his image. From this it also follows that in their essential being they are open towards and dependent upon God. Being religious is part of the human existence, whether they feel any religious need in themselves or not, whether they regard themselves as religious or not. This is not to say that through their religiousness they find their own way to God. But the Gospel touches them here and calls on them to respond. The Gospel is therefore a setting right and fulfilment of humanity. To deduce from this that the future of Christianity depends on the religious need of people, is to falsify hope. But it is legitimate for the Christian to hope that God has prepared the way for the Gospel in the religiousness of human beings and that the Church's labour of service is "not in vain in the Lord".

(d) The substance of our hope is the crucified, risen and coming Lord. The *parousia* of Jesus Christ towards which we move in eschatological hope with the world, unites all members of the Church in the prayer: "Come, Lord Jesus!"

2.2 The Eschatological Hope and Historical Hopes

(a) While as Christians throughout the whole world we share the one hope of Christ's coming, our historical hopes for our concrete situations today and tomorrow differ. We also have to ask ourselves whether our historical hopes are really related to the eschatological hope, and where we are projecting our own ideas and wishes into our hopes.

(b) In the gospels Christ speaks of the coming kingdom of God in parables. It is therefore impossible to translate the hope of the kingdom of God into political programmes or historical utopias. But the promises expressed in parables do not simply point beyond the world; they also relate Christ's eschatological coming to this world. The declaration that God "will wipe away all tears", for example, does not simply describe future blessedness but brings all who now weep because they are humiliated and oppressed, bewildered and desperate into the light of God's transfiguring *parousia*.

(c) Following a discussion between representatives of the Orthodox and Evangelical churches, we can describe the way in which the connection between the eschatological hope and our historical hopes is to be lived and acted on in practice as follows:

While in the Christian hope it is impossible to divorce the eschatological from the historical, we must distinguish between the two hopes. The Christian hope is based on the cross and resurrection of Jesus Christ and focuses on his return and the establishment of the kingdom by God alone. But, just as the kingdom of God has already "drawn near" (Mark 1:15) in Jesus Christ, so it is already present in the world today. It renews and transforms human beings and knits them together into a fellowship, especially in the Eucharist. Correspondingly, the Christian community establishes signs of hope in the coming kingdom: for example by its fellowship, by its ministry to the "least", the oppressed and the suffering, by its cooperation in social changes which benefit the weak and help to secure justice for the handicapped. Far from directing us away from the world, our eschatological hope strengthens our historical hopes for the world and enlists us in the service of God's creation. It is verified in the love to the least of Christ's brothers and sisters, who play a decisive role in the final judgment (Matt. 25:40).

2.3 Hope and Tradition

(a) On the basis of a discussion on tradition, memory and hope, theologians of the Orthodox and Evangelical churches are able to agree on the following statement: We remain certain of our hope as we call to mind the tradition of God's mighty deeds in Jesus Christ as authenticated for us in Holy Scripture and attested to us by the faith of the fathers. If we are to account for our hope we have to point to the promises communicated to us in the tradition. The reason for our hope is inseparable from the name of Jesus Christ risen from the dead and from his coming kingdom. By the operation of the Spirit, the kingdom and its promises become a present reality. This is the essence of the living tradition which continues in the Church from one generation to another. The promise of Christ's kingdom therefore carries the hope of the Church and Christians for themselves and for the world. Through all the changes of history it leads the Christian community into all truth (John 16:13).

(b) True tradition comes about as the remembrance (*anamnesis*) of what God has achieved in Jesus Christ for man's salvation. It thereby enters into believing fellowship with the fathers in the Church. But it does not remain there gazing fixedly at the past, as if it had to cling to an inert form of tradition, as if it were a keepsake. It could then become a "dead letter" which imprisons the Church in a "Babylonian captivity" and blinds it to the Spirit's continuing renewal and direction. In the case of true tradition, the remembrance (*anamnesis*) serves the continuing promise (John 14:25; 16:13) which leads to renewed hope. Where tradition is true and living, it is a matter of transmitting the flame. By the operation of the Spirit, the remembered tradition becomes a living hope for the present and future of the Church, of Christians, and of the world.

(c) The fruit of life based on the transmission of Christ's promises are historical forms of the Church in the world, historical forms of ministries, orders and institutions. These, too, are sometimes spoken of as the "tradition" of the Church. It is the tradition in historical form which must always be faithful to the apostolic tradition. In part it has been shaped by the historical and cultural environment into which the living Church once entered. Conversely, the tradition in historical form also reacts upon the environment and accompanies the Church's witness both as a blessing and as a burden. But Christ's promise that his Church will remain until the end of time (Matt. 16:18) is not a promise that the historical forms of the Church will continue for all time. In revolutionary times, these forms can experience a crisis, they may be destroyed completely or in part, or undergo radical change. The Church's continuity is grounded in the promise of Christ as attested in Scripture. On this, too, depend its hope for the future and its task in the world. As it hears and understands the promise anew, the Church may also recognize in the historical crises of its tradition the kind of changes which the Lord of the Church requires of the tradition in historical form. We also acquire a new understanding of ancient tradition and its historical relativity.

Under the guidance of the Spirit, we can also achieve a new understanding of historical tradition even without any critical revolutionary situation: for example, when the Church is led to new experiences of fellowship with other churches with different traditions yet trusting in the promises of the same Lord (ecumenical movement). True life, therefore, includes the hope of a renewed understanding of the tradition under the direction of the onward moving Spirit (John 16:13) and is therefore part of our ecumenical hope.

3. Our Contribution to an Ecumenical Account of Hope

It is in the socialist countries that we live out our Christian hope and it is there that we must authenticate it. The hope we have discovered fresh and new in our congregations, the hope which is based on Jesus Christ, Lord of the world and Head of the Church, at the same time opens our eyes to ecumenical horizons and teaches us to appreciate the importance and even the indispensability of ecumenical meetings. Out of the diverse historical situations and social contexts, diverse testimonies to Christian hope spring up. Yet all these diverse testimonies are focused on the one Lord who comes with the promise of his kingdom. This also binds them inseparably together as testimonies of the one Christian community.

When, on the basis of our hope, we work for peace and justice, we must even cooperate with representatives of other religions and ideologies. On the path of hope, therefore, we discover the true world-wide *oikoumene*.

We in our society are asked questions about our faith, to which we return an answer which represents our account of the hope that is in us. This "accounting" mostly is in the form of an explanation, an "apologia" (I Peter 3:15), which we have to offer "with modesty and respect".

We in the ecumenical fellowship do not willingly regard ourselves as on the defensive. We wish rather to exchange our experiences by way of questions and counter-questions, so as to be able to understand and confess the substance of our common hope in greater depth. In other words, we address each other as real brothers and sisters, all of us aware that we live by grace and justification, and that we are not at liberty to exchange our faith for cultural, social and historical values. We are exhorted by the apostle Paul: "Welcome one another, therefore, as Christ has welcomed you" (Rom. 15:7). "For now we see in a mirror dimly... now I know in part..." (I Cor. 13:12).

3.1 Our Situation in a Socialist Society

In the ecumenical fellowship we are often asked: How do you understand your situation in a country in which the Communist Party has the leading role and when atheism is part of the ideology of this party?

We regard this question, which does not cast any doubts on our Christian existence in socialist society, as a chance to speak about our experiences and thoughts. The communist parties in socialist countries combine socialism and atheism. This they regard as a sort of socialist humanism, as a liberation of human beings. That they should do so is no accident. The Christian churches were deeply implicated in the unjust structures of society. Christians neglected social issues, and this helped to bring about the situation in which communist parties see a necessary connection between socialism and atheism.

We believe, indeed, that this combination of socialism and atheism is historical in character and does not represent a fundamental necessity. It is not only Christians but also many progressive people and movements which are striving for justice and peace who do not regard this combination as fundamental. There are millions of Christians living in the socialist countries and involved actively in the development of their society. As citizens they are not obliged to be atheists. Religious liberty and freedom of conscience are guaranteed in the constitutions of our countries.

That even in the socialist society there are worshipping Christian communities is due to the resurrection of Christ, to the work of the Holy Spirit. He demonstrates his presence in the living witness of the Church and Christians. He is absolutely independent of the historical society in which we live as Christians, whatever its character and system. He is not tied to any so-called "Christian" society.

By going on living and working as Christian churches in our socialist countries, we bear witness that the ideological view of reality cannot be equated with the real historical reality, and that even the socialist society directed by the communist parties in Eastern Europe, despite their atheism, still leaves room for the churches.

3.2 Our Role in Development of Society

Another question is: How, as Christians, do you understand your cooperation in the development of the socialist society?

Our hope that the Church's future is in the hands of Jesus Christ saves us from letting ourselves be dependent on the ideological superstructure of our society, in our anxiety for the Church's future. It leads us to cooperate for the welfare of our neighbours and of society as a whole. In fact, the socialist society has been and is being built and shaped also with the help of Christians. We rejoice in its achievements, its difficulties are our difficulties, we suffer from its deficiencies. We consider ourselves as part of our society and take our share of responsibility for it.

In our experience, the cooperation of Christians is helping increasingly to dispel mistrust of Christians, to deepen mutual understanding, to develop human relations between Christians and Marxists, gradually to promote a growing recognition of the positive role of Christians and churches. The development of relations between the churches and socialist society is not free from problems nor is it yet completed. There is reason to hope that it will take a positive direction beneficial to both parties.

In the course of practical cooperation and common daily life there are many conversations with Marxist fellow-citizens. Although in socialist society the stress is placed on practical cooperation in real common tasks and goals and not on our different standpoints and ultimate aspirations, it is only honest to say that there are sometimes unsolved problems, critical questions and even real tensions. This is inevitable in collaboration between two such different attitudes to life and reality as those represented by Communists and Christians. How such situations are dealt with varies greatly from one socialist land to another. But we are all agreed that such situations should be resolved by frank discussion, without any pressure, with a sense of responsibility for socialist society and for détente in the world. The new forms of prophetic ministry in socialist society will have to be discovered in the light of the church tradition and of the various opportunities which have been offered by historical developments.

3.3 Our Christian Hope and Other Hopes

Another question which is asked can take various forms. We Christians in the socialist countries are often asked: *Do you not identify your Christian hope with the hopes entertained by your society on the basis of an optimistic view of the future?*

The question takes a different form when it is directed to those who directly identify their revolutionary hopes with the Kingdom of God on earth. In countries which are interested in the *status quo*, the question is as follows: *Can you really assume that the Christian hope can be fulfilled – even if not completely – in the secular hopes?*

In the light of historical experience, our answer to this question would be as follows: The hope which we have in Jesus Christ transcends all earthly hopes and will only be fulfilled at Christ's coming. In this present time, we are on the way to the coming of the Lord. This way also takes in the fulfilment of earthly hopes for justice, liberation and peace. Within history God uses not only Christian but even secular movements and ideologies, even when they are unaware of this, in order to bring humankind nearer to the goals of his kingdom of justice and peace. In our countries, optimism leads people to the view that the problems of the world must be tackled, that we must assume responsibility for these problems and deal with them with the aid of science and technology. We endorse the responsibility to tackle the problems but, as Christians, we certainly cannot go along with an optimism which expects everything from people and nothing from God.

In our socialist society we share in the efforts to realize earthly hopes but without abating or abandoning our Christian hope which in our services of worship we again and again reimbibe from the Word of God and which lifts our eyes towards the *parousia*. On the other hand, the Marxists themselves object strongly to any attempt on our part as Christians to "baptize" secular hopes and to secure a clerical monopoly of them.

3.4 The hope which is ours in Christ transcends all our ideas and expectations. "What no eye has seen, nor ear heard, nor the heart of man conceived, what God has prepared for those who love him" (I Cor. 2:9). In our diverse confessional and geographical situations, we are privileged in this time to see only part of the wealth of the hope in Jesus Christ. The ecumenical fellowship offers us the opportunity to bring our limited and often confessionally or historically coloured understandings of hope into discussions against the background of the whole world, the opportunity to ask questions and to listen. In this way the horizons of our hope are widened, its content deepened, and the conditions for a common confession created. We believe that it is the Holy Spirit which is leading us along this path to unity and to the common witness which we owe to the world.

Although in our ecumenical fellowship we have been given a foretaste of unity, our hope is directed towards the full unity of Christendom. In the Eastern European situation especially this hope of unity is very important. The challenges which we share lead us together as different churches in a special measure, even if differences also exist in the way in which we respond to these challenges and express our discipleship. Our hope empowers us to seek and to find methods which help us to keep growing into a greater and deeper unity. Our hope in the unity has a historical and an eschatological component. Both are linked together. The eschatological unity is being expressed in faith and in visible manifestations even now in history. It provides our common witness with credibility and missionary power.

Two conditions must be fulfilled if this witness of hope is to be a common witness and speak hope to the world: love among Christians, so that they are able to speak, live and celebrate together, without prejudices, without ideological systematization; and credibility, a credibility to be demonstrated by their solidarity with the oppressed, the hungry, the people denied their human rights, and the hopeless, a solidarity which sets the seal on their hope.

To express our hope together can only be a gift of the Holy Spirit who leads us into all truth. Our prayer, therefore, is: Come, Creator Spirit, come!

4. Testimonies to the Hope That is Within Us

Accounts of Hope from Latin America

It is perhaps clearer than ever today in Latin America that witnessing to the hope by and for which we live has little or no connection with abstract analyses of the ontological or terminological nature of hope "as such". In view of the alarming general dehumanization of our continent, a growing sense of the need for the survival of the human individually and socially on our continent prevents us from devoting much time to mere philosophical or theological speculation on prolegomena to hope. The desperate situation of our people makes it impossible for us to regard the vital and deeply humanizing fact of "living in hope" merely as a theological subject around which one can initiate an academic process of reflection whose purpose is to confront or discuss the various currently fashionable theological positions.

In recent years, especially, we have come to understand that "hope" and "liberation", which for us are so strongly synonymous, are not basically terms for wordy discussion or unrealistic utopian glorification, but deeply human experiences which, in spite of everything, exist among our Latin American peoples today and which call us to *hopeful community and commitment.*

This is probably why it is impossible for us to continue today the academic theological discussion of the "theology of hope" in which we participated not so very long ago. The oppressive forces of despair, rather than a change in theological fashion, have obliged us to turn our minds from an imaginary situation to the true reality of our people and our churches, seeking anew for ourselves the signs of living hope which are present among them.

This is why today's testimonies to the "hope that is within us" do not take the form of academic, theological language, but rather find expression in the song of the poet, the prayers of the priest and the witness of the prophet, the spokesmen of a people who maintain hope and perseverance — hope and perseverance which are the strength of a human life which opposes the oppressive despair of death and dehumanization. So we believe that the words of Don Pedro Casaldáliga, a contemporary Latin American prophet, in his introduction to a book of poems written in the prisons of Brazil, also serve as a valid presentation of the testimonies of hope which we have collected together here.

Like the poems in the book, the words spoken and the poems sung by our Latin American people, this imprisoned "people of the night" are life itself, "a shining challenge to death in a period spent underground in endless night".

Introduction by Don Pedro Casaldáliga to a book of poems written by Brazilian prisoners

To begin this conversation, I must first say that the words in this book are true: this poetry is life — the life of the poems, the life of a poet writing his verses in the darkness of the day, in agony, the final struggle, a shining challenge to death.

Has anyone in these past ten years of poetry and of night in Brazil published a book of poems which are so true, so committed to life, to death, to the people?

No hermetism, or any other frivolous literary "ism". "When I say stone, I don't mean bread." This poet achieved the "transparent poem" he was searching for.

This book has no borrowed humanisms, but it is almost human; it is direct and total, like a heart which is still on the way: day and night, life and death, struggle, hope, people. Ideology itself becoming naked humanity.

These brothers and sisters all show the human gestures of tenderness and pain and always of hope. "The rainy afternoons ... hair falling on shoulders ...", "doors creaking as if crying out for more affection ..." and shoes in a room without "the quiet presence of the one who is to return".

Fear, anguish, the suffering of distance and of torture speak in these verses with the neurological drama of "The Hood", as one poet puts it.

These written words are without superficiality, because life first of all chooses poverty. It is a "period spent underground", a notionless time, an "endless night".

Meanwhile, waiting and hope — the great Hope of the future of the People, as human History — flow through the whole book like persistent living blood.

The poet knows, from his own experience of life on the threshold of death (and never has that threshold — *umbral* — been so true to its etymology), that "the human creature resists". For him — and he has every right to make this claim — "it does not matter if the harvest of light is a long time coming". He believes that "the wounded hand sows the dark seed of liberty". And he sees the trains "wrapped in mist" hammering away "towards the dawn".

"We will survive", he cries with the experience of a survivor. With all the human faces he has never seen but still loves. Because the victory of the night "was not complete" but "left us the inextinguishable assurance of the forbidden tomorrow": the unforbiddable Tomorrow, brother-poet, poet-martyr, poet-prophet.

Difficult poetry, hard "material" of resistance and struggle, but this simply human poetry never loses its tenderness. This poet, the "blacksmith of the Day", never "hammered the anvil without tenderness". Just as in his eyes and in his hands, behind the bars and guards of the Shadow, the poet reveals in these written words the primitive gesture of a little child or a peasant. Whoever spoke to him came to love him as a friend. Whoever reads his words must love him too.

In the old classification of the poetry textbooks, these poems would rank as epic rather than lyrical. Clearly they are not narcissistic. They are the song of a people rather than the rhapsody of a moonstruck individual as he contemplates a rose or a woman.

The people are the poets of this book, "the people of the night", the people of the new Day, the people of this country, all the people of our America, the people of the World.

This book is a "general song" for America, against the "evil present", looking towards the "future which is ours".

A man committed to the People even to the extremes of torture and the everpresent threat of death could not sing any other way. This is why these verses are true, committed and calling for commitment.

This book is read and passed on like an emergency telegram, like a war cry. Or else it is secretly burned, with cowardice. The torture fire has often burned the flesh of the singer.

No one could read these pages as if scanning just another poem, the usual flower. This isn't a book of flowers.

"Here an act of love is always a challenge. A word of liberty is always a challenge." Merely holding the book in your hands is in itself a challenge.

None of us can permit ourselves the cruel luxury of leaving the poet to question himself in vain at the end of his poem. Let us answer him, with living gestures, that his "material" is legitimate. At this hour of the night in our country and in America, all of us should be made sufficiently literate by the silence of the dead, by the stars of hope, to be able to read and digest this book, which is as basic as life itself.

"Let us reject peace", when this means merely sitting "at the table of slavery". For otherwise, one day — that Day — we might be accused of holding out "clean" hands, "carefully manicured", "stained with the blood of the innocent".

Aren't we all, if we are still human beings, the "people of the Night", "defenceless beings", like all the defenceless? Aren't we "each in every one"? Aren't we all the "smiths" who forge this unforbiddable tomorrow?

Poet, friend, brother, as we join in your underground song with other wounds, and dogtired footsteps, we reaffirm with you the great Hope. And we also proclaim among the "fallen" whom you sing, among the nameless fallen of all the people of the night, the presence, perhaps anonymous, but always fruitful, of the glorious fallen One.

One day, brother, we will help you quench from your poems the painful words about weapons, the inhuman words about fear, the word of enforced silence, as inhospitable as exile. When the People of the night become the People of the day, when the open day becomes the common Fatherland of all men who are brothers.

Pedro Casaldáliga
Bishop of Sao Felix
Matto Grosso, Brazil

WE SHALL SURVIVE

We have lost the notion of time.
Light comes to us from the last lamp
filtered by a multitude of shadows.
Even the voice of our companions reaches us
slowly, as if coming from far away,
as if the shadow had robbed it of its edge.
On this still night we survive.
The word remains with us, even though repressed.
But the murmur reveals that the victory
is not complete. The silence increases
and an embrace is sent from someone whose face
we have never seen, but nevertheless, love.
On this still night we survive.
We shall survive.
Our faith remains with us, inextinguishable,
on this forbidden morning.

> For Jonas, a prophet whom death
> did not extinguish

I will till the field of morning.
With these hands
still shackled.
It doesn't matter if blood
blurts from my fingers
or from the wounded earth.
It doesn't matter if the harvest of light is late,
or if the stores of night remain intact.
It doesn't matter if the passage of the enemy
has left only ruins.
I will till the field of morning,
even though today I shall have to restore
the body of my brother, who is in pieces.
It doesn't matter if the harvest of light is late.

Letter from a Prisoner

From the Secretariat "Justice and Non-Violence"
of Sao Paulo we have received the following letter
which we publish herewith:

On the 28th April, we received a letter from Adolfo Perez Esquivel. The
letter was written on a napkin, which we are lovingly keeping ... May
the Lord grant him constant firmness until the end.

Mario, Alamiro, Carmen, Salvador, to all my friends, dear friends:

I do not want to talk to you of pain, but of Hope, of the Grace of our
Lord who can share and live with those brothers who suffer from injustice, with those who even after two or more years in prison still do
not know why they are suffering this punishment.

However, there is always a light to illumine the darkness. The presence
of God at each moment, in each act. The God of Love who forgave
while on the cross and at all times: "Father, forgive them for they
know not what they do".

Here, in this prison, I have lived through Holy Week with the grace to
understand more deeply the commitment, the sacrifice, the love which
Christ sheds over all men, over all humanity. What an Easter joy, that
of Christ triumphant through love, Christ risen and present, Hallelujah!

Prison gates cannot hold back the Spirit, the Love of Christ, which remains with its infinite presence in each of us.

Even those who doubt God receive his Grace.

The dungeons are full of inscriptions, of petitions, acts of faith, of hope.

To live, to share, to walk with those who suffer — they shall be blessed — we ask only to remain faithful to his word, and live in love.

Here everything disappears, we are naked before God, with fears, uncertainty and pain, but confident in his mercy.

This is my hope.

May the Lord guide you, and give you peace, strength and joy.

Adolfo

Buenos Aires, April 20, 1977
Letter from prison

I do not know what will happen, I wait confidently, but the work should continue, to be a Christian witness in spite of our limitations and weaknesses. United in prayer.

Homilies for Manuel Fiel, a murdered metal worker

HOMILY OF DON ANGELICO SANDALO BERNARDINO

Brothers:

We are here, united with Jesus Christ, the great victim of selfishness and violence. The crucified one, the liberator of the world, Jesus, the Carpenter of Nazareth, vanquished his own death through his resurrection. He had the assurance that no human suffering was in vain. Man does not suffer for nothing; his pain is transformed into liberation: "He who sows with tears will harvest with joy. He who goes out weeping to sow his seed will return with song to harvest his corn." Brothers, we are gathered here to meditate on the word of God. The Lord speaks to us, and his word is Jesus. He speaks to us in the Holy Scriptures. He talks with us; He knows what is happening around us. Is there anyone here who cannot see God speaking to us about the sad death of the metal worker, Manuel Fiel? Was he tortured like so many others? Did he die as a result of ill-treatment? Has torture ever been proved? And are some saying that the Department of Internal Order of the Commando of Operations of the Second Sao Paulo Army has become "a chamber of horrors" where prisoners are subjected to terrible sufferings and violence, to the shame of the decent people of this country?

97

Well, this shadowy situation has just been shaken up from top to bottom. The death of ordinary people, workers, shows this. And God must act through the humble to "put down the mighty from their thrones" (Luke 1:52), and David, the little shepherd boy, says to the Philistine Goliath through the ages: "You come to me with a sword and with a spear and with a javelin; but I come to you in the name of the Lord of Hosts." (I Sam. 17:45)

God says to us through present events that the meek, the workers, must not lose hope. With their companions in suffering, the downtrodden will build their own liberation and that of others.

God also says that the way of violence is deceitful and destructive. The violence of war, hunger, the exploitation of one man by another, assaults, abductions. The violence of the guerrilla, of the instruments of torture. An ocean of weakness and cowardice which conspires against men. Those who choose violence do not know that human rights and human dignity are above all other things, because man is a creature of God, and as such must be treated with dignity and his legal rights respected.

We recognize no one's right to use men as objects, not even in the pursuit of supposedly good objectives. Wherever human rights are not respected, for whatever reason — Russia, Cuba, China, USA, Angola or Brazil — we must be there to raise the cry: This is unlawful!

This is why, as bishops of Sao Paulo, we say once again:

— "It is unlawful to use methods of physical or moral torture in the interrogation of suspects, especially when it results in mutilation, the breakdown of health, and death, as has happened."

— "It is unlawful to deprive the accused of his right to full defence or to threaten him or to consider him guilty until he is so judged, or to prolong a normal trial indefinitely, when our laws expressly state that 'the law will assure the accused his fullest defence and the resources necessary for such defence' (Art. 153-15)."

— "No authority, of whatever nature, has the right to exert pressure on the consciences of the judges or to create obstacles to the free exercise of their functions."

— "We especially regret the suspension of the full guarantee of habeas corpus."

In a regrettable event like the death of Manuel, it is not right to place the responsibility on a particular prison warder or general when, quite apart from personal guilt which must be proved, the evil arises from the dual order (or rather disorder) in our country — the institutional order and the constitutional order — which under the present system has even been extended to the judiciary!

At this point, someone may well say in a gesture of frustration: "Manuel is dead. It's all over."

Indeed, a great wrong has been done. His wife and children are heartbroken. But he has become the seed of new life! He lives on, in a new dimension. He was called to see the Father's face. In dying, he spoke out aloud — a real cry of peace. He reminded us once again of the message of the Lord Jesus: "I am the hungry, the thirsty, the foreigner, the naked, the sick, the prisoner, who is at your side. Inasmuch as you do something for the least of my brethren, you do it to me." May we, brothers, each day see the face of Christ in the face of every man, and love him!

Let us now continue our prayer, brothers, interceding with God for Manuel Fiel and all those throughout the world who are falling victim to all kinds of violence; thus creating the seed which tomorrow will spring forth with the strength of hope, of the total surrender of love, of the ripe fruits of the liberation of our brother who walks, in spite of everything, in hope.

HOMILY OF FATHER ANTONIO HADDAD

My friends,

Manuel is dead. He is no longer here. We believe that man's life does not end with his death. We believe that the human person survives in a way which causes many people to speculate about it, for the human being is for us something truly sublime. It is inconceivable that we should return to nothingness. I am sure that Manuel is still alive. He is living in the fullness of life, the life he lost, and we can see the fullness of his life, and at this time his blood leads us to raise some questions.

Manuel has gone. We are here. History is in our hands. Manuel is part of our history inasmuch as we live in this moment of history when his life was ended, leaving us to raise questions — who knows whether they are signs of hope or signs of frustration. Let us think about ourselves, those of us who are here today.

One day, I don't know when, thousands and millions of years ago, God created man in his own image and likeness. Everyone knows this book — the Bible. The first book of the Bible is called Genesis. Genesis means "origin".

In Genesis, God tells us that man must work with the sweat of his brow. He must build his life. God created all things and gave them to men: this is for you; I give it to you in freedom and responsibility. Now, together with the others, you will build history.

Not on your own, selfishly, but together with the others. You know you are a person, you must be respected, you have your dignity. Brothers, I am not speaking of the UN Charter, the declaration of human rights, or any other document. I am speaking about Genesis — the first book of the Bible, of this history. We know that, in face of God's marvellous plan for freedom, responsibility, communication with others and for men building history together, man reaches a point where he says "Who me? No!" and breaks off the relationship. He breaks with the plan: "I dont't want to build community, I choose selfishness."

In today's Gospel (Luke 4 : 14-24) we have seen what Christ's mission was. Why did he come? The vague answer people always hear: "He came to save man from sin", is very abstract and ethereal. Here there is no problem; it scares no one. But when people take a closer look at that sin which Jesus came to overcome, they are afraid.

He came to bring a message to make men truly men. *He came as a human being, to teach human beings how to be human.* He came as an ordinary man. He was the son of a worker, like Manuel — good, humble, honest, a free worker.

He enters the Synagogue and defines his task, his mission: "I came to preach the Gospel to the poor." In the Bible, "the poor" does not mean only those who have no money, but those who are open, vitally concerned with human realization; those who are attached not to things, but to love and justice among men.

In our first reading today we heard the apostle St John say "God is love" (I John 4 : 8). He who loves can discern who God is. He who does not love cannot discern anything.

He who does all that was done to Manuel will find it hard to know who God is and will not have that basic experience of a God who is love. What they did to Manuel was not based on love. And God is love.

Christ loved the Church so that it could transform human lives and help realize their humanity. And the Church today still defends human rights. Why? Because according to the first book of the Bible man was created in the image and likeness of God, and to violate human rights is to violate God.

The human person is sacred. It is our divine duty to defend man. Again: Jesus came as a human person to teach human beings to be human. He, the Christ who realized his full potential as a man, came to show us how to "be people" in human relationships.

Which is the greatest commandment? "Love one another, as I have loved you" (John 13 : 34). My brothers, let us pray. I would like each of us present here to leave with remorse in our conscience: myself, you, us.

One drop of Manuel's blood which was shed: the guilt is mine, the guilt is yours, the guilt belongs to us all.

Let us pray and ask forgiveness.

100

The Priests' Movement ONIS
Takes a Stand in Peru

In the following translation we present a declaration of this movement, the text of which can be found in "Páginas Solidárias" of May 1977.

The start of a new year is the right time to evaluate the past year and to present our reasons for hope and concerns in the starting year, and which Paul VI defined as the year of peace for the defence of life. The priests' movement, ONIS, believes it is necessary, under the present circumstances, to say a word in public about its own position as a movement of priests; knowing that the mission of announcing the Gospel implies accepting the concrete consequences of witnessing our love to the Father and our liberation in Jesus Christ: "When you did it to these my brothers, you were doing it to me."

1. Faith and fraternity

As priests working in the poorest sectors of the country, we have witnessed this past year a serious deterioration in the living conditions and consequent daily suffering of those who do not have the minimum necessary to feed and dress themselves, do not have access to health care in case of sickness, cannot find work and who do not benefit from the minimum guarantees to defend their threatened rights. We are worried about the situation of the Peruvian people. As the bishops affirmed in a recent document, the economic crisis is at the same time a moral crisis. Starting with this situation of the poor masses of the country, and what this implies for us, we want to remind everyone that we have a concrete call to solidarity and fraternity to which Christ calls us, if we aspire to truly practising the Gospel.

The message of Christ implies, for those who accept it, the necessity of a profound conversion, as the answer to the gracious love of the Father in our life. That is why the practice of the Gospel is incompatible with the indifference to the fate of others, with egoism and with the invariable appeal to the law of the strongest as a norm for social behaviour. To pretend to live the experience of the gracious love of God and accept at the same time the exploitation of others is contradictory. Practising one's faith cannot thus be reduced to a set of beliefs and rites within the bounds of a restricted individual morality. Faith and hope should be present in all the dimensions of our relationships with others; they are always and necessarily expressed by a confrontation against injustice, and by the building of fraternity. It is in the exercise of our priestly vocation to announce Christ, to be a witness to him, that we call to mind the present living conditions of the people, that we reiterate our solidarity with them in their fight to transform a society whose dominating praxis is opposed to that which we as Christians seek to live.

2. The Gospel and economic order

The incompatibility between a capitalist organization of society and being effective in one's Christian witness is so evident that it strikes the eyes. The owners of financial and industrial capital are not only imposing at a fast rate their conditions for investing and lending, but have also recuperated the confidence to express, with all clarity, what they think and practise: individual profit as the fundamental motive of the economy, unrestricted ownership of property, total control of the workers by the enterprises, opposition to any significant action of social reform, refusal to recognize the most elementary demands of labour unions, their despotism in the face of the workers and of the country, the exaction of repression against all those who fight for a suffering Peru, in flesh and blood. The technical justifications for this kind of a system are not enough to hide its basic orientation, which is manifestly directed against the people and which is of dubious morality.

The social and economic context in which these affirmations are made is one of crisis. This crisis is another triumph for the rich. It is in reality the means by which they affirm that they are the legal representatives of the government, thus obtaining the elimination of the legal restrictions imposed on the most excessive forms of exploitation. Contrary to what they pretend to demonstrate, they are directly responsible for this crisis. Concealing from the workers the gains they are entitled to by law, hiding the surplus gains from the state as well as from the country, and refusing to reinvest them, has been normal practice during these last years. They are thus powerful instruments in impoverishing the country and in generating crises.

Figures tell us in an impersonal way what we see directly every day in our communities: that the minimum legal wage, which is not even enough for food, must be spent as well on rent, transportation, clothes, medicines, education, etc. Under these conditions, the deterioration of the real value of a salary becomes tormenting and inhuman, thus increasing hunger and the disintegration of the family. On the other hand, the situation of the under-employed, of the street peddlar, of the occasional worker and especially that of the independent peasant is even worse, as can be verified by the continuous reduction of their participation in the national income over the last years. If these tendencies continue, begging, child prostitution, robbery, and so on will all become inevitable realities.

All these aspects together form a coherent whole. Reformist tendencies and measures disappear, the effort of the State consists in creating better conditions for the investment of foreign and national capital. What has happened in other Latin American countries that have followed the same economic policy, with all the consequences of impoverishment and repression of the people, should serve as a lesson for us and keep us on the alert.

3. Christian love and defence of life

The objective cause of social antagonisms is clear. In this situation, the very least we can require is respect for freedom of expression, the right to organize the people, and human rights for all. We readjusted the institutionalized legal recourse through which political authorities feel they have the right to make judgments by themselves over the legitimate intention of any labour union statement which is contrary to their wishes. And besides, when they decide against an organization, this decision automatically qualifies the organization as subversive, illegal and criminal. This unexpected action, which occurs sometimes in less than 24 hours, has led to prison many leaders who had the courage to lay aside personal interest and assume the defence of the collective aspirations of their colleagues. The gravity of the economic crisis and the necessity to produce cannot justify actions of this type. Neither can it justify the suspension of job stability nor mass firings. What happens in our society is that the right to work depends on the way business goes for the owners.

For all this we ask, as have already done many important sectors of the country, that the state of emergency be lifted, as well as the suspension of individual liberties. This situation has caused us to lament the loss of many human lives. We ask for the restitution of the right to strike, of free circulation of objective information about the situation in the popular sectors, and for the right to debate the national issues.

Finally, we wish to express our preoccupation and our protest as to the destiny of the expatriated who have struggled for social issues, and especially of those in prison. Not long ago, a student died under these conditions. The explanation given by the Minister of the Interior was followed by many demands for an additional investigation, among them a demand from the highly placed governing board of the Catholic University; we still do not know the results of this investigation, which in itself is very serious. Popular protest can be heard in all cases where people have been threatened by death, by torture, and by intimidation, not only common and political prisoners, but their families as well. Institutionalized violence destroys peace, life and unity. For the good of the country, we think it is indispensable to have rapid investigations, that the results be made public, and that there be sanctions against those who are responsible, as the case is brought to light.

4. Good news and liberation

The God in whom we believe and whom as Christians we proclaim is one whose love prefers the "little ones", becomes involved in the destiny of the weak and oppressed, and calls us to participate in their salvation, in a fellowship without limits with the poor of the earth. We know that it is not the poor who occupy the important positions in our society, that they are mostly ignored by this same society and submitted to conditions not of their own choosing. We also know through our own experience that nothing and no one can kill their combativeness and hope. Human solidarity in difficult historic moments is the revealing sign of a love which does not die, because it is life itself which remains forever, which strengthens him who is weak, and guides those who trust in the God of the promise of liberation. Today our people show us that mysterious obstinacy of those who hope against hope, those who remain unswerving in the justice of their cause, and in the power of truth to transform history. Their struggle does not allow this hope to be suffocated, it reaches all the people, so that we can all be motivated to defend life, a necessary condition for peace. The peace promised by the Lord to all men of good will is the work of justice, and excludes any social system based on exploitation. It does not permit some people to wear themselves out sowing so that others can reap. It does not allow people to be treated as objects. Only in working together to build peace can we really call ourselves brothers and sons of the same Father.

Christian communities, and even the whole Church, are today being questioned by the concrete situation of the people who compose it, and are being challenged to engage in the defence of the rights of the poorest of the poor. But in order to do so, it is necessary to follow the situation much more closely, to be present with the masses, to speak for the voiceless. This would be our means of showing, under present conditions, our hope in the Kingdom, to be an active force in the fulfilment of the promise of liberation, and to open the way for an authentic, solidary society.

Lima, 17 January, 1977
National Executive Committee

Declaration Concerning Recent Events
by the Bishops and Prelates of the Southern Region
of Peru, 10 July 1977

"Miec-Jeci" (Spes), Nov. 1977, no. 33, pp 38ff.

Listening to the protests and aspirations of the poor as reflected in recent events in this country, and especially in our own region, we, the bishops, pastors of churches in Juli, Puno, Ayaviri, Sicurani and Cuzco, would like to share with the people our feelings as a Church in view of the present situation.

Events: The suffering of our people has become clear, in their way of understanding and with the means at their disposal, in a series of mass protests in Puno, Juliaca, Cuzco, Ayaviri, Sicurani, Juli and many provinces of the region and other parts of Peru.

This mass protest, the expression of justified complaints, has been violently repressed, and a fearful number of people killed, wounded, imprisoned or disappeared without trace.

Causes: For some time past we have been oppressed by a situation of violence made unbearable by recent economic measures: the continual rise in the cost of living, the wage freeze, the lack of labour stability, the low prices paid for the goods produced by the peasants, the lack of land for the majority of the peasants, the laws which discriminate against the workers, the prolonged suspension of guarantees and many other measures which in fact hit the people and benefit a minority.

We believe that the basic cause of this situation is a pattern of economic development and a social and political system which do not take account of the interests of the majority and are based on a doctrine of national security which subjects people to the power of the State and places them at its disposal. The people's lack of freedom puts them in a desperate situation; despair then becomes rebellion and unleashes violence.

These facts oblige us to give a response of faith as Christians and to take a stand in the desire to be faithful to the Lord and to his people.

Reflection of faith: From our experience of faith, we interpret this situation as a rejection of God's plan and therefore a situation of sin (cf. *Justice in the World,* No. 6).

The people of Israel discovered in their history a God who will not tolerate injustice, who defends the people's rights and calls them to full liberation: "I have come down to deliver them out of oppression and to bring them to a good and broad land" (Exodus 3 : 8).

God acts by condemning the violence done to his people: "Hear the word of the Lord, O King ... you, and your servants, and your people .... Do justice and righteousness, and deliver from the hand of the oppressor him who has been robbed. And do no wrong or violence to the alien, the fatherless, and the widow; nor shed innocent blood ... But if you will not heed these words, I swear by myself ... that this house shall become a desolation" (Jer. 22: 2-5).

Jesus tells us that his mission is the same: "The Spirit of the Lord is upon me, because he has anointed me to preach good news to the poor, ... to proclaim release to the captives and ... to proclaim the acceptable year of the Lord" (Luke 4: 18-19).

The Lord identifies himself so closely with the people that what we do to the poor we do to him. Thus we see the judgment of God – of salvation when our relationship with them is one of love and active struggle at their side; of condemnation when this relationship is one of exploitation, violence and rejection (cf. Matt. 25).

This experience of God, who chooses the meek, the poor and oppressed, clearly appears in the faith of the people of Israel, and Jesus Christ, from his own experience of poverty, requires our Church to be faithful to the Lord, and today this implies taking a stand for the poor of our time.

This is the point made by the Peruvian bishops when they urge the Church to "denounce energetically the abuses and unjust consequences of the excessive inequalities beween poor and rich, weak and powerful, accompanying their denunciations where necessary with concrete gestures of solidarity with the poor and oppressed" (XXXVI Episcopal Assembly of Peru, Medellin, Peace 23).

Denunciations: Therefore we denounce:

— the violence of repression and the efforts to frighten the people;
— the economic, social and political systems which do not take into account the interests of the majority;
— the fact that a privileged minority forces the masses to shoulder the weight of the economic crisis.

Proclamation: From our stand in favour of the poor and in solidarity with them, we declare our hope in the risen Jesus because we recognize his presence in this people who reject an unjust situation and proclaim a society ruled by love in accordance with the words of Peter: "But according to his promise we wait for new heavens and a new earth in which righteousness dwells" (II Peter 3: 13).

Petitions: In our longing to see peace in our land, based on justice and respect for human rights, we ask for:

— an end to repression and intimidation;
— exact information concerning the dead and missing;
— liberty for the prisoners;
— an end to the rise in the cost of living, especially as regards necessities, transport and petrol;
— fair prices and wages for peasants and workers;
— participation by all in the austerity required by the present moment and the suppression of economic privileges;
— full information and freedom of expression for the people;
— respect for the independent organizations of the people and their ability to make decisions on the main problems which affect us;
— the re-establishment of constitutional guarantees;
— a social order based on the interests of the majority.

Commitment: For our part, knowing that "without the autonomous organization of the people they cannot achieve their liberation according to God's plan, we commit ourselves to support organizations arising from the initiative of the people, not imposed upon them, and which help people to achieve greater dignity" (Abancay Regional Episcopal Assembly) and "to proclaim the Good News and help to give that message its historical and social effectiveness within its transforming action in the world" (Evangelization, 3.1.4).

We therefore repeat the words of the Peruvian bishops some years ago:
"In face of the adoption by any government of a policy of repression, and particularly by those which in the name of Christianity use violence and even torture against people struggling for the liberation of their people, we propose that the Church should condemn such repressive methods, recognize their right to struggle for justice, and show its solidarity with their ideals, while not always approving of their methods" (*Justice in the World,* No. 14).

> Luis Vallejos, Bishop of Cuzco; Albano Quinn, Bishop of Sicurani; Luis Dalle, Bishop of Ayaviri; Jesus Calederon, Bishop of Puno; Alberto Koenigsknecht, Bishop of Juli

"We Have Hope"

Congregational Song (tango)
(words by F.J. PAGURA, music by H.R. PERRERA)

Because He came into the world and into history;
Because He broke down silence and suffering ;
Because He filled the world with his glory;
Because He was the light in the coldness of our night;
Because He was born in a dark manger;
Because in His life He sowed love and life;
Because He broke hardened hearts
And lifted up dejected souls

> This is why today we have hope;
> This is why today we persevere in our struggle;
> This is why today we face our future with
> confidence, in this land which is ours.

Because He attacked the ambitious merchants
And denounced evil and hypocrisy;
Because He exalted the children, the women,
And rejected those who burned with pride.
Because He took up the cross of our suffering;
And tasted the gall of our afflictions;
Because He suffered our own condemnation;
And died for all mortal men.   *(chorus as above)*

Because the dawn saw his great victory,
Over death, over fear, over deceit,
Nothing can now hold back his history
Nor the coming of his eternal Kingdom.   *(chorus as above)*

107

I believe in God

HOMERO PERRERA

I believe in God, I believe that He lives
He is working among us,
in the trees, in the flowers,
in the people who can now see more clearly.
I believe in God, and that He will free us
from the oppression of Man,
in the factories, in the college,
in the people who today want to be human.
I believe in God, I believe in God, I believe in
    his liberating power.
He gave us life and light so that we too can shine.

I believe in God, and that He will free us
from self-destruction
through war, through hunger,
in the people who today fight for liberty.
I believe in God, and that He has power
to do many more things
in us, in the world.
How tremendous and glorious is His name!
He will free us, He will free us, He will free us!

Cancionero Abierto No.1
(ISEDET, p. 21)

The Centre and Basis of Our Hope

We have been invited to present to the Faith and Order Commission
not only testimonies to the hope that is within us, in other words,
within our people and our churches, but also to discuss the theological
problems arising from them and which relate to the present theological
and ecumenical discussion.

Because of the essential role played by our hope and perseverance in
the struggle for a truly human existence — which as we said at the beginning relegates merely academic discussion to a secondary place — we
must all reflect on the value and methods of this type of discussion.

We do not believe there is any point in purely speculative analyses of
supposedly relevant existential matters which have already been dealt
with on many occasions, probably too often, in so many academic and
theological discussions.

The testimonies of hope which we have presented in the first part of this paper clearly show that many of the subjects dealt with most frequently in the recent past are no longer — perhaps have never been — existential problems which occupy the hopes of Latin American men and women, whether or not they are Christians.

It is also very clear that there is little point in discussing the political dimensions of Christianity or the possibility or impossibility of the relationships between faith and ideologies. The answers to such questions are given to us each day in a continent where the powerful seem to have concentrated their efforts on defending the prevailing "Western Christian culture" by all possible means.

Just as clearly, it will be recognized that our testimonies of hope do not come into the debate on the problem of "faith and action": in a situation like ours in Latin America, the very concept of a *hopeful faith* which does not include *hopeful action which in turn creates hope* as an integral, inseparable part amounts to a contradiction. A faith which does not imply hopeful action is not, for us, a *hopeful faith*, but a *faith of waiting*, perhaps even despair.

At the same time, *action without hopeful faith* can mean *action without faith*, and therefore equally end in despair. We recognize, however, that in a situation of despair, action without faith can still be an act of love. By contrast, a faith without action is no longer the faith of which the Gospel speaks, since it lacks love.

Perhaps this makes it easier to understand a particular fact which springs to our attention from the most superficial reading of the texts we have presented. We had not discussed the once controversial subject of whether *Christian* hope is rooted basically in a pre-existent promise or arises from the promissory actions of love which people carry out in history.

We believe there is a common awareness that these are two inseparable dialectical poles: the "logos" of the promise generates hope only through its historical mediation in hopeful and promissory acts. "I believe in God, and that He saves us from self-destruction ... in the people who today are struggling for freedom", says the author of the hymn "I believe in God", and it is this same faith, which trusts in God and in man, while not ignoring the fact that man is a sinner, which is reflected in all our testimonies of hope.

We realize that the hope of liberation we have placed in the oppressed of today can claim for itself no kind of scientific basis: it is the hope of faith, otherwise it would not be hope. It is the hope of a total and integral liberation promised to us by God, who declared man his helper and co-creator. This is why we trust in the liberation promised by God — because we trust in man. And at the same time, we trust in those who today are oppressed by the forces of despair, because we trust in God.

We reject an "automatistic" vision of history, since automatistic conceptions, whatever their various characteristics, in the final instance deny the liberty of both God and man. Two extreme cases will clearly illustrate this: Christian interpretations of history ruled by a rigorous concept of divine predestination, and the theories of historical development of dogmatic communism. Both concepts in their final consequences deny the contingent nature of history and the possibility of free and creative action by God and men within it. The course of history is postulated *a priori*, and the changes in social structures are seen as automatic, so that hope, the central component of human creative acts, is reduced to mere waiting.

Contrary to this, we understand that there is one unique history, in which God and men co-participate in full freedom. A freedom of joint creation which is precisely the nucleus of the hope to which we witness. It is in this joint and continuous creation that we trust. We want to be hopeful participants in it.

Some time ago, theological discussion was concerned with a desire to clarify the relationship between a secular "principle of hope" and the Christian concept of hope; now, however, we believe that the texts we have presented show a shift in parameters, reflecting the changing situation in our continent; what we are now seeing expressed is not so much a "principle of hope" but rather a "perseverance in living". A "simple" and concrete struggle for survival as human beings, nurtured not primarily by a "principle of hope", a future utopia, but by perseverance, by protest against the "endless night in which we survive" and by the present experience that the "persistent murmuring proclaims that the victory of this night was not complete". We believe that it is in relation to this "perseverance in life" that we must question the place which Christian hope could or does occupy; not at the level of an abstract equation of concepts, but in relation to the daily reality in which our people live. The question facing us can therefore be formulated as follows: Is there a "Christian hope" which brings with it an extra contribution of humanization or the hope of humanization which goes beyond mere "perseverance in living"?

We no doubt tend automatically to answer this question in the affirmative, and the question itself seems to imply heresy or incredulity. But if we really take seriously the fact of joint creation and full freedom, the answer to our question about the humanizing contribution of Christian hope cannot be raised in the form of predetermined dogmatics but will arise from the hopeful and promissory acts of Christians in history.

We confess the death and resurrection of Jesus Christ as the centre and basis of the message of hope in which we believe — a message of hope which transcends all individual, situational hopes of Christians in history, as well as their mediation through the promissory acts which they carry out. We understand that the Gospel speaks to us of an integral and general salvation and liberation which includes both political and structural liberation, as well as liberation from sin and the fear of death towards a life in fullness. This message, however, only becomes the experience of hope through its historical mediation in a life of hope, in hopeful and promissory acts.

From this it will be seen that for us Christian hope is not simply something which we possess *a priori*, but a challenge which we must face. We cannot, then, really answer the question about its contribution of humanization or humanizing hope, since the answer to this question can only be given through historical experience. If Christians prove themselves through this process to be a factor of humanization and hope they will have mediated a contribution of hope which goes beyond the "simple perseverance" to survive.

The testimonies of hope which we have quoted clearly represent an integral human hope, even though for obvious reasons the hope of political and structural liberation occupies a basic place in our confession of Christian faith. We believe that these testimonies of hope are as such objective signs of true mediated Christian hope, since in the special situation of our continent they represent both a courageous, prophetic denouncement of dehumanization and institutionalized sin and a proclamation of the will of God for his creation and ours.

A Word to Those on Whom we Depend

From this perspective, we would like to indicate some possible lines of reflection concerning the possibility of a common witness to Christian hope which would try to take into account the hopes and fears of our brothers in other continents. Obviously in doing so we begin from our own situation and to some degree our thoughts are not impartial. We believe, however, that we can only speak about the hope and despair in which our people live by starting from the actual relationships which bind us to all human beings in our contemporary world.

As we see it, these relationships are determined first and foremost by the way in which some nations and certain national and international power groups and even continents keep other nations or regions of the world in various conditions of dependence or subordination — a direct or indirect state of dependence which affects all aspects of our existence.

Against this background, we would like to ask our Christian brothers in the countries on which we are dependent, quite sincerely: do you in your own hopes also take into account *our* hope of liberating ourselves from the dependence which creates the sort of dehumanizing conditions within our countries which the testimonies we have presented so clearly reveal? Do you share our hope of creating together a genuinely human world and of eliminating the existing structures of dehumanization as an indispensable step towards that truly human world?

We are saddened by one feature which we believe we discern in the realities of our world today, namely, the fact that people in the most powerful countries seem to be concentrating their efforts solely on maintaining at all costs the existing situation which favours them so one-sidedly and unjustly.

For many nations the unlimited growth and expansion of their own economy seems to have become the central and axiomatic focus of their corporate aims. In some extreme cases it is not even permitted to cast doubts on this false "hope" of unlimited economic growth. Anyone who refuses to share the prevalent technocratic superstition is dismissed as a utopian anarchist and as a destroyer of the blessings which have been achieved.

We urge our brothers – those who realize the danger threatening them and therefore us all – to recognize that the economic myth of unlimited technological growth means the end of all hope of a humanized world for us all. To invest all our "hopes" in the consolidation of present international structures will be to guarantee the despair of two thirds of humanity. Today that despair assumes the suffocating character of an ideology hostile to change and prohibiting any doubts as to the validity of the principles on which it rests, principles which are both aprioristic and unprovable.

This means that the hope or the despair of our Christian brothers and sisters in the most powerful nations affects our own hope and despair. If they fail to become hopeful and promising contributors to a truly human world, they will become agents of despair and perhaps signs of a spurious "Christian" escapism, utterly alien to a Gospel in which love finds expression in hope and hope is only real as it is expressed in love.

In the name of the message of hope which we all share together, we venture to ask our brothers and sisters in a spirit of friendship: Witness courageously to the hope that is in you by struggling against the forces of despair and dehumanizing stagnation in your own countries! These evil forces have their bases of power in your countries; from these bases they seek to destroy our hopes of a more human future in Latin America and the hopes of a more human and peaceful world. In making this plea we are not forgetting the forces of despair which are seeking to dominate the peoples in our own countries. But in the last analysis, we are convinced that these agents of evil could not continue to dominate without the support or at least the connivance of more powerful international forces.

We are messengers together of the one Christian message which is a message of hope. Let us become living agents of hope for our world in order that this world may be able to believe, in hope, in our message!

5. Giving Account of Hope

A Brief Report on the United States

ROBERT MCAFEE BROWN

Any account of expressions of hope in the United States must be selective; the items described are representative rather than exhaustive,
and many others could have been chosen. I have tried to present a
spectrum of different sectors of the notoriously pluralistic North American scene, including "mainline" Protestants, "evangelicals", blacks and
Roman Catholics. The report will summarize the main points of each
document, along with brief commentary. (For the documents see
Study Encounter, Vol XII, Nos. 1-2; Faith and Order Papers Nos. 81
and 85).

The documents included are:

1. The Hartford Statement — 1975
2. "The Boston Affirmations" — 1976
3. "The Chicago Call: An Appeal to Evangelicals" — 1977
4. "This Land is Home to Me: A Pastoral Letter on Powerlessness in
   Appalachia" — 1975
5. The response of the National Council of Churches to "An Open
   Letter to North American Christians" — 1976
6. "Message to the Black Church and Community" — 1977
7. "A Religious Response to the Mahoning Valley Steel Crisis" — 1977
8. Study Report by the Disciples of Christ — 1976

1. The Hartford Statement — 1975

Our starting point is the so-called "Hartford Statement" of January
1975,[1] a document not technically a "sign of hope", but mentioned
because it seems to have sparked some signs of hope. The "Hartford

---

●Prof. Brown is Professor of Theology at Union Theological Seminary, New York.
[1] "Giving Account of Hope in These Testing Times", *Study Encounter,* Vol. XII,
No. 1-2, 1976, pp. 41-43.

Statement", issued after a weekend of discussion, was initially signed by 18 Christian leaders and was offered to the wider world with the modest intention of opening a discussion. Its positive concern is to help American Christians recover from "an apparent loss of the transcendent". Its witness to transcendence, however, is indirect, since the body of the statement consists of thirteen antitranscendent themes the co-signers find "false and debilitating". The themes are couched in extreme terms, and one of the difficulties of responding to the document after its appearance was that there were few, if any, Christians who felt their own convictions were described by such claims as "Religious statements are *totally* independent of reasonable discourse", "Religious language refers to human experience and *nothing* else ...", "Jesus can *only* be understood in terms of contemporary models of humanity", "*All* religions are equally valid", "To realize one's potential and to be true to oneself is the *whole* meaning of salvation", and so on (italics added in each case). While the victory won by destroying such positions is mainly Pyrrhic, the drafters of the statement should be credited with achieving their stated intention, which was to start a discussion rather than conclude one, and they were indeed successful in spawning responses, many of which moved beyond negative polemics to statements more positively redolent of hope.

2. "The Boston Affirmations" — 1976

In January 1976, a group of theologians and lay persons in the Boston area issued a document that was the result of months of communal effort and is, at least indirectly, a response to the Hartford Statement. Called "The Boston Affirmations"[2] it deliberately set out to be positive rather than negative, as its predecessor had been. Twenty-one members of the Boston Industrial Mission Task Force worked on the drafting, and over 200 others were involved at one time or another in contributing to its development.

Recognizing that modern life is characterized by struggle, and that Christians often seem to retreat from specific struggles, the signers nevertheless affirm, "Still, we are not without hope nor warrants for our hope". They see "hopeful participation in these struggles" as the way to give an accounting of their faith. Strength to sustain such participation is found by them in the form of "signs of God's future and of ours" as revealed in both the past and the present.

This introductory statement is followed by eight areas of affirmation, most of them couched in traditional biblical terminology (Creation, Fall, Exodus and Covenant, Prophecy, Wisdom, The New Covenant, Church Traditions, and Present Witnesses). The testimony of hope predominates throughout the document. After recognizing the reality of creation and

---

[2] *Op. cit.*, pp. 44-47.

fall, for example, the signers go on to affirm, under "Exodus and Covenant", that "God delivers from oppression and chaos. God chooses strangers, servants and outcasts to be witnesses and to become a community of righteousness and mercy". In less majestic but perhaps more telling language, they affirm that "God forms 'nobodies' into a people of 'somebodies'", and that such an experience can call forth "celebrative response". The affirmation about "Prophecy" is not cast judgmentally, but rather states that "in compassion God speaks to the human community through prophets". Lessons from "the cultural insights and memories of many peoples and ages" are also affirmed as sources of insight, along with a recognition that they have a capacity to reveal human dependencies, the depth of sin, and so on. A statement on "The New Covenant" affirms that in Christ "Meaning and divine activity are incarnate in history and human particularity", thus making genuine hope possible. Such gifts are given communally, and those who receive them are to respond communally in a variety of ways. The gifts of the early Eastern church, the formers of doctrine, the monastics, the scholastics, the reformers, and the sectarians are gratefully noted as sources of insight and power for the Christian vision today.

The "affirmations" conclude with a powerful catalogue of "present witnesses" wherein "the transforming reality of God's reign is found today". These signs of hope are found in such areas as the struggles of the poor to gain a share of the world's wealth, the transforming drive for ethnic dignity, endeavours by women to overcome sexist subordination, the voices of citizens and political leaders demanding honesty and openness, the research of science, the arts, the Church, and other places as well. The document concludes with a call to others "who believe in the living God to affirm, to sustain and to extend these witnesses".

The strength of this document is its ringingly affirmative tone in an age of negation, along with its clear reliance upon the strength and resources of the past as they are brought into creative tension with signs of hope in the present. God's presence is affirmed, working in unforeseen places within the world. The document tries to open the ears of its readers to hear the voice of God in the voice of the times, and to recognize in those realities the ongoing activity of the God celebrated in Scripture and tradition.

3. The Chicago Call: An Appeal to Evangelicals

In 1977 another geographical area was heard from, represented by "The Chicago Call: An Appeal to Evangelicals",[3] issued over the signature of 43 Protestants in the "evangelical" tradition, a designation few of the Boston signers would have used. Recognizing that an astonishing "evan-

---

[3] See *Giving Account of the Hope Together*. Faith and Order paper No. 86, 1978, pp. 65-69.

gelical resurgence in the church" is taking place in the United States, the signatories immediately call upon their constituencies "to be especially sensitive to our weaknesses", lifting up eight themes that seem to them in need of special emphasis in a time of "evangelical resurgence".

(1) "A Call to Historic Roots and Continuity" notes the danger of becoming too independent of the past, also recognizing that while "the biblical limits of the Gospel" are sufficient, there is need to recognize that one can "learn from other times and movements concerning the whole meaning of that Gospel". (2) "A Call to Biblical Fidelity" warns against "individualistic interpretations of Scripture" and affirms the need to interpret the Bible "in keeping with the best insights of historical and literary study", as one way of responding to the guidance of the Holy Spirit. (3) "A Call to Credal Identity" reminds evangelicals that they have sometimes settled for "a credal church that merely recites a faith inherited from the past, and a creedless church that languished in a doctrinal vacuum". Affirming the value of the ecumenical creeds of the past, the document recognizes that all such statements are culturally conditioned and that the church must seek ever fresh ways to express the faith today. (4) "A Call to Holistic Salvation" warns against viewing salvation "as an individual, spiritual and otherworldly matter", while neglecting "the corporate, physical and this-worldly implication of God's saving activity". A holistic understanding will deal not only with personal salvation but will also seek "justice for the oppressed and disinherited".

(5) "A Call to Sacramental Integrity" urges a new recognition of "the sacredness of daily living", as well as "the sacramental nature of God's activity in the world". Affirming the two dominical sacraments is joined with a recognition that Christians are themselves to be "living epistles". (6) "A Call to Spirituality", affirms the message of freedom from guilt and the power of sin, sees preaching as a vehicle leading toward reception of this, and continues: "A true spirituality will call for identification with the suffering of the world as the cultivation of personal piety." Prayer, fasting, meditation, silence, Bible study and spiritual diaries are suggested as resources to these ends. (7) "A Call to Church Authority" notes two dangers: "We regret that in the absence of godly authority, there have arisen legalistic, domineering leaders on the one hand and indifference to church discipline on the other." After asking for "submission to one another and to designated leaders", there is a further call to "all Christian organizations to conduct their activities with genuine accountability to the whole church". The latter statement leads logically and naturally into (8) "A Call to Church Unity", which deplores the scandal of "isolation and separation of Christians from one another", as clearly "contrary to Christ's explicit desire for unity". Evangelicals are exhorted to "return to the ecumenical concern of the Reformers". Church unity cannot be merely spiritual, but "requires visible and concrete expressions".

The document is remarkable for its call to penitence and self-judgment, directed both to those who wrote it and those to whom it is addressed. Whereas Hartford concentrated on the shortcomings of others, Chicago underlines the sins of its own constituency. A time of "evangelical resurgence" is seen not as a time for victory communiqués but for a sober reminder of the dangers of the wrong kind of success. The document also exemplifies a concern for the world and for issues of social justice that is too infrequently associated with "evangelicals", and can help to break down stereotypes that "mainline" Christians often have about more conservatively oriented groups.

4. This Land is Home to Me :
A Pastoral Letter on Powerlessness in Appalachia

In February 1975 a remarkable document was issued by the Roman Catholic bishops of the mountainous "Appalachia" region of the eastern United States, one of the most economically depressed areas of the nation, in which the inhabitants have been systematically victimized by generations of absentee owners who have made inordinate profits from the coal mines and left the workers destitute. The document, entitled "This Land is Home to Me: A Pastoral Letter on Powerlessness in Appalachia", is the result of work by many lay groups, priests, and sisters, and was finally signed by 24 bishops of the region. It is written in blank verse and has been widely distributed within the region in an inexpensive newsprint edition. No summary can do justice to its power. Based on the theme of Psalm 72, in which it is promised that "the mountain shall yield peace for the people, and the hills justice", the letter responds to the psalmist's affirmation of hope that "[Jahweh] shall defend the afflicted ... save the children of the poor, and crush the oppressor".

The letter first analyzes the problems of the region, citing past exploitation, the beginning of new exploitation due to the "energy crisis", the acceptance by owners of the principle of "maximization of profit" at the expense of the workers, and the calls for "citizen involvement" as the only way to work for justice.

In the light of such realities, the letter turns to "the Church's social teaching", and after a review of the major papal social encyclicals reaches an unequivocal conclusion:

Thus,
There must be no doubt,
that we ...
can only become
advocates of the poor.

117

To this end, latter portions of the letter initiate a conversation to which the readers must respond, moving towards

> citizen control
> or community control.
> The people themselves
> must shape their own destiny.

Along with using tools of scientific analysis there must be "a steeping in the presence of the Spirit", for

> We know that if this renewed presence
> can mature into a convergence
> with a thirst for justice,
> a new Pentecost will truly be upon us.

The churches must establish "Centres for Reflection and Prayer" that will integrate social science skills and profound spirituality into the struggle for justice, and also become links in a nation-wide network for the sharing of such concerns. The bishops urge others to engage in the struggle — university people, economists, artists and so forth —

> provided they are open
> to the voice of the poor.

"Centres of Popular Culture" are needed in every parish,

> places where the poor feel welcome...
> so that if a new society is to be born
> it will emerge from the grassroots.

The centres are to be very practical and down-to-earth, teaching people about the power of multinational corporations and urging the development of a counterforce, "a corresponding multinational labour movement". The letter concludes with items on an unfinished agenda (twenty-one in all!) to which readers must begin to respond so that "solidarity with the oppressed" can commence.

The letter is truly a "sign of hope" for people in the region who have had reason in the past to wonder whether the Church was willing to do any more than bless the *status quo*. It also offers hope to the powerless by suggesting ways in which they can gain power for themselves against oppressively formidable odds. It effectively short-circuits the distorted notion that one must choose between "spirituality" and "justice", insisting that the two must and do converge in human lives. And finally, it demonstrates that concern for implementing the gospel can be initiated at the grassroots and unite Christians up to and including the hierarchy, for the bishops responded to the concerns spelled out in the letter, encouraged their articulation, and finally made those concerns their own.

5. The Response of the National Council of Churches

In October of 1976 the Division of Overseas Ministries of the National Council of Churches received "An Open Letter to North American Christians",[4] signed by eight Protestant leaders in Central America, along with five others who could not reveal their names for fear of reprisals. The letter is a plea to North Americans to realize what the oppressive power of their nation is doing to Central and South America — turning it into a prison and a graveyard, as North American business and government interests enter into collusion with Latin American oligarchies to provide fantastic profits for the few and repression, misery and death for many. After a poignant cataloguing of conditions in Latin America, the letter urges North Americans to make use of the franchise (the presidential election was only a few weeks off), and continues, "If in the past you felt it to be your apostolic duty to send us missionaries and economic resources, today the frontier of your witness and Christian solidarity is within your own country". The ballot can be used either to press the United States "toward paths of greater justice and brotherhood, or to accentuating a colonialist and oppressive policy over our peoples".

It is the brief reply of the Governing Board of the National Council of Churches to this letter that exemplifies the giving of an account of hope. Many North Americans, upon reading the letter (which was circulated through *Christianity and Crisis* and other journals), were either defensive or angry at having their sins of omission and commission spelled out so graphically. But members of the Governing Board responded, "We feel that what you have raised are the authentic and key issues impacting the relations between our nations and peoples". They went on to note that the same issues are applicable not only "in our inter-American relations but in our relations with other parts of the world as well". They noted certain piecemeal responses that North American churches have made in the past, that is, concern about human rights under repressive regimes, the relation of US foreign assistance and human rights, the Panama Canal treaty, and American corporations, such as Gulf & Western in the Dominican Republic and General Motors and IBM in Chile. But the response acknowledges that the "Letter to North American Christians" asks for more than this: "You are asking us to look at the more global and systemic nature of the impact of our nation and society on our brothers and sisters in Latin America". The Governing Board voted not to suppress the letter or restrict its circulation to church leaders, but to share it with all of its constituent members and request each denomination to circulate it, study it, and seek appropriate responses that move beyond statements into specific acts.

The Governing Board was giving an account of the hope within it — believing it possible to take on a "controversial issue", destined to anta-

---

[4] *Op. cit.*, pp. 69-73.

gonize many of its more financially fortunate constituents, who would feel themselves under personal attack. It was affirming that the churches could listen to cries of anguish from elsewhere, by which those same churches were implicated, and acknowledge that a relationship that has often been paternalistic must now be turned in new directions.

6.   Message to the Black Church and Community

In August 1977, a significant conference of Black Christians was held in Atlanta. Sponsored by the Black Theology Project of "Theology in the Americas"[5] (a nationwide coalition growing out of a conference of North and South Americans held in Detroit in August 1975), the Atlanta conference concluded with a widely distributed "Message to the Black Church and Community" that is a signal example of how black Christians are giving an account of the hope that is in them.

The document is couched in the powerful and vivid rhetoric that characterizes black preaching at its best, abounding in sharp images, biting denunciation and compassionate hope. The theme of the document is liberation based on Luke 4 and Isaiah 61. "Black theology understands the 'good news' as freedom and Jesus Christ as the Liberator." Throughout the gospel the note of deliverance abounds, and today, "the blackness of Jesus is a religious symbol of oppression and deliverance from oppression".

A strong indictment of "traditional Christianity" follows, highlighting "its failure to comprehend the physical as well as spiritual nature of human being." Disposing of such piecemeal Christianity, the message affirms that the gospel "must deal with the issues of life here and now as well as with the transcendent dimension of the proclamation". In powerful imagery, it exhorts the Church to "come out from behind its stained-glass walls and dwell where mothers are crying, children are hungry, and fathers are jobless". Not only "must the gospel be heard in judgment against the disorder of society", but the Church has a responsibility to help the oppressed "overcome their powerlessness, rise up and take charge of their lives".

The black church is seen as the necessary vehicle for achieving this. The black church has power; furthermore (as the document later states), "it is the only institution over which black people have total control". The black church must re-assert its power. Gospel power must be translated into community power, "for there can be no authentic community in a condition of powerlessness".

After calling attention to the difficult bind in which the black middle-class finds itself, the message turns to "The roots of the crisis", stating

---

[5] *Op. cit.*, pp. 74-78.

that "The root problem is human sinfulness which nurtures monopolistic capitalism, aided by racism and abetted by sexism". Racism and capitalism are seen as setting the stage "for despoliation of natural and human resources all around the world". "Exploitative profit-oriented capitalism" is scored for being fundamentally alien to human values in general and black humanity in particular.

Rather than rejecting the disinherited ("for they are us"), the message affirms that "we embrace all of God's children who hunger and thirst for justice and human dignity". The document ends on a note of great hope. Recognizing that at Atlanta the participants have felt themselves "surrounded by a great cloud of witnesses" (that is, black participants in the freedom struggle in the United States, and those who came before cited in a paraphrase of Hebrews 11 that brings the list of "witnesses" up-to-date) the message concludes:

> In their company and in the company of generations yet unborn, whose life and liberty will be shaped by our deeds, we call upon our church and our community to join us in the warfare that shall know no end, until we shall be perfected together in that kingdom of justice, love and peace which moves relentlessly toward us by the dominion of Jesus the Christ, our Lord and Liberator.

The document is utterly realistic, and yet it breathes hope. It recognizes that power is a necessary vehicle for implementing the struggle for justice, and it sees hope in the power of the black church. Placing its trust in God, it exhorts all who are concerned for justice to enlist in God's service. Acknowledging that a certain kind of "other-worldliness" can be a moral cop-out, it calls for concerned action here and now, yet always rooted in the power of a God who transcends the here and now. And at a very important point, it registers a significant advance over previous black thinking. Up to now, Black theology has focused understandably on racism as the social root of subsequent evils, giving little attention to the ways unjust economic structures perpetuate injustice and compound racism. But the Atlanta message clearly acknowledges that racism, sexism and monopolistic capitalism must *all* be understood as "the roots of the crisis". The document furthermore opens the way for a new level of cooperation between blacks and non-blacks. "*All* of God's children who hunger and thirst for justice and human dignity" are embraced. A necessary period of "separatism", as blacks recovered a sense of their own dignity and worth, may be drawing to a close with the implementation of this message.

7. A Religious Response to the Mahoning Valley Steel Crisis

A further instance of "giving an account of the hope that is in us" can only be reported in tentative fashion, since the issues germane to it are not yet resolved. On 19 September, 1977, a steel mill in Youngstown,

Ohio, was arbitrarily closed down by a Board of Directors meeting a thousand miles away. Five thousand people were thrown out of work, absolutely powerless in determining their destiny. While this is a familiar story in capitalist society, the sequel is not so familiar for the people of Youngstown have refused to accept the decision lying down and have been formulating alternative courses of action. Involved at every step of the way have been the religious leaders, who on 22 November, 1977, issued "A Religious Response to the Mahoning Valley Steel Crisis".[6] The document is an ecumenical triumph in that it is the product of Roman Catholic, Protestant, Orthodox and Jewish cooperative thinking and action. The religious leaders challenge the decision of the Lykes Corporation for engaging in "a way of doing business in this country that too often fails to take into account the human dimensions of economic action". They cite relevant facts, and give the clear impression that they have done their homework and become cognizant of all the factors involved. Their reflections on the "Moral Dimensions of the Crisis" are drawn from relevant scriptural materials in the Psalms, the Prophets and the Gospels. They stress the Judaeo-Christian tradition's "highly developed social teaching with direct relevance to issues of economic justice", and its concern for basic human rights, which include "the right to useful employment and to decent wages and income, the right to participation in economic decisions and even ownership, the right to bargain collectively, among others". Governments must preserve and defend these rights, and economic institutions must serve the common good: "We are convinced, in short, that corporations have social and moral responsibilities." They will not accept a system that forces persons to make harsh decisions in secrecy, and they affirm that "economic decisions ought not to be left to judgment of a few persons with economic power, but should be shared with the larger community which is affected by the decisions." They see these adverse decisions as not solely the responsibility of the Lykes Corporation, but as reflecting national patterns and attitudes that must be questioned.

The balance of the document is "A Response to the Crisis". It moves to specifics which propose plans for community cooperation, education programmes, and finally an exploration of "the possibility of community and/or worker ownership of the sheet and tube plant or other positive alternative use of the facilities to employ the workers". A feasibility study is to be funded to explore such alternatives. A challenge is issued to other major employers "to pledge publicly, community and employee consultation in future economic and investment decisions affecting employment and community life". The Lykes Corporation is challenged to respond to the outpouring of community concern and outrage. Beyond these local concerns, more far-reaching issues are

---

[6] *Op. cit.*, pp. 78-86.

raised "to advocate an effective national policy to retain in our region basic steel and the jobs related to it." This will involve investigating federal aid for modernization, government purchasing policies, changes in economic policies at the national level, and so on. Citizens of Youngstown are called upon to help create a model of community response to economic and other challenges so that other communities similarly affected need not lose hope. A long passage from Isaiah 58 concludes the document.

Perhaps the most notable sign of hope in this document is the fact that in a situation of desperate economic deprivation for thousands of people, the religious communities have been able to combine forces — across Catholic, Protestant, Orthodox, and Jewish lines — and work together on issues that concern them all. In many other communities, similar closing of factories has left the victims stunned and powerless. Marshalling the resources of Scripture, the authors of the present document offer hope rather than despair. Another feature of the document is that it offers hope through specificity. The notion of community ownership of a steel plant is a bold concept, and yet one that could rally citizens towards new levels of cooperation, as well as striking a blow against the concept that the few, sitting in a board room, should have power to determine the destinies of the many. The concluding words from the book of Isaiah move beyond rhetoric, affirming that if people seek to do justice, "Then will your light shine like the dawn and your wound be quickly healed over". It is possible to "rebuild the ancient ruins, build up on the old foundations". When and if that is done, those so engaged "will be called 'Conciliator', 'restorer of households'." (cf Isaiah 58)

8. Study Report by the Disciples of Christ — 1976

An example of an official ecclesiastical reflection on "Giving an Account of the Hope that is in Us" is found in a document prepared over a two-year period by the Commission on Theology and Christian Unity of the Council on Christian Unity of the Christian Church (Disciples of Christ).[7]

Affirming that "Christian faith gives rise to hope", the authors also recognize that "Christians must never suppose that hope is the unique accompaniment of Christian faith". Nevertheless, while being attentive to what others can teach them about hope, Christians have an obligation to indicate what is distinctive about their own hope.

The *basis* for Christian hope is a proclamation about Jesus Christ that moves beyond statement to "a new determination of the lives of those

---

[7] See *Giving Account of the Hope Today,* Faith and Order paper No. 81, Geneva : WCC, 1976, pp. 10-17.

who believe". Truly to believe is to be a different person, whose life is turned outward "on behalf of the world and humankind". While such faith is never a fixed and firm possession, there can nevertheless be a constancy upon which life is founded because of such faith. Such a life is a life "that is lived in this world", and God is known "in and through the actual affairs of this life". The faith that God is trustworthy is a confidence embodied in the "here and now", although trustworthiness refers to the future as well.

These considerations lead to a discussion of the *character* of Christian hope, based on "the confidence and trust in God that applies to the future as well as to the present". Christian hope is belief in the coming of the Kingdom of God. Initially such a claim seems to lack specific content, for we possess no blueprints of God's kingdom even though "we are led to entrust the future to him". However, there are "imaginative pictures of the end" that help us develop a significant content. The God who gives the Kingdom is manifested in Jesus "who was the friend of the poor and oppressed, the outcasts and those who suffer". So the Kingdom will actualize justice, righteousness and mercy; it will bring liberation and peace. Images can be found to evoke this faith all the way from Isaiah to Martin Luther King. No one image is exhaustive, and various images can correct one another.

Further specificity is found by relating images of the end to more proximate statements of Christian hope: "Those who starve will hope for food;... those who are tortured will hope for an end to torturing..." Hope must be expressed in concrete ways since faith has its locus in the here and now. It is conceded that while hopes must be "boldly concrete" and "immediate", they will also remain "complicated and ambiguous". There is always need, therefore, to search for coherence, relating images of the end to realities of the present by finding "their foundation in the God who is known in his gift and claim".

The final section, "Christian Hope and Christian Activity in the World", stresses that Christians not only hope, they also strive. The questions "What shall we do?" and "What do we hope for?" demand the same answers, because hope and the impulse to act are both founded in the Lord of Creation. While full knowledge of how God acts is withheld from us, in the light of the actions of Jesus Christ in the here and now, we receive guidance on how we must act in the here and now.

A creative tension between "hope in the activity of God" and "the determination to work vigorously" is crucial. While Christians, working under grace, will not try to take credit for their accomplishments, neither will they, under that same grace, conclude that human effort is absurd. Hope and activity go together.

This reminds us that hope is not only an orientation to the future, but is itself a mode of life; in addition to hope for God's kingdom, there are lives already characterized by hope. Christians thus live with "confidence in the face of the unknown future". Neither stoic resignation nor precise knowledge of the future provide the Christian's marching orders, but rather "a courage founded on trust in the living God".

The Disciples' statement is important because it holds together things that are often too easily put asunder. Faith and hope are insufficient without each other; Christians and non-Christians can share in hope, even when Christians insist on distinctive dimensions to their hope; hope has a specific reference to the world of the here and now, even though it promises for the future as well; imaginative pictures, poetic images, of the "end" are needed to give us a charter for the present, but specific concrete images for the present must be derived from them and held in tension with them; a variety of pictures are needed since no picture, no conceptualization, can encompass all the truth; hoping and doing are seen to need one another, and hope in what God will do must not negate what human beings can do; a future that is unknown can be embraced with confidence because that future is God's, even if we do not know the precise terms in which God will claim it, mould it, and finally redeem it.

[Note: Some time ago it was hoped (sic) that a proposed new confessional statement of the Presbyterian Church in the United States (that is, the "southern" Presbyterian Church) could also be included. The confession was a church document in a new *genre*, proclaiming the faith by "telling the story", that is the biblical story, in narrative form rather than the "propositional" form so dear to generations of Calvinists. Because it was the biblical story, it was the story of hope, imaginatively retold for today, in ways that could have sparked a new confrontation with the "old, old story". However, as if in reminder that not all hopes are realized, the confession failed to secure necessary ratification by the two-thirds of the presbyteries that was needed to make it a constitution document.]

Conclusions

There are some common threads running through the documents cited above. In addition to the brief comments after each document, we add some summary conclusions that emerge from our study:

1. The Lord is a *living* Lord. This means that even in discouraging and apparently hopeless situations new things are always possible.

2. Concern for personal sanctity and interpersonal justice always go together; hoping and doing are two sides of the same coin.

3. Those who examine themselves critically in the light of the gospel can receive new power from that same gospel. Put another way, in grappling with *present* perplexities ("hearing the voice of God in the voice of the times"), the resources of the *past* (through Scripture, tradition and human wisdom) can empower persons for the *future*, by opening up new possibilities for the achievement of hopes as yet unanticipated.

125

4. Abuse of power — ecclesiastical and political — can be an effective roadblock to hope; ways must be found to use power creatively rather than destructively.

5. It is increasingly clear that all must work together if we are to give an account of the hope that is in us — blacks and whites, Appalachian laity and bishops, "evangelicals" and "liberals", Jews and Orthodox, Catholics and Protestants.

6. Hope must be described by specific and concrete instances and not just in generalized terms.

It has been said that a number of instances cited above are more "signs of hopefulness", that is things in which we can take heart, than they are "accounts of hope", in other words, self-conscious articulations of what it means to hope today. That may be true, and it may not be all bad. It is, I presume, the standard sin of North Americans to appear as activists who reflect very little about their activism. It may be that what we mean by hope will be found more in various "signs of hopefulness" than in straightforward theological utterances. It may also be that the places where hope emerges in our situation will be more in the formal and informal coalitions that arise from time to time than in the official statements of mainline denominations. One way, indeed, in which many of us give some account of the hope that is in us, is through alignment with the sorts of groups represented in a number of the above statements, even as we stay within given denomination structures. There are ways in the United States to do both, and it may be part of our peculiar ecumenical vocation to witness to that possibility.

I conclude with some reflections of my own, for which no other United States delegate should be held responsible. I am not sure that hope can be the appropriate first word for us today in North America. Unless we distinguish what we mean by it very drastically from a culture-faith that equates hope with America remaining "Number One", or defines hope in terms of an ever-rising GNP, we will be misunderstood, and our church talk about hope will be eventually coopted and defused of transforming power. Our cues will come from documents like the Atlanta statement or the Appalachian letter, and by exposing ourselves more sensitively to what is said by Chicanos, Asian-Americans, and other minority groups, so that we can be domestically sensitized to the international reality of our inordinate wealth in the face of such poverty and despair elsewhere. Hope for our nation will be born out of looking national pride in the face, cringing at what we see, recognizing that as long as our national hope rests on political and economic and military power we doom ourselves (and most of the human family along with us), acknowledging that only out of some deep purging, penitence and striving for a renewal on the far side of diminishment, can we receive a hope that is other than illusory. To affirm hope too quickly, too easily, to be so afraid of being perplexed unto despair that we refuse to be perplexed at all, can only lead us to confuse the gospel hope with a vain hope.

To the degree that our churches could begin to see that the local church is only a specific instance of the entire global family, our churches might become communities where a modest hope could begin to be reaffirmed — a hope that would first come as judgment but only to pave the way for grace and empowerment.

I do not know whether we have it within us as a nation to embody a global perspective, beginning to see the world through the eyes of the dispossessed, beginning to realize that whereas others have the problem of having too little power, we have the problem of having too much. Indeed, I do not know whether we have it within us as churches to do those things. But I do know that if we do not, hope is indeed far from us. So I am forced back to the bedrock of the Scriptural belief that, in spite of all appearances, this is still God's world, and that in spite of all our efforts to thwart the divine intention, that intention will at last prevail. I only hope and pray that we do not produce too many casualties before we learn what God — and so many others — would teach us, if we could be still and listen.

6. Three Accounts of Hope from Western Europe

ELLEN FLESSEMAN-VAN LEER

Though Christianity is one of the main factors which has shaped the present-day culture of western Europe, the time when the Church was a dominating influence in public life is definitely past. Defection from the churches, already begun before the Second World War, has greatly increased since then. Disillusion with sterile school-theology has caused many committed Christians to turn away from Christian doctrine and engage in social and political action. These facts, combined with the empirically oriented general climate of thought which permeates western society, have caused a crisis of identity for many Christians and churches. However, over the last couple of years a reversal is clearly noticeable. Action-oriented individuals and groups are asking for the Christian motivation of their engagement. Theologians and church bodies are trying to set forth the meaning of the Gospel. New statements of faith, Christian manifestos and catechisms are drawn up. In many quarters a longing and new openness for Christian faith-reflection is being found.

In this situation the Faith and Order study "Giving Account of the Hope that is in us" found a relatively widespread echo at different levels. It is true that quite a few attempts to cooperate in it did not produce clear results. Some of them did not get much beyond analyzing the general situation. Others, trying to give a comprehensive survey of Christian doctrines, were bogged down by the immensity of this task at the very beginning. Even so, the very fact that attempts were made is significant. A number of contributions have nevertheless been received. Among those which have been published by the Faith and Order Commission is a paper which records a conversation of four participants from different churches in West Germany, testifying with great honesty to the experience

---

● Dr Flesseman-van Leer is a well-known Dutch theologian.

of a "deficit" of hope; and another paper in a more traditional, orthodox vein, made by an interdenominational group of ten persons in
Hampstead Garden Suburb, London.

I. Analyses

A. *A Conversation About Hope*[1]

This is the resume of discussions held by a small group of people from
various denominations in Bristol, England. Bristol is a city of 412,000
inhabitants who live mainly from industry and also a fair amount of
commerce. The group consisted of 9 members, 4 women and 5 men; 4
of them were theologically trained. The group had in mind to make but
a simple and modest contribution to a world-wide enterprise.

The fact that this document consists of actual conversations, reproduced in a condensed form, gives this account a personal and lively
touch. The common summaries which conclude each round of discussions counteract an otherwise too individualistic approach. The result
is that in this document the group has certainly given a *common* account
of its hope. In the first round, the group members stated what salvation
meant to each of them. All spoke in terms of personal experience or
personal relationship with Jesus Christ. Though the various viewpoints
could not be put under a single heading, all, in their different ways,
pointed to: "... something given to us, or breaking through to us ...;
... a personal encounter with Jesus ...; ... something involving each of
us, yet reaching out to 'all that is' ...; ... not something once-for-all,
finished, but growth...". Next, the members pointed to specific events,
which had triggered or confirmed their faith-experiences, such as an
emotional and difficult friendship, a church service in a foreign country,
or a trying time of major illnesses. Drawing together these various
experiences, the group leader summarized them and thereby moved
them to more universally applicable dimensions of salvation: "Again,
notice that we talk about something *on-going,* a growing relationship, a
growing up. Perhaps that's it: *growing up to be truly human, towards
Christ and with Christ.* He is God's new creation, and our salvation
means becoming linked with him so that we are drawn into the making-
of-all-things-new in him". Then, each member chose a particular passage
from the gospels which seemed to him or her particularly relevant.
Mentioned were Matt. 25:31-46; Mark 10:35-45; Luke 19:1-9 and
John 19:1-9. The conclusion of the group's conversation on salvation
was that "both in the gospels and in our own experience we see salvation
as God, in Jesus Christ, bringing all people and all things into the community of his love, freed from guilt, disease, division and death, into
the fullness of life with others and with God; where, on the way to

---

[1] *Study Encounter,* vol. XI, No. 2, 1975, pp. 10-16.

becoming the persons God intends us to be, we share in the family joy of all creation. *But we insist: this salvation is not a 'thing', nor a doctrine, but a happening, always on the move..."*

But this might still seem too abstract. Therefore, the group tried to translate its thought into a poem:

WHAT A HOPE!

For peace,
peace between nations,
peace between races,
peace between sects,
peace between neighbours,
peace of mind.
What a hope!

For community,
community at home, work and
school, where all are accepted
and loved,
community giving children security,
community in which the old are valued,
community — reconciling, giving,
forgiving,
community with others and the universe.
What a hope!

For freedom,
freedom from oppression and torture,
freedom from hunger,
freedom from materialism,
freedom from fear, fear of death,
freedom from self.
What a hope!

In Jesus of Nazareth,
He taught love to all,
His goodness challenged evil,
His love overcame it,
He suffered torture without bitterness,
He showed death was not the end.
What a hope!

The equivocality of the title should be noted. The phrase, generally being used as a cynical exclamation, expresses the startling nature of Christian hope, which hopes in the midst of the cynicism and despair of the world.

After having thus described the content of their hope, the group went on to lay bare the basis on which it rested. They were convinced that

130

no human being "can create peace, freedom and community. God alone can bring in these things, and we work with him". Compared to the rest of the document, this part of it is comparatively short and even a little meagre. Easter and the resurrection are mentioned, the resurrection not merely as assuring us of salvation after death, but as "the real life" which begins now. "Heaven spills into the present, giving us strength here and now." Some thought was given to the relation between Good Friday and Easter, and the conclusion reached was: "We have the assurance of Easter, but we must remember that resurrection comes only through the torment and anguish of Good Friday. Keeping the two together, we shall be saved both from naive optimism and cynical despair".

But the group did not just want to speak about the hope of salvation in their personal lives or the world in general. The question had still to be answered what bearing their hope had on the life of the city in which they lived. Three areas of problems were singled out: (i) An apparently run-down neighbourhood, with bad housing, racial tension and prostitution. Bad as these things were, the group felt that the really alarming aspect of it was "that we have drawn a circle round the area"; thereby, "the people have been marginalized" and as it were pushed out of the community. (ii) The smarter suburbs of Bristol. There too people were marginalized and cut off from real community, because they "hardly know how to talk and listen to one another and act together". (iii) But the real isolation in present society the group saw in our attitudes to death. If anywhere, there the lack of community is revealed. "It has become a terror, and a guilty subject; ... death, by picking us off one by one, exposes so ruthlessly the underlying truth of our condition: that we are alone. True community does not exist. It exposes the barrenness of much of our western society."

Left still was the question in which way this hope could be brought to other people. In this relation the Church was mentioned, which should be a sign of hope in the world, "a real community, pointing the way to what real community means". But the Church as it actually is "seems ill qualified to be a sign of hope". However, the members admitted that they themselves were part of this Church. Therefore, they could not just denounce it, but had to begin by confessing and continually seeking forgiveness for their own failures. In this way the group was brought to the insight that "the only source and 'proclaimer' of hope is God in Christ, through the Holy Spirit". "Our hope is that, even in the most unlikely situations, the God, whom we know in Christ can build bridges. Our calling is to discover them, and work with God in strengthening them, wherever and however true community needs to be built."

This account breathes such a spirit of honesty and is so devoid of all pretentious sophistication that it is not easy to make analytical observations without doing it an injustice. The foremost impression it

131

conveys is one of piety and personal commitment. It is written in a clear and unpresuming style, simple and straightforward without ever being banal; theological language and doctrinal terms are avoided.

Its central point is the hope and longing for true community (communion), which only God can build, but for which he will use human beings. Closely linked with this hope of the new community is the certainty that through personal relationship with Christ men and women can become new beings and that a new life is imparted to them. In theological terminology: the main emphasis is not placed on justification — though it is not absent — but on the process of regeneration and sanctification. However, basic in this process remains the initiative and continuing activity of God. In view of the above, it is not surprising that sin, guilt, and forgiveness are comparatively marginal thoughts. It is significant that in the central poem "What a Hope!" they are only obliquely mentioned. The new life is marked by its outgoing attitude: a concern for human issues and the wish to witness to the Christian hope of salvation in words and actions. Attention is primarily directed to small-scale personal attitudes, though worldwide problems are not forgotten, as is evident from the poem.

The context of this account is the comparatively limited one of Bristol. However, the structural problems which undoubtedly will exist in that society too are not explicitly dealt with. When its suffering is mentioned, it is primarily the personal suffering of alienation, illness, death and lack of communion. "Worldwide concerns" and "the grim realities of the world" are by no means negated, but one does not get the impression that they form a serious challenge to the faith of the group members. And the same is true for the challenge of secularization; apparently, it is not felt to constitute a threat which can make it difficult for believers to keep their faith. Thus, the whole tone and colour of this document is uplifting, positive and joyful.

It is remarkable that the Spirit apparently plays no conscious role in this account. It is mentioned only in a thoroughly traditional formula. This fact can probably be explained by the undoctrinal character of this document. For, theologically speaking, the work of the Spirit is really the one and all in this account. Prayer is not referred to in the abstract, but the conversation recorded ends with a prayer of dismissal.

The personal and experiential approach of this account furnishes probably the explanation of the fact that the more "objective" aspects of Christian faith do not seem to have much existential meaning. The mentioning of the resurrection and crucifixion is comparatively traditional and even superficial. Hope of the Kingdom of God is not named, though it seems unlikely that the group would deny it. Though a certain importance is attached to the notion of personal life beyond death, the wider eschatological dimension does not seem to be an important living reality. Or perhaps it would be more correct to say that in the poem on hope some form of realizing eschatology is envisaged – but it is a this-worldly eschatology: the goal of true community in Christ, which is to be realized on earth and within history by the World and the power of God in and on us.

B. *Witness and Discipleship: A German View*

The second document "Our Hope: A Confession of Faith for this Time"[2] represents a carefully formulated statement of theological principles, drawn up at the Joint Synod of Catholic Dioceses, held in Würzburg, West Germany, 1971-75. The Synod consisted of a kind of "upper house" of bishops with a veto-right, and a sort of "lower house" of priests, representatives of the orders and lay people. The members of the "lower house" were for the greater part chosen, only a minority was appointed. The Synod, at its eighth and last general assembly in 1975, adopted our document as a "resolution" (Beschluss) with a large majority. Thereby, it received the status of an official synodal document, which carries a certain, not fully defined semi-magisterial authority. In some places this well-balanced and well-thought-out statement shows its Roman Catholic origin by a particular emphasis or thought, but it is so truly ecumenical that also other Christians will have no difficulty in recognizing it as an expression of their faith and hope. Though it seems evident that much theological thinking went into it, it is written in a clear and decidedly non-doctrinal language. When biblical texts are quoted or biblical wordings explicitly used, it is done in a functional and exegetically sound way. The words of the title "a confession *for this time*" are taken seriously. There is a clear recognition that the state-ment is drawn up in a secularized society, dominated by presuppositions, "axioms" as they are called, which are often "a counter-current" to Christian faith, and which consequently "make it extremely difficult to correlate this message of hope with people's experiences". This insight is hardly ever lost sight of. In this way, the claim is substantiated that this confession is not merely aimed at the renewal of the Church and as such addressed to Church people, but also to those outsiders who are "searching for meaning in life".

The document is divided into four parts. *Part I: Witness to hope in our society* is the most weighty one and considerably longer than the other three parts taken together. Out of the richness of the Church's faith, eight theological subjects are selected, namely those which are consi-dered to be essential in view of the situation to which the document speaks.

---

[2] See "Giving Account of Hope in These Testing Times", *Study Encounter*, vol. XII, No. 1-2, 1976, pp. 65-87.

1. The first of these subjects is "God of our Hope". There is a clear realization that this belief runs counter to the general trend which views society as "a network of wants and their satisfaction". It also has to contend with the criticism that God is "a code-word for a dangerous appeasement or an over-hasty reconciliation with our painfully torn world". Actually, however, hope in God "awakens in us again and again the hunger for meaning, the thirst for justice for all people ... and prevents us from settling down exclusively within the truncated dimension of our world of wants".

2. The second theme deals with the "Life and death of Jesus Christ". The new interest in Jesus as human being is fully acknowledged and it is pointed out that it can offer a valuable stimulus for the conduct both of individual Christians and the public life of the Church. But equal stress is laid on his eternal divine sonship. Otherwise the radical character of his love would seem to be "a grotesque overtaxing of human capacity". But the main point made in this section is that the life of Jesus Christ was no success-story but "a history of suffering"; therefore in a society which is "becoming increasingly the helpless victim of a widespread indifference, a growing insensitivity to suffering", belief in him should induce us to "recover our capacity to suffer in order to be able to suffer also in the sufferings of others". And these "others" are not only to be looked for in the realm of the Church. Christians should be alert "to hear the dark prophesy of suffering" in the secular world too. Only then can they "confess aright the hopeful message of Christ's suffering".

3. The most prominent feature of the third theme "Resurrection of the dead" is that main attention is not given to the hope of our personal resurrection (though that notion is expressed also), but to the resurrection of those who died before us. Also communion with them is strongly advocated. It is manifest that this runs counter to our general social consciousness, in which the thought of death and grief are repressed. Actually, however, the message that there is a future for the dead is one of hope and justice, for it affirms that the sufferings of the past were not pointless. Therefore, it "liberates us for a life which resists the pure self-assertiveness whose meaning is death" and makes us into " 'Easter' men and women" who are prepared to live for others.

4. The fourth subject with which the document deals is "Judgment". At first glance, it might seem surprising that it is counted among the essentials and that it is considered to be an expression of our hope. But the statement highlights its liberating dimension in pointing out that "it tells of God's power to establish justice" and that it "brings news of an imperishable hope to all those who suffer injustice". Therefore, it "frees us to work for justice in season and out of season", and impels us "to oppose structures of injustice". Though the dark side of the message of judgment is not left out, the emphasis is put on its hopeful aspect.

134

5. In an account of hope "Forgiveness of sins" cannot be omitted. Here it is developed against the background of a society hallmarked by "the secret illusion of innocence" and a "self-exculpation mechanism". Hope of divine forgiveness makes it possible to accept oneself and to deal realistically with one's guilt and one's sin. It makes man[3] free and gives him the courage and joy to accept concrete responsibility. It is in line with the character of this account that it addresses itself not only to individual guilt, but also to "that structural involvement in guilt in which we find ourselves at present because of human dependence and interdependence at the world level and in face of the needs and the oppression of far-off foreign peoples and groups". It also draws attention to the danger that Christian doctrine is used to strengthen the status quo: the doctrine of guilt and sin can be misused in such a way "that the powerless are loaded with still more guilt and the powerful with still more 'innocent' power".

6. Under the heading "Kingdom of God", the hope for the "new man" as well as the "new heaven and the new earth" are comprised. The Kingdom is conceived as "an eschatological event whose future has already begun for us in Jesus Christ" and whose consummation will be exclusively the work of God's transforming power. Hope of the Kingdom gainsays public consciousness with its naive evolutionary optimism and its implicit trust in science and technology, and fosters "sober realism" about the possibility of man. This realism "does not paralyse our concern with personal and social suffering", but it liberates us from too extravagant standards. For the Kingdom certainly transcends the world, but is not indifferent to it.

7. In most confessions of faith and theological treatises, the subject "Creation" precedes that of the Kingdom. Here the order is reversed. By thus placing it in the light of its consummation in the Kingdom, the hopeful, forward-looking aspect of the world as God's creation is affirmed. The key notions in this section are praise, thanksgiving, joy and especially celebration. These notions gain credibility, because they do not entail an "uncritical endorsement of existing conditions". On the contrary, belief in the goodness of creation sensitizes us to its pains.

8. The last subject dealt with in Part I is the "Fellowhip of the Church". A clear differentiation is made between the Church and the Kingdom. In that light the definition of the Church as "the community of hope" must be understood. But it is not only a fellowship of hope, it is also "a school in which living hope matures, where we can learn it together and celebrate it together". The document is realistic enough, however, not to pass over the deficiencies of the Church; in particular, it points to the dangers inherent in its "official structures and administrative machinery".

---

[3] Note: in the German language the word "man" (*Mensch*) refers to both male and female.

The much shorter *Part II: The one witness and the many messengers of hope* and *Part III: Ways of discipleship* spell out how the foregoing confession of faith can become a force of renewal in the life of the Church. Here all that has been confessed before receives its concrete working out. It is one exhortation to become conformed "to him in whom our hope is anchored".

In Part II attention is focused on the Church as the people of God. The same critical world-openness is found which characterized the treatment of the subject in the former part. The Church should on the one hand avoid withdrawal in a separate religious world and on the other hand an over-accommodation to the world and its latest fads. The attitude of the document is in no way apologetic or defensive. It is admitted that the Church is a Church of sinners and even "a sinful Church". Again one is struck by the little emphasis on the institutional side. It is stated emphatically that the Church is not so much a Church for the people but rather of the people, and that all in their different ways are responsible for its renewal. In speaking of the ministry attention is focused on its "duty to seek the Spirit and constantly to allow for his incalculable and often disturbing spontaneity".

Part III mentions some concrete ways of discipleship, which all derive from Jesus' obedience to the cross. Therefore, in our obedience, "we shall ourselves experience the cross too". In order to bring home the radical character of this thought, the statement points to church life being so conformed to society that Christian faith is in danger of becoming "a religion of prosperity instead of a religion of the cross". According to the document, discipleship is not merely an inward attitude, but it demands also an outward societal and political realization. Beside the way of obedience, the ways of poverty, of freedom and of joy are mentioned. Most of what is said here has already been indicated in Part I, but here it receives a particularly pungent expression. The one really new note, not found elsewhere in such an explicit way, is the emphasis on joy. "The ultimate aim of all renewal of our church life is that this joy should be reflected in countless ways in the countenance of the Church and thus the witness of hope will become in our society an invitation to joy".

Part IV: Programme for the whole Church and Society as a whole spells out what distinctive çontributions the Church in the Federal Republic of Germany can make to the Church universal. Four specific points are mentioned:

1. Living in the country of the Reformation, the Church in Germany has a special obligation of trying to overcome the great religious divisions of western Christendom and "of striving for a new and vital unity of Christians in truth and love".

136

2. In view of past history "one of the special obligations of the German Church within the universal Church is to work for a new relationship of Christians to the Jewish people and to its religious history".

3. Being the Church "of a comparatively rich and economically powerful country ", it has a special ecumenical obligation and mission to share its wealth with the churches of the Third World, not as an act of charity but as the price of its catholicity and orthodoxy. For "the one world Church cannot simply be just one more reflection of the social divisions of our world".

4. Careful stewardship of the natural resources of the world is needed, if the future will be fit for human beings to live in. Germany being a highly developed industrial and technical country, the Church there has to mobilize its moral forces to develop "a radical change in our patterns of living", new forms of "collective asceticism".

I am not sure whether this too short summary of the document can convey something of the spirit which permeates it. The main emphasis is laid on the particularly hopeful aspects of the Christian faith and on the specific ethical implications and actions which follow from these aspects. There is moreover a clear awareness that the climate in which witness to Christian faith and hope has to be given is no longer favourable to it; the forces in the world which are counteractive to it are specifically described. In this way, this account is an example of how faith and action are to be held together and how a confession of faith and a formulation of ethics has to take into account the situation, the "milieu" in which it has to function. This statement is, in the best sense of the word, contextual, with the understanding that the particular and the universal contexts are both kept sight of; this is particularly evident in the fourth part of the document.

The document shows a keen awareness of suffering, personal suffering, but even more the suffering of others and of society at large. Another of its pivotal thoughts is that of solidarity, in particular with those who are poor and powerless. There is also an intimation of the structural aspect of many problems. Another strong point is that in speaking of the tasks and actions consequential upon Christian hope, the document combines their corporate nature with the claim put on every individual believer.

There is never a triumphalist tone; on the contrary, there is a fair amount of Christian self-criticism, which, however, nowhere degenerates into a form of self-deprecation or pessimism.

Because of its nature, this document has a theological richness which is far greater than that of most accounts. It is perhaps noteworthy that the Spirit is not considered to be one of the essential subjects. Certainly he is mentioned a few times, not very emphatically, in connection with the Church, not in connection with discipleship. Nor do the sacraments

137

receive marked attention. There is one mere reference to the sacrament of penance. Baptism and the eucharist are not mentioned under the heading of the Church but under that of the Kingdom. That is to say that they are placed in the eschatological context of the new life and the coming glory instead of an institutional context. That is in accordance with the observation made above that the institutional side of the Church is played down. It is perhaps strange that prayer is referred to explicitly in only one or two instances, and that not very emphatically.

Due to the "undogmatic" approach of this confession, there are several doctrines which are, probably purposely, omitted. The eternal divine sonship of Jesus is mentioned but the concept of incarnation is not; the notions of Trinity or Triune God do not appear; the affirmation that Jesus Christ liberates us from sin and guilt is in no way doctrinally developed. Other doctrines may have been omitted because of the ecumenical spirit of the document. The papacy is passed over in silence and mariology is only hinted at. And when the saints are mentioned and communion with the dead even emphatically advocated it is done in such a way that even staunch protestant believers may wonder whether they too should not include those thoughts in their Christian hope.

C. *Country-wide Study in the Netherlands*

The third document[4] consists of two parts: the actual account, entitled "Giving Account of our Hope in an Ambiguous Existence", and a second more formal part "Criteria for an Account" which gives general guidelines to which an account should conform and by which it can be judged. This twofold document is the outcome of a rather extensive study process, set up by the Council of Churches in the Netherlands. About 400 persons, men and women, theologians and non-theologians, representing a variety of religious, social and political outlooks, divided into 25 groups all over the country, took part in the study. The document was accepted unanimously by the Dutch Council, sent to its member churches for consideration and recommended as basis for further reflection.

The first part of the report, the account proper, is so short that it even could be quoted in full here. It seems preferable, however, to give an analysing summary of it, because in reading it through, it appears initially to lack a clear outline. It seems to express more a certain mood than give a clear-cut argumentation. The general spirit which it breathes could be called one of "getroste Verzweiflung" (consoled despair), to use a term of Luther. Here speaks a "nevertheless" faith, a faith "notwithstanding everything". That comes to the fore already in its

---

[4] See *Giving Account of the Hope Today,* Faith and Order paper No. 81, Geneva: WCC, pp. 1-9.

very title: account *in an ambiguous existence*. The climate and situation out of which and to which this account speaks is determined by a "feeling of ambiguity. Light and darkness, sense and nonsense are inextricably entangled. History is a mixture of banality and grandeur. Man[5] is capable of the greatest sacrifice and of the most bestial, sadistic practices". This might seem to be a rather timeless description; the very existence of man is always characterized by ambiguity. However, the clear *realization* of this ambiguity is specific to the Dutch spiritual situation. Moreover, this ambiguity is occasioned by specific present-day phenomena, such as technology, which "has brought us progress and prosperity", but also the threat of "becoming alienated from ourselves, from our fellowman and from nature"; or the increasing complexity of society, which frustrates "every simple and straightforward choice", though such choices are necessary, "if we are not to end in social as well as in human deadlock".

Thus, this account is decidedly not a timeless one. It speaks to a situation which in its "openness" is threatened by hopelessness and lack of meaning.

If one analyses this account, a precise train of thought appears. After a description of our situation of ambiguity, it is argued that only faith can break through this ambiguity and give the courage to affirm that life is meaningful. "To believe does mean the conviction that this ambiguity does not have the last word."

Then a paragraph on Jesus follows, on whom the certainty is based "that God has intended man for happiness and not for suffering". It is to be noted that Jesus is seen specifically in his humanness, though not primarily as example but rather as the one in whom "we have seen the face of God illumined". In his life and obedience unto death, Jesus vindicated the rights of "the defeated, the weak and the discarded". Thereby and also by this forgiveness of "those who had run aground", he has shown what God's will is. And God, "by raising him from the dead, has once and for all made it clear on which side he is", and that "his love has the last word to the point where it will not allow itself to be forced out of existence".

From this it follows that "for us hope has become ineradicable and with it the fight against despair". This fight takes concrete form in discipleship, or, as it is called here, "following after Jesus". It "will be reflected in the big and small decisions which we have to take from day to day". The strong point in this paragraph is that the decisions which it mentions are those which confront every man and woman in the Netherlands, such as the way in which money and leisure are spent; the

---

[5] Note: In the Dutch language the word "man" (*means*) refers to both male and female.

political party voted for; the attitude towards migrant workers and people who are redundant; "and particularly how we can live with our failure and guilt".

After having thus dealt with faith, the account turns to hope, though this is not a clear-cut differentiation, for, as the account itself maintains, "our hope is a form of faith". The hope the account has in mind is the final hope of God's Kingdom, though the term Kingdom is not used. It is described in such biblical thought forms as "God himself, who shall live among men and who shall wipe every tear from their eyes". "Then at last everything will happen in the way which is God's will and life will become good in all its dimensions."

This hope of God's Kingdom is worked out in two directions. On the one hand, it has a critical function. "Our society and our whole life and work are judged by this future. Much of what we think of as important proves to be of no importance in that light, and a great deal of what we name progress is called into question. And at the same time we also learn to discern which tendencies and developments may be called fruitful." On the other hand, this hope spurs us to action, for when we believe in this future "we cannot leave things as they are". This paragraph is a sort of parallel to the former one on discipleship, but there the more personal decisions and attitudes were considered while here rather the more worldwide problems are viewed; "the fight against exploitation and suffering, against violence and meaningless destruction of men, against hopelessness and resignation, against pride and egoism". In this way the account points out how belief in God's Kingdom "implies that we try step by step to translate our fundamental choice into our deeds".

In the following paragraph the statement deals with the Church, for, as it is said, "believing is a plural thing". The Church is primarily considered as a community in which believers find mutual support and where Christian tradition is kept alive and passed on. Moreover, "there we also learn to pray, for ourselves and for our world, and we try to express our hope for the world by working towards the future, always supporting each other. In this way the community can become a segment of hope made visible through its worship, its teaching and its action".

The account ends by affirming that the eschatological hope for the future is a light which "plays over our world and causes light patches here and there, even now". This "is enough to encourage us to go on", for it assures us that "the future is no chimera". And so the last words of this account are: "In spite of everything, our life is marked by the joy of expectation."

The main scope of this account is the affirmation of meaning in a seemingly meaningless existence. It speaks more of suffering and futility than of sin and guilt. Its main search is for meaning, not for forgiveness.

The statement cannot be described as being pessimistic, but the Christian joy which it expresses is a muted joy. The language is in no way traditional or doctrinal, and sometimes even rather moving. But I am not sure whether this account will easily find resonance in people who do not share its general mood.

It is so strongly future-oriented that one can question whether the newness of life, given already now, is not underestimated. In this respect it might be significant that creation is not mentioned. However, too much weight cannot be given to such observation. The statement is short and many aspects of Christian hope and faith are mentioned only in a single sentence and some not at all. In any case, the account is certainly not other-worldly; in its future orientation it remains faithful to the earth and expresses emphatically the interrelation of faith and works. Micro- and macroethical considerations are kept together too; equally, both the immediate and the worldwide context.

Still, the account is richer in theological content than it might seem to be at first glance. This first impression is due to the fact that all theological concepts are avoided and even many biblical notions often translated (for example forgiveness: cutting man free from his guilty past); also the intentional brevity of the account plays a role. Even so, it is noteworthy in view of its eschatological focus, that individual life after death is not even hinted at. As already indicated above, Jesus' humanity is developed, his divine Sonship or divinity not mentioned, though probably presupposed. The account is rather theo- than christocentric. God is confessed in his love for man; the thought that he is Judge too is not at all or only very indirectly expressed ("With an appeal to God's will, (Jesus) took his stand against the powers of Church and society which threatened ... to crush life to death"). The Spirit is referred to as working in the Christian community; in the context of the community a reference to prayer is found also. Baptism and eucharist are not named, though they are surely meant in the words that in the commuity "salvation is celebrated".

Turning to the second part of the Dutch report, *Criteria for an account,* the very term "criteria" might cause some initial misunderstanding. Therefore, the Dutch paper sets out to define what it means by this term. An account, it explains, is not the same as a confession of faith; it is less formal and comprehensive, has not primarily a teaching, catechetical function, and mentions only "what now, in our time and situation, is relevant and functions". Given this framework, criteria cannot be conceived of as being hard and fast requirements which an account has to meet in order to be acceptable; rather, they are general "guidelines in the service of a mutual dialogue, and not measuring rods to judge each other's orthodoxy".

The document goes on to formulate seven criteria:

1. An account has to be *contextual*, in other words, it "has to pay attention to the climate and situation in which it has to function primarily".

2. It has to be *biblically* justified, not in the sense that it quotes biblical texts, but in the sense that it relates to main themes of the Bible.

3. An account should be *related to society* and should point "to ways of critical and constructive action" in it. This applies to interhuman relations and to structural and worldwide problems.

4. The *Christian community* has to play a part. Though an individual believer can give a personal account, there is a limit set to his subjectivity, because his hope and faith are nurtured by the tradition of the Church.

5-7. The three remaining criteria deal with the *form and language* of an account. Its tone, it is stated, should not be too self-assured; its language should be clear and understandable and "no more should be said than can be answered for".

II. Common Problems

1. The three accounts we have dealt with are different in form and in scope. Also, their status is different. The British paper does not claim to be more than a personal expression of hope of a small group of committed Christians. The Dutch paper purports to be an account of a cross-section of Dutch Christians, and the national council, by accepting it, has made it into a document which should be heard in its member churches. The German account has a higher status. It is an official document of an official, representative church body.

2. This difference in magisterial and ecclesiological status points to the problem of the relationship between a confession of faith and an account. The Dutch paper tried to define the difference between them. Irrespective of the question whether one agrees with its description, it seems clear that the borderline between the two is not a hard and fast one. The German document, which calls itself a confession, states that it is in line with the giving account study to which Faith and Order has summoned all Christians. The one thing which can perhaps be said is that an account seeks to state what needs to be stated today and therefore can be intentionally selective. An account may be characterized by a certain theological imbalance, proper to its concrete situation. This observation is borne out by the three accounts considered. Even the German statement consciously makes a selection of the themes with which it deals (though in the second reading of its first draft in the

Synod the remark was added that "the whole richness of the Church's creed shines through").

3. All three accounts have come up against the problem of language. There is a realization that traditional Christian and even biblical language will no longer do, because it is no longer understood or its meaning has been drained out of it by familiarity. Therefore, they have looked for a new, communicative language. All three distrust highsounding and big words. Doctrinal notions, as for instance Trinity, incarnation, atonement, are not used. They also try to speak of such concepts as sin, forgiveness, justification in a new way, meaningful to people of today. The same applies to the concept of the Spirit; because many have no picture of what is meant by it, the Spirit is comparatively seldom mentioned by name, though his work is emphatically acknowledged.

Also the form of an account has come up for scrutiny. The form which the continental accounts have chosen is not the only one possible. The conversation form of the Bristol paper gives it a particular liveliness and its short poem and dismissal prayer are perhaps its most compelling features.

4. The European accounts are written in a pluriform, secularized and "post-Christian" society. All three show a clear awareness of this fact. This poses the question to whom these accounts are addressed. The two continental documents explicitly deal with this question: they state that their accounts are aimed primarily at themselves and at people like them, that is believers, but often doubting and questioning believers, in or on the fringe of the Church, and furthermore to those who are seekers. Language and content of these accounts – and that goes for the British one too – are not really geared to fully secular "outsiders". But is one single account which can speak to all people feasible in a pluralistic situation as the one in western Europe?

III. Faith and Praxis from Different Perspectives

1. A statement without any apparent consciousness of the contemporary climate in which it has to function will make it sound flat and unconvincing as an account of living faith and hope. It has to be contextual. The immediate context of the two continental accounts is a secular, technological, rich society with its egoism and greediness; in the Bristol account human isolation and lack of community receive a stronger accent. To speak to the western European situation, an account should show awareness that faith and hope have to contend with a climate of indifference and shallowness as well as cynicism and hidden despair.

2. The European accounts, in their different ways, describe how faith goes together with praxis. To various degrees they show a critical attitude towards society. Also, all three show awareness of major world problems, but concentrate on what is demanded in terms of possible,

143

personal action. An account that only points to what is amiss in society at large or concentrates on the world problems which beset mankind without indicating what sort of concrete action or way of life discipleship demands from ordinary men and women in their actual situation, will give most Europeans a feeling of frustration rather than strengthen their Christian hope.

3. Beside the more personally geared actions and attitudes, the German synodal confession describes four specific tasks for the German Church on behalf of the whole Church. The four tasks mentioned would most likely be recognized as valid by the other two European documents too : to strive for Christian unity, to work for a new relationship with the Jews, to share its wealth with the poor of the Third World and to develop forms of collective asceticism. It would be a good thing if, following the example of the German confession, Christians of the various churches and regions would state in their common account which specific obligations their particular churches have to fulfil for the sake of the universal Church.

4. We have noted that there is a selectivity of biblical themes dealt with in the European accounts. Though no exact check-list of such themes can be given, for continental Christians the eschatological Kingdom to come is certainly among them ; an account of hope which does not focus on it would seem seriously inadequate to them. Judging from the Bristol account, this hope does not seem to be equally important to British Christians. Any account of hope will surely have to speak about God and Jesus Christ. According to the ones we have considered particularly the human life of Jesus has become important; it is notably his suffering which is a cause for hope. The accounts witness to a personal God. Compared to their emphasis on his love, the notion of God as Judge recedes into the background. However, the very impressive treatment of the theme of judgment in the German account should be kept in mind.

5. The three accounts express a longing for the Church to be a real fellowship and a place where hope is strengthened and takes shape. They also take a rather critical stance towards the Church institution as it exists today. An account of hope which will speak to the European mind has to honour this longing for Christian community in an increasingly atomizing society, combining it with a realistic acknowledgement of the failures of the existing Church.

The theme of the Conference of European Churches held in Geneva in 1967 was "European theology challenged by the worldwide Church". In order to get a still clearer picture of our accounts and their specific emphases, we might view them in the mirror of that challenge. Four points of critique were particularly brought forward by the non-western churches.

(a) It was maintained that in matters of faith too much value is attached by Europeans to the human intellect and to doctrine. We saw that the tone of the European accounts is decidedly non-doctrinal and can hardly be called intellectualistic — though clarity of thought and intellectual honesty are valued. Might it not actually belong to the special province of European Christianity to be watchful that sound theological thinking and scholarship are not lost sight of?

(b) It was said that not enough attention is being paid to the socio-political context, the concrete situation in which the Gospel addresses men and women. We saw that our accounts are manifestly contextual. They show a clear awareness of the injustice, suffering, oppression and poverty in the world. It should be realized, however, that today the situation in western Europe is not marked by big social and political problems which demand an immediate, unequivocal solution. Moreover, compared to non-western accounts, the European ones speak probably more deductively to their situation than inductively from their situation. But this is not an ultimately tenable distinction: there is a back and forth from account to situation and from situation to account.

(c) European theology, it was stated, does not pay enough attention to creation, nature, its own culture and history. In a way, this point is indeed borne out by the three European accounts, although creation is one of the themes of the German one and the ecological problem is referred to by the three of them. But none of them gives a positive, theological evaluation of nature, culture or history, and it might well be that any European account would hesitate to do that. Mindful of the "blood and soil" ideology of Nazi-Germany, European and particularly continental Christians have become very sensitive indeed to the danger of giving a halo of sacredness to natural givenness.

(d) The fourth point of critique concerning the intimate connection of reflective thinking and committed Christian action is clearly met by the European accounts, with the understanding that in them theological reflection is seen to precede action, and not *vice versa.*

1. Towards Fuller Community of Women and Men in the Church

Introductory note

At the meeting of the Commission on Faith and Order, a week was devoted to discussion of accounts of hope from different parts of the world and the formulation of a "common" account of hope. The commission members and other participants first met in groups to discuss different aspects of the hopes in people everywhere. One of the working groups was on new community between women and men, the working paper entitled: "Towards an account of hope from women", which the group had read in advance. It was a collection of statements and reflections from women in various parts of the world about their hopes for the future. Most of these accounts were contemporary; one was almost a hundred years old, indicating that the hopes of women today have been carried by previous generations. The working paper is appended to this report.

The seven women and thirteen men members of the group, drawn from different countries and cultures and holding a variety of theological positions, reacted in different ways to the statements. After considerable discussion, there was agreement that what was said in the preparatory paper was not inclusive enough, but was indeed expressive of the reality which many women in various parts of the world experience today. Having come to this working agreement, the group examined various segments of "Towards an account of hope from women" to see which elements might be appropriated for both women and men, and which expressed distinctively or exclusively a woman's experience.

The common concern of the group was over the brokenness of community between women and men, and the group's shared hope is for "full partnership of women and men in the Church which clearly presents a sign of true community in the world". The report is really a collection of reflections on what the group regards as full partnership in a community of women and men, providing "clues and new items for further study and discussion".

The importance of these materials lies in the methodology, the process of reflection. Confronted with the sensitive issues of feminism in the churches and of the new consciousness of women, the group first responded defensively. But after their own theological reflection, and after they got to know one another, the members entered into a creative dialogue, resulting in a common account from women and men. The documents show a way for women and men to get into discussion together about a potentially divisive and often threatening issue. They also indicate that the commitment to stay with the issues can open up new horizons of both personal understanding and theological creativity for both women and men.

Response from the Working Group on Community of Women and Men in the Church

to
"Towards an Account of Hope from Women", a Faith and Order Working Paper

Those of us who worked together in the group on the "Community of Women and Men", did so with the conviction that in God we have the promise of new life that can change the alienating and disrupting contexts of human existence. We found in the Gospel message the "hope of God" for the full restoration of all aspects of human life to the purposes of God's Kingdom.

I. Our own community of women and men

As women and men meeting to share the problems and promises of living in true community, we were determined that we ourselves should grow into that community of mutuality which we intend for all.

We came from different parts of the world, representing almost all continents and many cultures; we reflected the major traditions of the Church — Catholic, Orthodox and Protestant, and held a variety of theological positions among ourselves; we varied a great deal in our historical experiences and cultural heritages. In some of our churches women have already been accepted into the ordained ministry of the Church; in others the question of even greater participation of women in Church life was yet to be opened.

We felt, however, that in our societies, as in our churches, there is "brokenness" in the community of women and men which distorts our life. We found ourselves sharing with each other our own hopes and aspirations for a truly human community.

One of our African participants pointed to the saying in St John's Gospel: The harvest is plentiful, but the labourers are few. "The Church is losing much of its harvest", she said, "because of its unwillingness to use committed women in the ministry. I hope," she continued, "for the day when all the people of God can be fully used in the service of his kingdom."

An Orthodox among us was equally dismayed at the lack of community, and wished "that the Church makes a study of all those customs that limit women's participation on account of their 'impurity', a notion which seems alien to the New Testament". Another among us had come with the hope that all the churches would present their problems and difficulties on this question "and discuss together their differences with a view to arriving at common solutions".

Many of us were able to give concrete examples of brokenness from our own lives. Even those women among us who have become pastors and professors witnessed to the lack of community in professional life, and hoped for the change of attitudes and structures that will liberate all men and women in need of liberation. One of us felt that this is possible only "when true partnership develops at the local congregational level and at the lowest strata of society". We all shared the hope of a Roman Catholic participant that this community should be established "on the basis of love and sacrifice".

We were also able to voice together some of our common concerns:

— that we should respect diversity and listen to each other as we wrestle anew with questions of the full participation of all the people of God in the life of the Church, having courage to hear the Spirit as it speaks to us, and to speak the truth to one another in love;

— that we recognize that the search for new ways of working, worshipping and living together as men and women will cause controversy, confusion and pain, and that we be prepared to pay the cost of living out this hope;

— that we need to give serious theological, ecclesial and liturgical attention to the development of language and metaphors that enable the people of God to speak of God in a way that is inclusive of both women and men;

— that we should examine those practices that limit women's full participation in Church life with the view to identifying the alien influences that are not conformable to the spirit of the New Testament;

— that our aim should be to become communities "where love casts out fear", and to glimpse a new vision of wholeness of women and men in the humanity of Jesus, the Christ.

In this search, we felt that the place of our meeting — Bangalore — was significant. Here, in India, we are confronted not only by traditions and religious values developed over centuries, but also with the stark reality of poverty and deprivation, and the need for social change. We realized that in our struggle to realize the community of women and men we were involved in the larger struggle to make the whole of life more human.

Our common hope as a working group was for full partnership of women and men in the Church which clearly presents a sign of true community in the world. We began our search for community by listening with sympathy and with patience to voices from different situations which speak of the brokenness of community between women and men.

II. Learning to listen to accounts of hope

Our working group tried to listen to the accounts of hope provided in the working paper entitled, "Towards an Account from Women" (appended). We had *no choice* about the texts which were the basis of our discussion. In fact, some of us would have preferred other texts that might have lifted up different types of accounts from both women and men or the more balanced text found in the "The Community of Women and Men in the Church Study." Our first reactions as a group were very mixed. Some were hostile to the texts and found them offensive. Others felt that the texts were inadequate for expressing and furthering the task of the working group in assisting the WCC and the churches to rebuild community of men and women. Still others were excited to hear the voices of the women speaking out. However imperfect or unrepresentative, these accounts of hope from women confronted us with the reality of *broken community :* we realized our first task was not to "correct the text", but to grow in our awareness of the broken community expressed and the ways the churches might respond.

As a representative community of women and men from churches around the world, we found our experience of listening to the texts provided insight into ways of hearing their message. We could not discuss all the texts in depth, yet we found a certain pattern of discussion and response developed as we *listened critically.* The elements that emerged were:

First, the *questions* we heard raised in the particular text and the questions we brought out of our own context.

Second, discussion of the *biblical materials* used by the writers as well as other materials about our theme of community and hope. This led us to many questions and to a recognition of need for further biblical study on the topics.

Third, increased attention to the *life situation* out of which the text was written and efforts to understand its own context. This also led to many further questions about social, political and historical contexts as they interact with the thinking of the Church.

Lastly, *clues and new items* for further study and discussion kept emerging and we saw our task as an unfinished process in which we were learning to listen.

The following material refers to texts from "Towards an Account of Hope from Women" and responses of the working group. These reflect the process of critical listening by members of our group and invite the readers' own responses as a basis for new dialogue.

A. Response to "The Woman's Creed"

Our first questions were centred on terminology. Why *The* Woman's Creed and not *a* Woman's Creed? This caused us to discern that all the statements given to us for discussion had a common context, namely that of brokenness — a broken relationship between men and women in the community of Christ, a common cry that the community is not the whole it should be. We also asked why this document was called a creed, and this led us to compare it to the traditional Apostles' Creed. It was fascinating to go through the articles of the Apostles' Creed that had been left out in "The Woman's Creed" and ask why they were omitted and why presumably they did not bear a message of hope to the author. It was noted that in the Apostles' Creed only two articles cover the public ministry of Jesus "born of the Virgin Mary and suffered under Pontius Pilate", while the whole of The Woman's Creed centred on the ministry of Jesus.

As we struggled to hear and respond to the feeling of brokenness that underlies this document, we saw certain possibilities for further reflection. Why do some women feel the need to write "new creeds" where the aspirations of women are more clearly vocalized? How might the Church present its traditional creed and its articles in a way that would bring out liberating possibilities for a community of women and men?

In this creed (and in several of the other accounts we read) the Gospel stories of Jesus' dealing with women were the basis of women's hope, and we saw that this was absent from the traditional creeds. What does this tell us about presenting the scripture as a basis for hope and about the elements of the Christian tradition to which people appeal in time of need? It would be interesting to ask for a man's creed to see to what a male might appeal. Part of the hope for a community of men and women is to see the precise way in which the Christian message can help us understand our respective identities.

This woman in her anguish composed a creed, a statement of belief, and not simply a complaint or statement of grievances. Her Christian faith caused her to seek out what could confirm her rather than simply what oppressed her in the tradition. What does this tell us about our grounds of hope and the role of the Christian heritage for a community of women and men?

B. Response to an account from a Latin American woman

Whereas we joined together in reading *The Woman's Creed* at the closing of our session, we began our listening together to this account by having it read out loud.

Much of our response was centred on the latter part of the passage referring to Mary the mother of Jesus. The first question centred on Mary as "the new woman" and whether this did not represent a confusion about Christ as the new Adam who is the new human person, both male and female. "Is not Mary better seen as a type of the Church", was one question asked. But quickly we moved to the biblical image of Mary as a lowly person, a nobody who was made very important in God's plan of salvation, and the liberating power of this image for the author. In this sense, downtrodden men and women not only in Latin America, but throughout the world might identify with her, and she might appeal to our times far more effectively than when she is placed on an exalted pedestal removed from humanity.

As we reflected on the role of Mary in the New Testament, it was pointed out that we know little of her historical life, and that the passage quoted in the Latin American woman's text is really almost the only common Gospel memory about her. In Mark the passage about the mother and brothers contains the question"Who are my mother and my brothers?", and Jesus points to his disciples and says: "Here are my mother and my brothers – whoever does the will of God is brother and sister and mother to me" (Mark 3: 31-35). In Luke, while Mark's emphasis on the importance of God's word is kept, the atmosphere is more favourable to Mary and the brothers as actually meeting Jesus' criterion: "My mother and my brothers are those who hear the word of God and do it" (Luke 8: 19-21). Thus Mary becomes a model disciple and her response at the annunciation already vocalizes by anticipation Jesus' criterion for discipleship: "Be it done to me according to your word" (Luke 1: 38). Then she begins in the Magnificat to anticipate the Gospel proclamation of God's salvation for the poor, the lowly and the outcast (Luke 1: 46-55).

151

From this we saw certain possibilities for further reflection.

— Not Mary as *the* new woman but as *a* new woman and a possible model of liberation. In history she has had a certain plasticity embodying for different people an aspect or value that they treasured (as Virgin, as mother, as lady, as helper of the poor, as intercessor). We should not sit in critical judgment on other generations but ask how she might be of help to a community of men and women in our time, precisely in fidelity to her biblical image as a disciple, as one of the lowly who is more important in God's plan than the worthy and powerful, and who tells forth the good news of God's liberating action in Luke's gospel.

— The Markan emphasis that Jesus' true family is not based on blood kinship but on fidelity to the will of God is helpful to the notion of Christian community. In certain areas it is important to stress that real community is not established by heredity, by race, by economic ties, by tribal ties, or by marriage when they are pressed to exclusivity, but by *discipleship.*

— The century-old disputes among Christians about the image of Mary may begin to be healed if all sides can take as a common agreement that Mary's real dignity springs from her role as a disciple — as one who heard the word of God and kept it — and that this is a dignity which she shares with all Christians. That *a woman is held up* by Luke as the first to meet this criterion suggests already the Pauline dream that there be no distinction in the community of Christ because one is male and female.

C. Response to a woman's voice from Korea

In responding to the opening section of this text which is an interpretation of the biblical message from perspectives of men and women, some persons raised the question of accuracy in exegesis. The group felt that biblical interpretation ought to be in dialogue with the tradition and context of the community involved. The concern of Jesus for women and their inclusion into the community with men is an important message. It could be stressed as a sign of self-worth in communities where women have a low status. Such stress on Jesus' openness to women might be especially important in areas where the Bible is accepted literally.

The group was again reminded of the context of suffering out of which this story arose, and of its dramatic and forceful description of the changing roles of the men and women in the face of political oppression. The closing statement by the Korean woman that "As long as there are any oppressed women in this world, there will not be any salvation for men," raised many questions not only for the Korean context but also for our own. There were those who could affirm that this text was simply intended to speak of solidarity in liberation – that when one person is not free, no one is free. But we also wanted to affirm as a group that Christ has already set us free in community together and that the message of this text is found in its description of the way this becomes a new reality in the face of new situations.

D. Response to a poem from a South African woman

After a few preliminary comments, we felt that this was a message in poetic form and should therefore not be analyzed in purely intellectual terms; the message comes through facts and ideas as much as through imagery, song and rhythm. We came to understand or feel that the messages does not speak to women alone. "My sisters" is not to be understood as a restrictive term. The poem was understood to be connected with all human suffering; although it is contextual, it is not space- or time-bound. It teaches us to seek information about suffering in many forms which we feel called upon to bear in our communion. This communion is understood to be "sharing" in every sense of the word. In connection with this our group accepted the invitation of one of our members to go with him to visit a village where he and his wife, who is a medical doctor, work among the poor. The poem is a strong expression of hope in the risen Christ. In this connection we saw that we must envision the presence of Christ in our midst as the basis of our community, and of the hope for overcoming all forms of oppression.

In sharing our response with churches and groups we invite you to search out these and other accounts of hope and to join in a shared process of listening. Our work together in reading the texts in an attitude of critical listening was for us a school for learning to live in community.

III. Accounts of hope for community of women and men

As we worked together we were aware that cries testifying to the brokenness of community can be heard coming from different cultural situations, from nations and people rich and poor, from many churches, from women and men, from married and single people. We have received a number of testimonies which might be listened to as the study on the community of women and men in the Church continues. The following documents witness, in spite of brokenness, to the search for new community and show how, in the process of that search, new community is realized. We include the following statements coming from a number of groups belonging to our churches as well as statements from members of our group written here in Bangalore. We invite others to search their documents or to compose responses and to share them with us.

A. Statements from church groups

1. Extract from Mother Thunder Liturgy: The "Mother Thunder Liturgy" is the composition of a group of lay persons of the Episcopal Church in the USA who are attempting to formulate their worship in a non-sexist language that is theologically and pastorally responsible to the whole Christian community of women and men. The Eucharistic Canon calls each of us to consider anew our relationship to Jesus the Christ.

We give thanks to you, O God, for the
goodness and love which you have made known
to us in creation; in the calling of Israel
to be your people; in your Word spoken
through the prophets; and above all in the
Word made flesh, Jesus, your Christ:

Whom you have sent, in these last days,
to be incarnate from Mary, our sister, to
be the saviour and redeemer of the world;
in whom you have delivered us from evil
and made us worthy to stand before you;
in whom you have brought us out of error
into truth, out of sin into righteousness,
out of death into life.

On the night before He died for us, our
Saviour Jesus Christ took bread, and when
He had given thanks to you, He broke it,
and gave it to his disciples, and said,
"Take, eat: This is my Body, which is given
for you. Do this for the remembrance of me."

After supper He took the cup of wine; and
when He had given thanks, He gave it to them,
and said, "Drink this, all of you; This is
my Blood of the new Covenant, which is shed
for you and for many for the forgiveness of
sins. Whenever you drink it, do this for
the remembrance of me."

Therefore, according to his command,
O gracious God,

We remember his death.
We proclaim his resurrection.
We await his coming in glory.
And we offer our sacrifice of praise and
thanksgiving to you, Maker of all; presenting
to you, from your creation, this bread and
this wine.

We pray you, gracious God, to send your
Holy Spirit upon these gifts that they may be
the sacrament of the Body of Christ, the
Blood of the new Covenant. Unite us to Jesus,
our brother, in his sacrifice, that we too
may be acceptable, being sanctified by the
Holy Spirit. In the fullness of time, bring
all things into your Christ's rule, and bring
us, together with (   ) and all your
saints, into the everlasting heritage of your
sons and daughters; through Jesus Christ,
our Saviour, the first-born of all creation,
the head of the Church, and the author of
our salvation.

By whom, and with whom, and in whom, in the
unity of the Holy Spirit, all honour and
glory is yours, most Holy One, now and
forever. Amen.

2. An Affirmation from Women: Because words are a way by which
we reach out to each other, a group of women in the United States
have formulated this affirmation of faith as a means for women and
men to begin to express together their common Christian witness. The
statement issued by the Lutheran Women's Caucus is reminiscent of
"A Woman's Creed", refined and reshaped to express both a "woman's
affirmation" and to move towards an affirmation for the new community of women and men in the Church.

An Affirmation

By creating female and male
in his image
THE CREATOR GOD gave
wholeness
to all human beings;
by setting woman and man
together in the garden
to care for each other
and for the earth,
He made women and men
equal and sharing partners.

By treating women
as full persons
(a radical attitude for his time)
THE SAVIOUR GOD demonstrated
the positive value
He placed on women;

by giving himself
for each and all,
He restored women as well as men
to wholeness
and mended
the togetherness broken by the Fall.

By rebirth
and renewal,
through Word and Sacrament,
THE SPIRIT OF GOD calls
men and women into the
One body of Christ, the Church;
by giving full gifts
to all Christians,
the Spirit equips
women and men
for Christian service,
and moves women and men
together
into full participation
in the life and work
of the Church.

3. Proposals from Metropolitan Timiadis: "The Concern for Women in the Orthodox Tradition: New Challenges", by Emilianos Timiadis, Metropolitan of Calabria (now of Silivria), offers one summary of hopes for the community of women and men from the Orthodox East. We believe the following excerpts from the Metropolitan's "Proposals: New Roles" are especially noteworthy.

It is not the debate on the sophisticated and contentious subject of women's ordination which is of primary importance. It is more expedient to see what the ministry of the Church, in its wider sense, suggests for women.

Men and clergymen do not assume the exclusive responsibility for the apostolate and evangelization, as was the practice for a long time. A woman, a baptized and full member of the Church, assumes the same responsibility. This witness to others must be preceded by an evangelical life which continues the true preaching of the Gospel. Whoever wishes to deliver a message, must first himself or herself become a living message, full of courage, accepted and believing and entrusted with the confidence of others.

Just as a pastor has a sense of fatherhood (patrotis), reflecting his care, his affection and his love for others, so every woman has a sense of "sacred motherhood" (metrotis), embracing not only her own children

156

but all the people surrounding her, bringing comfort, kindness, and tenderness. Fatherhood and motherhood in family must be seen in complementary terms.

The qualities springing from the nature of motherhood should be explored more deeply. Motherhood should not be interpreted only in the narrow sense of child-bearing. If we extend the concept of motherhood to the spiritual, social, and cultural fields, woman may well be defined as mother of all. This constitutes her mystery and her grace. This grace can make her a paragon of strength because of her amazing power. She conveys life. She is a source of life. She incarnates the self-emptiness, the Kenosis, the sacrifice, by standing against death for the sake of her children.

Nuns should participate in the matters concerning their interests in the decision-making councils of the Church.

Women play a prominent part in education and should continue to do so.

We have to contend with the exclusiveness of the word "man" by extending the meaning of "anthropos" in the Bible and elsewhere.

When we consider the situation of women in our present-day society, we see that though some women have understood the extent and the new dimensions of their responsibilities, a great many others are not at all interested in the question. Today we are at the meeting-point of two civilizations, two worlds, and to refuse to accept the fact of the evolution of certain mentalities and customs is at the same time to refuse to accept progress and to see its relevance and challenge for the Church.

4. An Account of Hope from India: In August, 1978, sixty-five women and men, across the generations from various parts of India, representing churches — Protestant, Orthodox, and Roman Catholic — gathered in Bangalore for an Asian consultation on the "Community of Women and Men in the Church". It was the first of many regional, national and local consultations to be held on the study. Six members of the Faith and Order Commission were participants, adding an international presence to issues lifted up by a community of women and men in India.

The introduction to the final statement of the consultation begins, "In the recent past many voices have been raised from various parts of the world on the status of women in the life of both Church and society. The growing consciousness of women of the injustices perpetuated on them have resulted in many forms of study programmes and movements for action." The following materials are excerpted as an offering of an account of hope from Christians in India.

The full proceedings of the report are being published by the consultation and copies will be available through the community study office in Geneva.

Church in the society

We recognized that the distortion of the community of women and men is not a malaise of the Church only, but of the total human condition. The society in which we live has perpetuated and institutionalized the subjugation of women in all fields of life – social, political, economic and religious.

Our task is not simply to remedy the situation in the life of the Church but indeed to strive for the transformation of our society, to seek the eradication of all forms of fetters. Some among us felt very strongly that it would be impossible to deal with this question at the level of the Church, because the Church is very much conditioned by the life in the society. The liberation of women can only be effected with the liberation of all other forms of subjugation. Many of us, however, felt that the Church should not reflect all the brokenness of the society, and that by perpetuating the same evils of caste, class and the oppression of the weaker sections of society, the Church makes an absurdity of the Gospel message and its calling to the ministry of reconciliation; unless the Church at least in some measure is able to overcome the evils that beset the society it cannot exercise its prophetic ministry or be the "light" or "salt" of the earth.

Again the Church, as the community that follows Christ, has been called to stand alongside the poor, the oppressed and the marginalized in society. There is no justification of the situation where the Church itself develops institutions, practices and theology that inflict further oppression on women and others who are already suppressed in society.

The injustices perpetuated on women, like self-inflicted wounds, affect the humanity of men themselves and destroy the possibility of genuine corporate life as males and females.

Roles of women in the family

In this context we wanted to deal firstly with a fear that might be immediately raised in many people of our churches, namely, that the call of community is in some sense the denial of the role of women as mother, wife, and so on. We would like to affirm the God-given vocation of the woman as the child-bearer (mother) and co-partner of man (wife). This is not to minimize the evils of sex-based exploitation. These functions in human relationships have been greatly distorted and misused. We seek to strive to rediscover the ways in which women can, in freedom and in joy, perform these vocations in the context of a corresponding readiness of men to share the responsibilities as well as joys of life in the family. In many cases these vocations and the sexuality of women have been exploited to the extent that they have become a burden and a curse to the woman. We believe that we need to rediscover the nature of the corporate parenthood and the meaning of marriage.

158

While for most women marriage is the form of fulfilment of their lives, the choice of some women to be single is a God-given calling for their vocational fulfilment. We need to develop attitudes which would affirm the life of women in many roles, and to work for the removal of prejudices and unjust treatment of mothers, single women, widows and divorced women.

The question of the community of women and men should be considered in the context of what is happening to the family under the pressures of modernization, urbanization, industrialization, resulting in the breakdown of the traditional patterns of extended families and the widespread acceptance of the so-called nuclear families. A responsible corporateness of human community cannot be preserved merely by accepting the concept of nuclear family as against the extended family. What we need is to seek ways of preserving the values of both, recognizing that in a healthy community, children, youth, married couples and grandparents, all live together playing mutually supportive roles.

5. An account from the Roman Catholic Church (Extract from the Report of the 1976 Plenary Session of the Roman Pontifical Biblical Commission): At a plenary session in 1976, the Roman Pontifical Commission (consisting of twenty scholars appointed by Pope Paul VI) agreed unanimously that the New Testament by itself does not seem able to "settle in a clear way and once and for all" whether women can be ordained priests, and by a vote of 12 to 5 that scriptural grounds alone are not enough "to exclude (the) possibility" of ordaining women. In a third vote (also 12 to 5) the international team of biblical scholars agreed that, if the Church were to open up the priesthood to women, it would not be contradicting Christ's original intentions. The following sign of hope is excerpted from the conclusion of the Commission's report:

The masculine character of the hierarchical order which has structured the Church since its beginning thus seems attested to by Scripture in an undeniable way. Must we conclude that this rule must be valid forever in the Church?

We must however recall that according to the gospels, the Acts and St Paul, certain women made a positive collaboration in service to the Christian communities.

Yet one question must still always be asked: What is the normative value which should be accorded to the practice of the Christian communities of the first centuries?

The ministry of leadership and the sacramental economy

One of the essential elements of the Church's life is the sacramental economy which gives the life of Christ to the faithful. The administration of this economy has been entrusted to the Church for which the hierarchy is responsible.

Thus the question is raised about the relationship between the sacramental economy and the hierarchy.

In the New Testament the primordial role of the leaders of the communities seems always to lie in the field of preaching and teaching. These are the people who have the responsibility of keeping the communities in line with the faith of the apostles.

No text defines their charge in terms of a special power permitting them to carry out the eucharistic rite or to reconcile sinners.

But given the relationship between the sacramental economy and the hierarchy, the administration of the sacraments should not be exercised independently of this hierarchy. It is therefore within the duties of the leadership of the community that we must consider the issue of eucharistic and penitential ministry.

In fact there is no proof that these ministries were entrusted to women at the time of the New Testament. Two texts (I Cor. 14: 33-35 and I Tim. 2: 11-15) forbid women to speak and to teach in assemblies. However, without mentioning doubts raised by some about their Pauline authenticity, it is possible that they refer only to certain concrete situations and abuses. It is possible that certain other situations call on the Church to assign to women the role of teaching which these two passages deny them and which constitute a function belonging to the leadership.

Is it possible that certain circumstances can come about which call on the Church to entrust in the same way to certain women some sacramental ministries?

This has been the case with baptism which, though entrusted to the apostles (Matt. 28: 19 and Mark 16: 15f), can be administered by others as well. We know that, at least later, it will be entrusted also to women.

Is it possible that we will come to this even with the ministry of eucharist and reconciliation which manifest eminently the service of the priesthood of Christ carried out by the leaders of the community?

It does not seem that the New Testament by itself alone will permit us to settle in a clear way and once and for all the problem of the possible accession of women to the presbyterate.

However, some think that in the Scriptures there are sufficient indications to exclude this possibility, considering that the sacraments of eucharist and reconciliation have a special link with the person of Christ and therefore with the male hierarchy, as borne out by the New Testament.

Others, on the contrary, wonder if the Church hierarchy, entrusted with the sacramental economy, would be able to entrust the ministries of eucharist and reconciliation to women in the light of circumstances, without going against Christ's original intentions.

160

1. A POEM

We must tell stories, both old and new, to get an imaginative vision of what could happen if we only tried. This is why one of the group members started to write down this poem in a language that wasn't her own, just to give it a try.

There is God's people
in the midst of oppression —
now who is giving hope
to those who are slaves?

> There are the Egyptians,
> in dread of these people
> 'cause the more they oppressed them
> the more they became.

There is old King Pharao
the man who's in power —
now who's gonna have the courage
to challenge this man?

> And there are the midwives
> named "Beauty" and "Splendour"
> who soon will discover
> the power they have.

The King wants to use them
for further oppression:
you kill all the sons!
the daughters may live.

> Yet they weren't submissive
> but rather subversive
> they didn't fear Pharao
> they did fear God.

They felt with the people
and with the oppressed
they felt with the women
and this was their strength

> They felt they had powers
> they resisted the King
> said "no" to oppression,
> took sides for the poor.

And thus these two women
named "Beauty" and "Splendour"
became the first agents
in God's story of liberation.

Now look at God's people;
this groaning creation —
it's still the old story:
God's waiting for us.

2. DIALOGUE: WOMEN AND MEN IN THE GREAT HARVEST

(Created by Veronica Swai and J.N.K. Mugambi)

Jesus: The Harvest is abundant,
            But the reapers are few:
            Come, you all,
            Come and join in this heavy task
            Of gathering the harvest
            Back to the side of God.

Women: Are you calling only women
            Or only the men?

Jesus: The hands of women
            And all those of men
            Are all needed in the great work of God.

Men: But why do you include us all?
            We, the men, can do the work —
            Do you not know that the women are responsible
            For the fall of men?

Jesus: You have ears and you do not hear,
            You have eyes and you do not see
            The limitations of your power.
            Man without woman is incomplete,
            A world of only men is inconceivable —
            Why do you discriminate?

Women: We too would like to serve you
            For you are the Son of God
            And it is God who empowers and calls
            Both women and men
            To become reapers on his farm.

Men: But how do you expect
            We men to work with women
            When they are already fallen?
            Was it not Eve who spoilt the garden of Eden?

Jesus: Adam and Eve shared the first paradise,
            And today man and woman both share
               the joy and sorrow,
               the courage and fear,

the faith and uncertainty,
the hope and the despair,
Both in unison share
The predicament of humanity
Therefore, let no man think himself complete,
Let no woman shy from responsibility,
Let each person male or female
Contribute to the totality of community
With clear conscious mind and unity
Not that of fear and hostility —
But with cheer and vitality.

IV. Our hopes and recommendations for the study of community of women and men

A. We recommend the recently published study guide on *The Community of Women and Men in the Church* for widespread use in all of our churches and other Christian groups, believing that its methodology is helpful, open-ended, theologically responsible, and ecumenical.

B. We recommend that the Faith and Order Commission bring together a group of scholars representative of Orthodox, Roman Catholic and Protestant traditions to examine the evidence of scripture and tradition as it relates to the role and participation of women and men in the Church.

C. We recommend that a document be prepared on the stated positions regarding ordination of women in the various church bodies over the past few years. The document would print the actual texts and compare the texts, so that these may be more clearly understood, openly discussed, and readily available.

D. We recommend investigation of the implications of Marian doctrines as part of the hope of Christian women and men in the community of the Church, within a particular question as to whether Protestant, Anglican, Orthodox and Roman Catholic teachings may in fact be converging in this area.

E. We recommend that a collaborative study be initiated between the community of women and men in the Church study and the sub-units on Church and Society and Dialogue to examine the relationship of women and men in the Church as it compares with those found in other religions, and non-religious cultures.

F. We recommend that all churches begin now to consider seriously the elimination of all exclusively masculine language in biblical, liturgical and other official texts where the inclusion of both sexes is clearly intended and no doctrinal point is involved, inasmuch as such exclusive use of masculine terminology, even if unintentional, may hinder the full participation of the community.

G. We recommend in regard to the study on "The Community of Women and Men in the Church" that a study be undertaken on *community* itself to clarify the nature and marks of the community we seek.*

Towards an Account of Hope from Women

CONSTANCE F. PARVEY

I. Introduction: The Case Against Us

As a contribution to the study "Giving Account of the Hope that is within us", I have been asked to collect and present to the Faith and Order Commission "accounts of hope" from women. Evaluating the study process launched in 1972, the Commission, meeting in Bangalore, will consider a great variety of accounts of hope. What could be a contribution from women to this process? It is not easy to write such an "account of hope" for the following reasons:

1. Women are not all the same. We inhabit all the continents of the world and come from a great variety of church and cultural backgrounds.

2. The churches have not asked women to give an account of our hope. It has been assumed that the hopes for the faith and life of the Church as expressed by men were also the hopes of women.

3. The case against the hope of women in the Church, as expressed in both scripture and tradition, is formidable. In *scripture* it is taught that women should keep their heads covered and their mouths shut in the churches. They are subordinate to the men in Church and society. In *tradition* women are below men in the orders of creation. They are the B to the male A. And, as Karl Barth has said, "B always follows A", so women follow men. In the worship life of the Church, though the women outnumber men in all Christian churches, the worship life of the people is predominantly led by men. The priestly, teaching and administrative authority of the various churches is predominantly wielded by men — even in those churches which have a more inclusive teaching on the

---

*The "Study Guide for the Community of Women and Men in the Church" is available from the Faith and Order office, WCC, Geneva.

●The Rev. Dr. C. Parvey is study secretary for the Community of Women and Men in the Church.

"priesthood of all believers", or a more congregational and egalitarian polity, or in those churches which ordain women.

This being the situation, how can one begin to speak of an "account of hope" from women in the Church? The ancient Christian roots of patriarchal "headship" in the cultures of pre-Christian times, both Jewish and Roman, and the continued patriarchal shape of all the churches in Western culture and their missionary outreach have given to Christian life the ancient patriarchal image of women as subordinate to men. Women are subordinate in all areas of practical life: church, family, society. The Church has been the chief teacher, and, in general, women have been "well-taught". Our secondary place in relation to men has been firmly established.

In spite of this patriarchal tradition, there are some accounts of hope from women. A change is taking place. Women are rejecting these patriarchal views and their subordinated position. Certainly the status of women in society has changed — partly through the education of women for leadership in society. But the churches are still reluctant to see women deviate from our long-socialized role of subordination, silence and silent service. Many women are still modelled more after the Martha who fussed in the kitchen than like the Mary who sat at the feet of Jesus, the rabbi, wanting to pursue truth.

Women as the *diakonia* of God have been traditionally more interested in the healing ministry of *diakonia* (healing the sick, caring for the wounded in battle, feeding the hungry, housing the homeless) than in political and social action that can prevent sickness, war, starvation, destitution. We have been more concerned to soothe the battered wives and children than to work to stop them from being beaten. And we have given little attention to "dreaming the dreams" that might make a better tomorrow and a more responsible shaping of today. As women, we have had centuries of socialization to know "our place".

II. Renunciation and Affirmation

Part of the new hope for women today is expressed in daring to dream. Mary Daly, an American theologian, offers us her dream as the end to the preface of the second edition of her book, *The Church and the Second Sex:* "I dream of these, my sisters, as drawing from the vision of our past and future foremothers, waking the human species to glimpse still further stars."[1] Men reading this may find it utopian and idealistic. But to women, it is a voice in the wilderness, daring to break a new path.

When I looked for accounts of hope from the regions of the world, I was struck by how many of them begin with a renunciation of conventional Christian teaching. But it is renunciation that is also affirmation;

---

[1] New York: Harper & Row, 1975.

165

it does not throw out scripture and tradition, but claims within scripture and tradition a new *space* for women. The new hope of women does not declare that "God is dead", but rather that God is alive and well, beyond only God the Father, as Mother, creator, divine power and as the origin from which all life springs, forms, develops. The new hope of women does not abandon the fatherness of God, but adds God's motherness.

The Woman's Creed, by Rachel Wahlberg, an American, is a poetic sample of how different tradition could be if women's thoughts were involved:

(Upon pondering The Apostles' Creed and wondering what it would have been like had some women written it)

I believe in God
who created woman and man in God's own image
who created the world
and gave both sexes
the care of the earth.

I believe in Jesus
child of God
chosen of God
born of the woman Mary
who listened to women and liked them
who stayed in their homes
who discussed the Kingdom with them
who was followed and financed
by women disciples.

I believe in Jesus
who discussed theology with a woman at a well
and first confided in her
his messiahship
who motivated her to go and tell
her great news to the city.

I believe in Jesus who received anointing
from a woman at Simon's house
who rebuked the men guests who scorned her
I believe in Jesus
who said this woman will be remembered
for what she did —
minister for Jesus.

I believe in Jesus
who acted boldly
to reject the blood taboo
of ancient societies

by healing the audacious woman
who touched him.

I believed in Jesus who healed
a woman on the sabbath
and made her straight
because she was
a human being.

I believe in Jesus
who spoke of God
as a woman seeking the lost coin
as a woman who swept
seeking the lost.

I believe in Jesus
who thought of pregnancy and birth
with reverence
not as punishment — but
as wrenching event
a metaphor for transformation
born again
anguish-into-joy.

I believe in Jesus
who spoke of himself
as a mother hen
who would gather her chicks
under her wing.

I believe in Jesus who appeared
first to Mary Magdalene
who sent her with the bursting message
GO AND TELL...

I believe in the wholeness
of the Saviour
in whom there is neither
Jew nor Greek
slave nor free
male nor female
for we are all one
in salvation.

I believe in the Holy Spirit *
as she moves over the waters
of creation
and over the earth.

---

* The Hebrew word for Spirit is feminine.

I believe in the Holy Spirit
the woman spirit of God
who like a hen
created us
and covers us
with her wings.[2]

The Woman's Creed, as a woman's hope, is not so much a protest against fathers, as a protest against a language about God that is too small, too limited, too restrictive, not expansive enough for the spirituality and life experience of women. This woman's "account of hope" envisions a God of tenderness, compassion, nurture; a God who longs to provide an environment that encourages acceptance and growth; a God that speaks out of the wholeness of experience; a God that does not leave out the unclean women because of ancient laws and taboos about menstruation; a God that sees woman not only as a complement to man, but as a full and equal person in the care and stewardship of the earth. Wahlberg's work is a creative enlargement of conventional theological categories. It expands the tradition.

Such is the hope also expressed by women about scripture. Beginning one hundred years ago, when Elizabeth Cady Stanton and her committee wrote *The Women's Bible,* they affirmed their faith in scripture, yet brought a new perspective. Beginning at the beginning, Stanton introduced a hermeneutic based on her own self-understanding and her own exegetical skills. The writers of *The Women's Bible* knew that they had to begin with the first descriptions about God and human persons and deal with the double question of (1) the male and female nature of God, (2) the "image of God" as including both women and men. In her commentary on Genesis 1 : 26-28, she writes:

> Here is the sacred historian's first account of the advent of woman, a simultaneous creation of both sexes, in the image of God. It is evident from the language that there was consultation in the Godhead, and that the masculine and feminine elements were equally represented. Scott in his commentaries says, "this consultation of the God is the origin of the doctrine of the trinity". But instead of three male personages, as generally represented, a Heavenly Father, Mother and Son would seem more rational. The first step in the elevation of woman to her true position, as an equal factor in human progress, is the cultivation of the religious sentiment in regard to her dignity and equality, the recognition by the rising generation of an ideal

---

[2] Wahlberg, Rachel Conrad: "The Woman's Creed" published in *Women and Worship,* ed. C.F. Parvey, New York: LWF/USA National Committee, 1977, pp. 67-68 (also published in *Jesus and the Freed Woman,* New York: Paulist Press, 1978).

Heavenly Mother, to whom their prayers should be addressed, as well as to a Father. If language has any meaning, we have in these texts a plain declaration of the existence of the feminine element in the Godhead, equal in power and glory with the masculine. The Heavenly Mother and Father! "God created man in his own image, male and female." The masculine and feminine elements, exactly equal and balancing each other, are as essential to the maintenance of the equilibrium of the universe as positive and negative electricity, the centripetal and centrifugal forces, the laws of attraction which bind together all we know of this planet whereon we dwell and of the system in which we revolve.

In the great work of creation the crowning glory was realized, when man and woman were evolved on the sixth day, the masculine and feminine forces in the image of God, that must have existed eternally, in all forms of matter and mind. All the persons in the Godhead are represented in the Elohim the divine plurality taking counsel in regard to this last and highest form of life.

Who were the members of this high council, and were they a duality or a trinity? Verse 27 declares the image of God male and female. How then is it possible to make woman an afterthought? We find in verses 5-16 the pronoun "he" used. Should it not in harmony with verse 26 be "they", a dual pronoun? We may attribute this to the same cause as the use of "his" in verse 11 instead of "it". The fruit tree yielding fruit after "his" kind instead of after "its" kind. The paucity of a language may give rise to many misunderstandings.

The above texts plainly show the simultaneous creation of man and woman, and their equal importance in the development of the race.[3]

In the first chapter of *The Women's Bible*, we have not only a dream, a vision, but a new affirmation of faith that springs from an expanded experience and with it, a fresh hermeneutic. Early Christian feminists did not simply leave the Bible behind as part of the "religion of men", but, even a century ago, claimed it for themselves with a hermeneutic that expresses their own situation and selfhood. They did not renounce their participation in the people of God. They expanded the vision of the people of God to be more inclusive — to reflect the experiences, learnings and contributions of women.

I find it intriguing that so many women today, in their accounts of hope, start from the same beginnings as the feminists 100 years ago. Yet it is unlikely that women in Asia and Latin America who focus on the same scriptural roots have ever seen or heard of *The Women's Bible*.

[3] Stanton, Elizabeth Cady, *The Women's Bible,* Seattle: Coalition Task Force on Women and Religion. April 1976 (first printing 1898), pp 14-16.

Henriette Marianne Katoppo, an Indonesian theologian, reflects on the issue of partnership between women and men. As the editors of the Pentateuch saw human anthropology as the foundation stone upon which societal life was built, so Katoppo looks back to Genesis for an anthropology, an affirmation of what women know about themselves, but have not found confirmed in the conventional teachings of the churches. Commenting on Genesis 2:21, she addresses herself to the issue of partnership:

> Now this, at last—
> bone from my bones,
> flesh from my flesh!
> This shall be called woman,
> For from man was this taken.

Women and men may read a great deal into this verse. Both male chauvinists and radical feminists may use it to denounce the opposite sex, in which case it seems to me the point is missed altogether.

Surely the point is that women and men were created together, as well as to complement one another. Servanthood, not sexuality, is the primary bearer of God's image. The principal focus of the creation story is on the possibility of *reciprocity,* on the fact that "Adam is not supposed to be *lonesome,* but *twosome.*"

Togetherness, partnership, belonging, indeed *love* is the essence of the beautiful verse quoted above. Translated into human relationships, actions, institutes — what has man made of it?

Throughout church history, men have been depicted as the norm, women as the deviation. "Women are misbegotten males" is one of the kinder references. The fact that women, too, were created in the image of God (Genesis 1:27) seems to have been obscured somewhere, somehow.

All societies rest on the twin pillars of production and procreation, in which women occupy a central place. In agricultural surroundings, the family is still the main production unit, work association and property-holding unit. In this connection, we may find it easier to understand the emphasis on marriage which prevails in Asia, which is largely agricultural.

When the family has moved to the city, the pattern changes, although basic attitudes do not — and the team-work is not always evident. Men go out to work, while women stay home minding the children. The welfare of the family is the woman's first obligation. It is generally accepted that primarily the woman and secondarily the man should be concerned with the children.

A man who spends a lot of time away from his family is a dedicated worker; a woman doing the same thing is an unnatural mother. A man who enjoys spending his time with the children and taking an interest in them, may be called "womanish". A woman who is averse to doing housework is beneath contempt − so deeply ingrained are the stereotype roles of women and men. We talk about the reversal of sex-roles. Complete reversal is, of course, impossible. Women are the privileged sex who bear children. However, we can go a long way by challenging the validity of certain sex-roles. We might ask ourselves to what extent they need to be maintained, especially in the light of the historical perspective.

In an Asian setting, we should also bear in mind that in many of our traditional Asian societies women have actually occupied positions of importance and respect. In at least one Indonesian tribal society, the wife's family is referred to as "the visible God". There is also a saying that "Paradise is under the soles of mother's feet".

All over the world, women and men are becoming increasingly aware that *women's liberation* is *human liberation,* in so far as it is concerned with the liberation of *all* people to become full participants in human society. As Christians in Asia, let us, women and men together, reflect upon the experience of oppression, and act for the new creation of a more humane society − a society where women and men will encounter each other in love, joy and hope, as God intended them to do.[4]

The main theme of Katoppo's essay (too extensive to quote in full) is against the sexual exploitation of women. From a constructive point of view, she develops her theological argument that woman is not something divinely other, distant and apart from man, subject to man, but women and men are both subjects of God. Together they are corporate, fashioned in "the image of God" − of the same bone and flesh that God, the Creator, has made.

III. The Search for a Usable Past

Through these accounts of hope one can see that in all parts of the world, women are struggling to meet the future as human persons (made human in God's image), and yet to survive the present as women. Excerpts from the following affirmation of faith, inspired by Deut. 6, illustrate one such hope:

"A wandering Aramean was my father" was a confession of the Israelites which spoke of their identity − of *who* and *whose* they were. My father was a wandering Aramean − but who was my mother?

---

[4] Katoppo, Henriette Marianne: "Women and Men", *Testimony and Asian Suffering,* ed. T.K. Thomas, Singapore: Christian Conference of Asia, 1977.

171

We are mothers and fathers and friends
and grandmothers.
We are different and we are alike.
We belong to and are responsible for
the earth, ourselves, each other,
and that which we cannot name.
We are believers in a future
that goes forward from our past
with hopes and fears and courage
We are children of the Mother-Father-God.
We are creatures in a struggle
to be co-creators.[5]

Women search for and claim a usable past — as women, side by side — not subordinated to, or subsumed under men's hopes. This journey to the source is integral to the journey ahead. The Aramean mothers are being found. Women in the Church bring a new past, tradition in new content and form, as they look forward. It is obvious from a number of sources that women have to renounce a false hermeneutic, a false teaching about their identity, and with this begin new discoveries and make new assertions about human wholeness, mission and service.

Marta de Groot, a Dutch theologian, expresses some of the joy of this search for a usable past through her re-discovery of this prayer of St Anselm, 11th century:

And Thou, Jesus, sweet Lord,
art Thou not also a mother?
Truly, Thou are a mother,
The mother of all mothers,
Who tasted death,
in Thy desire to give life to Thy children.

Reflecting on this prayer, de Groot writes: "It is liberating and surprising to find a prayer as Anselm's. These are the words of a theologian on the way to prayer, who discovers the secret of birth and death, which is as female as it is male, in the person of Jesus, the giver of life. In Jesus, Anselm experiences being mother and woman as a reality which gives life and reconciles. The bearing, the upbearing of God and human being, reveals human life to us in all its fullness."[6] Like the woman searching for the lost coin, women are finding "a usable past". As the future moves towards us, the past unearths new sources of inspiration and support.

---

[5] Excerpt from "Out of the Garden — Womanspace, Womantime, Womanspirit", Loveland, Ohio, Grailville, 1975, p. 43.

[6] de Groot, Maria: "Moeder Jezus", Hervormd Nederland, October 1977. Translated by H.M. Katoppo in unpublished essay, "The Role of the Theologically Trained Woman in the Ministry of the Church", given at the Ecumenical Consultation of Theologically Trained Women, Sibu, Sarawak, East Malaysia, March 1978.

IV. Up from Oppression: New Prophetic Voices

As the hopes thus far referred to reclaim the past and enrich the tradition, women are also identifying, out of their own experience of subordination, with what it means to be oppressed, to be rendered silent. Perhaps women oppressed and subordinated through conventional Christian teaching are now serving the plan of God in our time as new prophetic voices.

Olga Alvarez, a Latin American theologian, addresses human liberation in terms of women and men. She takes Jesus' attitude towards women as the model for human liberation, and suggests that we take a new look at Mary. She writes:

> Knowing the gospel stories that tell us of the attitude of Jesus towards the women of his time, we realize that it is he who initiated the elevation of the status of women. He allowed women to hear his teachings and accepted women's company as he travelled "from town to town and village to village, proclaiming the good news of the Kingdom of God. With him were the twelve and a number of women ... Mary, known as Mary of Magdala, Joanna, Susanna, and many others" (Luke 8:1-14). In many ways the gospel stories show us Jesus breaking the stereotypes of women's role and place. He broke the taboo of sex when he treated women as full human beings. He initiated the appearance of the new family, giving death to the traditional family, when someone advised him, "Your mother and your brothers and sisters are outside and would like to see you," and he responded, "My mother and my brothers are those who hear the word of God and practise it." (Luke 8:21) What did Jesus wish to show with all of this? He presented a new image of women, incorporating them in history, recognizing their human dignity and their rights; he broke with all discrimination that negates women and their realization as persons. And if Mary in the New Testament is the model of the New Woman, that model has been obscured by patriarchal views of women as a false image of innocence, beauty and submission. The meaning of Mary as the New Woman is yet to be discovered.[7]

Alvarez then relates this "New Woman" to many courageous Latin American women of the past and ends her essay with a hope for a new society based on both new men and new women.

> We can cite countless women of our pueblo committed to the struggle for change. They deserve our respect and support because they have begun to understand that liberation is a conscious and consistent

---

[7] Alvarez, Olga Lucia: "Latin American Woman, The Church, and Liberation Theology", *Radical Religion,* vol. II, no. 1. Berkeley, Calif.: Community for Religious Research and Education, p. 20.

participation in the process of liberation in each one of our countries. It is integration into the revolutionary anti-colonial struggles of our America.

Liberation is not only the liberation of women. Liberation is to awaken and open the eyes of others, and together with them to construct a new society, and with it the new man and new woman.[8]

In some parts of the world, women are more conscious of *how* they experience oppression: mental anguish, lack of a past, lack of role models and fore-mothers, sexual exploitation, etc. In other parts of the world, women are so overwhelmed by the total oppression of their people (racism in South Africa, political oppression in Korea, poverty in Latin America) that they give their primary attention to *what* oppression means to a human people.

A voice from Korea combines both:

Men are always reciting St Paul's teaching about women. It looks like they are following Paul instead of Jesus. Throughout the teaching of Jesus we cannot find any degrading of women. Jesus liberated women 2,000 years ago but man's patriarchal interpretation of Paul is followed more strongly. Men use the Bible verses which are convenient for them. Read the Bible carefully and you will find the words of advice for women almost invariably follow with comparable words of advice for men. When women read the Bible their message is different form the message men receive.

The World Day of Prayer meeting was the beginning of Church Women United. A few women gathered from different denominations ten years ago. After a chairperson was selected, she became involved in the human rights movement. It was the time so many ministers, professors and university students were arrested. Through their activities working together with all the women were different denominations and other organizations, women's conscientization and leadership has developed. It would have taken years and years of training projects to raise their awareness. A real sample of "learning by acting" is happening.

All the wives, mothers, and sisters of prisoners who had never been outside working (except going to church as ordinary women) became very active. Most of them never had a chance to speak in public, especially in front of men. Of course, they did not want their husbands, sons, or daughters involved in any kind of trouble. They persuaded their husbands, sons, and daughters not to be involved, begging them to think about their families. After they were put in jail, families came out of the house and had to run here and there to help the prisoners. Meeting people, confronting police and secret

---

[8] Ibid, p. 21.

police, the more pressure on them, the braver they became. Day after day, month after month, all the concern was on the prisoners and their eyes, ears, and mouths were opened for our country.

After prisoners were released the husbands were astonished at how their wives had changed. They appreciated their wives' activities and realized how big a role their wives had played. Men did not think that women could do so much work outside the home. Now men and women have become co-workers and sex barriers have been broken. All these activities have brought about the big change in the church concerning women's role.

A great step for the human liberation has been taken. Jesus was the the only one who treated women as human beings, made in God's image. We have a long way to march, not just for women, but for men as well. As long as there are any oppressed women in this world, there will not be any salvation for men.[9]

Like the account of the Korean woman, a Latin American woman combines both:

Juanita grew up in a village in Guatemala. When she was eight, she went to the city to work to support her family. She went to school and learned to speak Spanish. "Life in the city is better", she said, "but you lose a lot. Jesus is commercialized in the city, but he lives with us marginals." After the earthquake, she went back to her village, to help the women there. These are some of her comments:

A woman in the rural area has a very difficult life because she is deprived of so many things. She cannot say what her problems are or share her experience or work for solutions. People tell her she has no ideas and besides it is not the custom for women to go to meetings. So she becomes accustomed to keeping silent. Men believe a woman is only good for working in the kitchen and no one pays any attention to her. This is an exploitation of human dignity. These women have good ideas, but sometimes they are unsure of what they want to say and they are afraid to speak out. It is very difficult for them to speak . If one does and no one listens to her, then she thinks that what she has been told is right, that she isn't capable of saying anything useful. So she doesn't try again.

A woman who has not reached the age of majority is not allowed to speak when older persons are present. Generally it is the boys who go to school. Women are considered inferior beings who have to learn to cook and weave and do domestic work, but not to use their brains as men do. When a woman marries, she is like an object, something without much value. She obeys her husband and does what she is told because since childhood she has been taught that a man must be

---

[9] Excerpts from an unpublished essay by a woman from South Korea.

obeyed because he is a man. What must be done is to make these women aware, so that they wake up a little and realize that their situation is not good. The poverty and indignity they suffer is not God's will, but the will of other human beings.

It is other human beings who exploit them, who benefit from their work, pay them unjust prices and exploit their human feelings. Sometimes people use the words of the poor to find money for them, but afterwards everything remains in the pockets of the small world which is called "the powerful". I am only 19 years old, and perhaps you do not believe me, but I discovered this when I worked with the emergency after the earthquake. Contributions were sent from many countries, but often they didn't reach the people who needed them. I thought, if these things happen now in an emergency, what will happen with money sent later? The best thing I can do is to open the eyes of these people, as mine were opened. Once teaching begins, it never stops. They can learn to read and write. They can learn to put roofs on their houses. They can learn to speak out.[10]

A voice from South Africa speaks to her sisters not about the particular problems of women, but of the pain of all South Africa. The poem is a re-enactment of the scene at the foot of the cross.

We are still waiting

My sisters tell me
how people die of hunger
because there is no food to eat.

My sisters tell me
how people die of lack of hope
because they do not see a way out.

My sisters tell me
how people die of fear
submerged in silence, the silence of death.

My sisters tell me
how people die of sadness
because they have heaped treasures
and have lost their souls.

My sisters tell me
how people die of courage
because they have dared to speak up
to shout out against the oppressors.

---

[10] Cited as Juanita, Guatemala. *Half the World's People,* a report of the Consultation of Church Women Executives, Glion, Switzerland, 1977. Geneva: World Council of Churches, p. 17.

Jesus Christ, the Son of God,
called the Prince of Peace
and (by mistake of the Roman authorities)
King of the Jews,
was executed
according to the fashion of the
occupant forces;
and died on the cross.
He had no army.
He had no resources.
He had no connections with the elite.
He did not turn stones into bread.
He did not establish the Kingdom.
He had no power.

My heart is trembling.
Couldn't He have turned those
stones into bread?
Couldn't He have jumped from
the temple walls?
Couldn't He have declared
Himself ruler of the earth
and established the Kingdom?

Why those millions of bitter sighs?
Why those tears of anger?
Why those broken hopes and dreams?
Why that naked despair
   in the eyes of the little boy
   – my boy –
as he tried to escape the machine guns?

We are still waiting for the miracle.
The devil is still tempting us.

As if Christ were not risen,
As if the promise were not ours,
As if we could not have the courage to dare,
As if we had to be afraid,
As if the power of the Lord
were not present in our weakness.
We are still waiting for the miracle.

   As if...[11]

---

[11] Excerpts from "We are Still Waiting", South African. Author unknown. *Half the World's People*, op. cit. p. 52.

An "account of hope" from women means more than liberation from subordinated status. The new equality that women envision is based on an expanded vision of God coupled with new insights about the care and stewardship of the earth, society, family and Church. An "account of hope" from women touches every area of human life.

Women who have known the experience of not having a voice, or an identifiable, usable past, are a new voice in support of, and among the poor, the politically and socially oppressed. Women are not only concerned with injustice in society, but with shifting their attention to injustice in the Church. They are not only interested in building a more complete partnership between women and men in society, but also in building a more complete partnership between women and men in the Church. An essay on Pentecost by the Danish theologian, Anna Marie Aagaard, evokes some of this hope for the renewal of partnership in the Church. Following a reflection on the ministry of Lydia to St Paul, she writes:

> Two thousand years of church history separate us from the worshipping women at the riverside outside Philippi. A long history has given us the churches in which we now live. Our present reality comprises churches where blacks are excluded from white congregations, and where class and sex distinctions alienate us from each other. Our reality is a host of different denominations, and church structures heavy with the burden of many centuries. Our reality is a Catholic Canon Law more influenced by Roman Law and Gratian's limited perspectives than the new law of Christ. Those who lived the Gospel before us have marked the Church, and we cannot join hands with Lydia and her friends across the ocean of history. But still we are called to dream God's dream — still we are called to live the hope of "ochlos" comprising ethnic, social and sex differences. Let us then take courage from Lydia's story: as truly as we believe, so truly *we* are the church. Also *we* are the minds, the hands, and the feet of the church, and let no acquired roles quench that belief in us. Let no one destroy our hope of one holy people where women are again recognized as God's witnesses, and let no one destroy the love with which we women are also called to make the Kingdom real on earth. Let us take courage from each other and oppose all theology and all church structures which make us less than we are: women are loved enough by God to embody God's own visions.[12]

---

[12] Aagaard, Anna Marie: "Women and Proclamation", LWF International Consultation for Women, Colombo, Sri Lanka, 1976. Geneva: Lutheran World Federation (quotation here cited is from the second edition and adaptation of this essay under the title: An "Account of Hope for Women and Men: From Ethne to Ochlos", unpublished).

V. The Theopoetic

The accounts of hope from women referred to up to this point are rooted in scripture and tradition, associated with the prophetic role of justice in society, and with renewal in the church. They draw on the experience, perspectives, resources and lives of women. But women's hopes have another dimension. They bring to theology a new language about God — new modes of doing theology, and new language forms. Much of what women write is written in a descriptive way — not in the rational, systematic typologies of theology in an "age of science", but in the language of experience, expression, poetry and drama. In this descriptive mode, coming from the roots of women's *psyche,* there are no polarities or dualistic language structures. Theology is experienced and expressed as an integrated imagery of wholeness; of head and body, heart and spirit. As women are doing theology out of their experience and longing for wholeness, they are tapping new sources of power within themselves, and this power is reflected through the written word. Some of the new theological language has great vitality, resembling public, spoken language. It is more the language of liturgy than the language of theology. An example of this "liturgical" writing is called *Bakerwoman God,* by Dr Alla Bozarth-Campbell from the United States. To me it could be a reflection on the anamnesis; it is a poem that speaks not only about "Do this in remembrance of me", as something past, but also as something present, shaping the "becoming".

Bakerwoman God,
I am your living bread.
Strong, brown, Bakerwoman God,
I am your low, soft and being-
shaped loaf.
I am your rising
bread, well-kneaded
by some divine and knotty
pair of knuckles, by your warm
earth-hands.
I am bread well-kneaded.

Put me in your fire, Bakerwoman God,
put me in your own bright fire.

I am warm, warm as you
from fire. I am white
and gold, soft and hard,
brown and round.
I am so warm from fire.

Break me, Bakerwoman God.
I am broken under your caring Word.

Drop me in your special juice in pieces.
Drop me in your blood.
Drunken me in the great red flood.
Self-giving chalice, swallow me.
My skin shines in the divine wine.
My face is cup-covered and I drown.

I fall up
in a red pool
in a gold world
where your warm
sunskin hand is there
to catch and hold me.
Bakerwoman God, remake me.[13]

In scripture one finds a baffling, elaborate and sometimes explosive compounding of realism, fantasy, history and myth. The new theology, coming from the experience of women, speaks from such an imagination. It is a language that compounds new imagery. It is the language of the theopoetic, defined by Amos Wilder as "the vision before the message, the hymn before the sermon, the poem before the prose".[14]

An account of hope from women today goes beyond equal rights and inclusive language. These are only the necessary pre-conditions. Accounts of hope from women go backwards and forwards in time, stretching towards new words for women to give witness to the more inclusive expression of God's redemption and reconciliation in our time.

VI. Implications for "a common account of hope"

In brief, what insights do women bring to an account of hope today? As I re-read these accounts, among the contributions I find are as follows. What would you add?

— a human anthropology, not individualistic or androcentric, but corporate and inclusive of the experience, wholeness, and full equality of women and men

— a personal and historical experience that critically re-examines and re-appropriates the past, enlarging conventional norms and teaching of scripture and tradition

— a sense of stewardship and mission not "over against Creation", not man over against woman, or persons over against each other,

---

[13] Alla Bozarth-Campbell: "Bakerwoman God", *In God's Image: Toward Wholeness for Women and Men,* New York: Division for Mission in North America. Lutheran Church in America, No. 3, p. 235.

[14] Wilder, Amos Niven: *Theopoetic,* Philadelphia: Fortress Press, 1976, p. 1.

but working in cooperation with God, also as creators, as part of God's creation process, with it rather than against it

— out of women's own experience with subordination, a recognition of oppression among those who suffer and a feeling of solidarity with them against all structures in Church and society (of hierarchy and domination) where some serve and others are served

— an exciting re-birth of theological language — of the fundamental expansive, dramatic descriptive and poetic nature of language related to God

— a recognition of the nearness, the intimacy, the subjectivity of God, not merely God as objective, distant, holy-other.

Experiencing these voices of "women's hope", I am reminded of a simple statement from Nelle Morton:

No longer do we look *up* to bring *down* the Spirit — the life force — but *down,* then *up* from *down under.* Working out of pain, rather than out of sin, leads to a realistic dealing with pain as over against persistent suffering and guilt ... Thus, we free ourselves to live out of the solidarity in which we seek Presence and Grace for one another, out of which we connect with a past to recover woman's history, and which creates new words and new language ...[15]

And, finally, I am reminded again of how many women's voices are unidentified, or silent.

---

[15] Morton, Nelle: "Being Heard to New Speech", *There is No Road Ahead,* Loveland, Ohio, Grailville, 1975, p. 43.

2. Christian Hope and the Natural Sciences

Addressed to the Church and Society Conference at Cambridge, Mass, July 1979.[1]

1. Scientists and Christians

We live in a world largely dominated by science-based technology. As Christians, called to serve that world in the light of our faith, we must examine the resources of our tradition to see what positive contribution we can make to this growing technological civilization. Of course, Christians of other eras have participated in important ways in the development of science and technology, but the record of the Christians' influence is complex and the subject of much historical dispute. On the positive side it has been argued that the scientific and technological mentality appeared and flourished in Christian lands and thus apparently was favourably affected by Christianity. The Christian doctrine of creation meant that nature itself was not sacred and might be approached as object, not subject. Nature also was the handiwork of God, and studying it was an act of piety. The medieval scholastics' conviction of the rationality of God fostered the notion of order and intelligibility in the universe, prerequisites for scientific exploration.

On the other hand, Christian lands did not everywhere give rise to a scientific culture, but only in the west, and there only after a millenium. Other influences seem to have been important. Perhaps the barbarian incursions of the first millenium, which destroyed the old order, predisposed the mind to receive new ideas. Trade routes with the Middle East brought innovations with cultural repercussions. Even accident and

---

[1] For summary of recent events, see the preparatory paper for this study by Jan Milic Lochman, "Trends in the Ecumenical Dialogue on Faith and Science", in *Giving Account of the Hope,* for the Bangalore Conference.

chance may have played key roles. In any event, the Church itself was not regularly a patron of free scientific inquiry; and in the long run the rise of secularizing movements and philosophies after the 17th century produced a scientific culture at some distance from active Christian influence.

These examples are only suggestive of the complexity of the debate. The relations between Christianity and the origins of scientific and technological society are ambiguous, and we must be cautious about our claims. We cannot accept, for example, the thesis currently popular in some quarters that Christian faith is the direct cause of a disrespectful, reckless technological exploitation of nature. This view is untenable on the evidence of history.

Perhaps it would be wisest to say that Christianity was not a sufficient condition for the appearance of science and technology, but that certain Christian ideas and attitudes may have been necessary to this result. In any case we look now for ways in which Christian faith in our time may engage constructively with scientific and technological culture. And the first and most basic thing to say is that we affirm the presence of these skills as a positive good for humanity. Withdrawal from technology is a romantic notion which would deprive millions of people of any viable future. Technology, and the science which underlies it, are essential to human development and well-being, making it possible for God's gifts in creation to be widely shared.

Christians might contribute usefully by encouraging a realistic understanding of the work of scientists and technologists, refusing to yield to exaggerated expectations or fears. The researchers and engineers are neither devils nor saviours, neither the agents of doom nor the creators of utopia. Such polarized attitudes are dangerously unreal and in the long run, through fear or disillusion, will poison the atmosphere in which these people pursue their tasks. Their work is, rather, amenable to human control and, of course, has its human failings.

Both Christians and scientists could further improve matters by repenting of and abandoning the triumphalisms which have disfigured their past. For scientists this has taken the form of promising endless progress and the fulfilment of all human hopes. For Christians it has meant the arrogance, or complacency, of thinking that their self-contained theological systems say the only important things about human life and destiny. For both scientists and Christians, triumphalism has meant a claim to know too much, to explain reality comprehensively and definitively. Self-criticism and an openness to constructive criticism from others would help both communities, improve their relations, and allow them to serve the human race together.

II. Creation and Purpose

When we turn from basic attitudes and intentions to substantive matters, we discover at once a serious problem of understanding between scientists and Christian theologians. The latter focus on a particular event, the life, death and resurrection of Jesus Christ.[2]

In that event they see God revealed, so that their knowledge of God has its centre and content in a particular history. Then when they turn to a matter like the origin of life and of the world, they in effect understand it in the context of what they know from their historical experience: if God has given us life in Jesus Christ, it must be his power as creator which is manifested there. Similarly, for the ancient Hebrews the event of the Exodus in which they felt themselves claimed by God was definitive. It was this experience which formed the basis of their subsequent conclusion that this God must be the one God, the Creator of all that is. And to express this idea they developed the creation narrative with which the Bible opens and which the Church inherited.

Obviously this is a process of reasoning quite unlike that of the scientists, who look first at the world of nature to see what is happening there. Their observation of the universe is the basis for their theories, their interpretations. They hope to discern there a nexus of events that is intelligible — and this hope has been increasingly fulfilled. If they do move from their observations to theological statements, they are engaged in "natural theology", rather than the theology of revelation. It may be unwise to take this step, to deduce theological affirmations from scientific observations; but the two are not necessarily unrelated.

It has been commonplace in recent years to say that there is no real conflict between scientific and traditional theological views of creation. They belong to different realms of discourse. The former discusses the behaviour of matter and energy, the latter the meaning of our existence. Creation for the theologian is not cosmology, but a confession of the dependence of our lives on God. There are other reasons, too, why the two disciplines are alleged not truly to interact. But this separation must not be pushed too far. An integrated world view would find both scientists and theologians interpreting the significance of human life and the natural world (and thus how they are to be treated) and scientists helping us all to understand the ways of God's creation (and thus possibly enriching our knowledge of God). They would become open to each other and, quite properly, vulnerable to each other's critique.

Whether or not the scientific approach can help us to understand the "mind of the maker" is a subject of dispute. But without entering

---

[2] The terms "resurrection" and "acts of God" (below) are themselves part of the methodological problem between theology and science, but the present group did not discuss them.

again the problem of natural theology, with which many of us have difficulties, we may consider some illustrations of the interaction.

It has been a popular Christian notion that "creation" means the beginning of the universe at a moment in time; and thus piety has been attracted to the "hot big bang" theory of origins, finding it a reinforcement for theology. But time itself is an aspect of creation along with space, energy and matter, as scientists remind us; and it is meaningless to think of creation "in time", or at a moment. Creation is a far more radical and profound concept. Science thus puts useful limits to religious language and in fact affects, as it has throughout history, the way believers appropriate the Christian message.

Again, recent investigations have enabled scientists to piece together a remarkably comprehensive view of cosmic development, from primordial particles through the appearance of organic matter to the self-consciousness of *homo sapiens*. The picture is that of a continuous process in which new and more complex forms emerge from simpler levels. There is also much death and destruction in the process, but the scientist is apt to be impressed with the way new existence continually emerges from the demise of the old. Overall one gets the impression of fecundity, of endless creativity. It is, in short, "continuous creation". And theologically minded scientists have seen there a correspondence with the intention of Christian doctrine to describe God as the sustainer and preserver of the world. They do not claim to *derive* the doctrine from their science, but rather let their science enrich their understanding of doctrine.

Does this continuous cosmic process have a purpose? The scientist in his professional capacity does not ask questions which look for purpose. Some actions, for example in biology, may *look* purposeful, but they do not require explanations involving purpose. The presence of purpose in the development of the universe cannot be read off directly from science. It is, however, a permissible interpretation of the data, if anyone should choose so to interpret them. Chance, the random behaviour of particles at the micro level, does not rule out this interpretation; for patterns frequently emerge at the macro level.

For the theologian, on the other hand, the idea of purpose is a central conviction which is not derived from observation of the natural world, but from the history of the acts of God. It is an anthropocentric statement, focused on human destiny, not on the natural history of the cosmos. It would be dangerous for theology to find its own concept of divine purpose in scientific discoveries, for the direction of nature could be the result of an innate *telos* in things — in the classic illustration, as the oak tree is the *telos* of the acorn, and contained within it. Such an idea is of no help to human beings who would act "purposefully". Purpose as giving meaning to our lives belongs to the theological concept, where we can anticipate our future, and anticipate giving an account of our lives before the God of history.

Yet despite the difference in the nature and intent of these concepts of purpose, the Christian who looks at the cosmic development, observing particularly the emergence of the selfconscious person who is capable of responding to God, may find some confirmation and enrichment of what he knows on Christian grounds. Of course, this contingent universe will one day die, and time with it. But a Christian who reads its history may yet find encouragement in its direction, in its linearity, in its evolution of ever higher forms, to trust the significance of his life to the providence of God.

III. Nature and Hope

Science and theology have also evaluated nature from different perspectives. For natural science nature is non-moral. It is simply given, a brute fact. But there is a theological tradition that nature is somehow "fallen" and awaiting its redemption. It cannot be fallen as man is, for it can hardly sin. Its fallenness seems rather to be in its ambivalence in relation to humanity — life-giving, but also life-destroying. Tidal waves and microbes are not evil in themselves, but they are certainly threatening to human beings. This "natural evil", as it is usually called, is different from "moral evil", which humans do and for which they are responsible.

It is useful for Christians to be reminded that for the sciences nature is intrinsically non-moral. That will focus our attention on human concerns and save us from anthropomorphizing the natural world. This is not to say that God may not have purposes for nature quite apart from humanity, as the book of Job says so eloquently. But we cannot know these purposes, and our responsibility towards nature concerns its relation to people, present and future.

The problem of "natural evil", however, remains. It is not easily disposed of by calling it a human interpretation of non-moral events. We confront the problem in its most acute form in death, in the perishableness of nature which we share. In nature death brings forth new life; but for human beings death is an *affront* to life. We do not accept it passively, nor should we; for we have a degree of self-consciousness which enables us to contemplate our death, ritualize it, and aspire to transcend it. It really does affront our nature as human. Perhaps it is not surprising that traditional Christian faith has found a link between sin and death, knowing that evil is always more than moral evil. Nor is it surprising that the concept of "new creation" has included the conquest of death, though obviously in a way which we cannot now understand, a transformed existence to which the sciences do not speak, but to which faith testifies. It is in that theological sense that nature with all its ambivalence is included in the Christian proclamation of resurrection.

And so we come to the question of hope, the subject of the conference from which this report is written. The basis of hope for the creation is laid, theologically speaking, in the resurrection, in the new creation which God has inaugurated in Jesus Christ. Hope is based on what God has already done. The new creation, God's new age, is thus already in one sense in being, accomplished in the work of Christ. It continually breaks into and transforms our existence. But it is also not yet, awaiting a final fulfilment. Our hope in it depends on both actuality and anticipation.

The new age will, nevertheless, be a radical break with the present. It cannot be thought of as a temporal paradise. Here again science may offer to theology a contribution which is informative and confirming, though not, of course, determinative. The scientific certainty of the eventual disappearance of Earth, to say nothing of the heat-death of the universe, must put firm limits to our speculation about God's kingdom as an extension of this world. We know only – and it is enough – that we will experience his presence in ways which will exceed our present imaginings.

IV. The Human and the Natural

The discussion of death has already pointed to the distinction of man from the rest of nature. *Homo sapiens* has an extra dimension which Christians have popularly called "spirit", not so much a separate element in his constitution as a heightening or enhancement of his total being in relation to God. He is "person" in the full sense of that very biblical concept, the one who is called by God and is capable of responding. And insofar as he is transformed by the act of God in Christ, he is a new being, that new *anthropos* of the new age.

The contribution of science to this theological picture of the human, the backing of confirmation it brings to Christian anthropology, has become quite intriguing in recent years. New understanding of the workings of the evolutionary process have shown how more complex forms – theology would say "higher" forms – have emerged from simpler ("lower") ones, with quite new properties. Thus organic matter has evolved from inorganic, and the self-conscious creature *homo sapiens* from the simplest organism. Man is an "emergent being", something distinctively different from the rest of the creation.

Human beings have, moreover, achieved a relation to the process which is different from that of any other stage. Through deliberate action on their environment, they are able to alter their own evolution. It is not so much that they change their physical constitution, although public interest in such as-yet-unaccomplished feats as genetic alteration or cloning may reveal popular aspiration for a new humanity. It is, rather, that in evolution self-conscious creatures appear who are purposeful, and so turn evolution into history. They understand and henceforth direct the process which has produced them, responding to purposes which they design — or discern. It is to this human history that Christian faith is addressed.

Of course all this is not the *Christian* meaning of human uniqueness, but there is an interesting parallelism which adds breadth to our understanding. The freedom of decision and the power over nature which man has acquired have even led some theologians to speak of him as "co-creator" with God. This phrase may at first sound arrogant, an example of the sin of pride; but we may receive it positively if we understand it to refer to special human responsibility before God and with God for the rest of the world. We are called to be God's stewards, responsible for the creation with which he has entrusted us, and for the use of the special powers with which he has endowed us. We could say, theologically speaking, that scientific and technological man was intended in the providence of God, meant to become an exploring discovering — and creating — being.

Another aspect to the discussion of human uniqueness concerns the danger of reducing this emergent being to simpler, lower levels. Here we may find theology offering a contribution, or admonition, to certain kinds of science, or to the way some scientists interpret their work. There is a multi-dimensionality to man which must not be lost. Entirely materialistic and deterministic descriptions of the evolutionary process would be a mistake and a danger. The human personality cannot be so reduced. Its openendedness must be defended against any who present themselves in their own work as the authors of a comprehensive view which explains all human behaviour. Scientists themselves who are investigating one level of complexity, for example biology, frequently resist on logical grounds the reductionist claims of the disciplines relevant to levels lower than their own, for instance physics and chemistry.

V. Hope and the Future of the Technological Society

Any Christian account of man must consider another theme, which deals not so much with scientific theory as with the uses of science and technology. This is the realistic assessment that, until the ultimate fulfilment in the new age, human beings are sinners. Creation may be the outpouring of God's love, and new creation the final triumph of that love; but we have to reckon with an interim, this age, in which love is marred and obscured by sin. One must expect, therefore, that people will continue to use science and technology primarily to serve their own personal and social interests. And yet we know, as surely as we know anything in Christian ethics, that such enormous power must be disciplined to the service of all humanity, not to private greed or to exploitation or to war or to the power of particular states.

Is there any hope for such a redirection? Because the new age, in which God transforms our lives and frees us from sin, is already active, we are enabled at least to act towards this goal. The new being in love is not just a future possibility but a present actuality. It speaks of human unity, of mutual responsibility, where all justly share in the benefits of science and technology and in the decisions governing their use.

This is the Christian intention we bring to the public debate about the direction of the technological society. It is true that science and technology have been great boons to humanity, and have the potential for still greater and more widespread good. But potential is not actuality, and in point of fact we find this great power embedded in economic and political systems[3] which often use it for harmful ends, like the arms race. Potentially, it is free; actually, it is bound.[4] Decisions about its direction are not made mainly by researchers themselves but by political and commercial agencies who control the flow and use of support funds. Naturally enough, the people who do the work are often not very happy at such outside control, arguing that decisions taken there are frequently ill-informed, based on irrational fears or hopes. Nevertheless, to avoid the elitism where those who know decide for those who do not, some sort of public accountability seems desirable. It is not, then, a question of freeing science and technology from the service of ends, but of making sure that those ends are compatible with the common good. In some countries movements for formal public assessment of the effects of proposed technological developments are already well advanced. (For example, the British Council of Churches' representation at the Windscale enquiry.) Christians can and should support these movements so that their humanistic concern for the general welfare will be influential.

It should be acknowledged that not everyone believes that science and technology can be made to serve humane goals. Some critics discern there an evil which is inherent, inevitable. It has been argued, for example, that technology *necessarily* bends natural biological rhythms to the discipline of the mechanical clock, to our detriment; or that technological society *must* expand its use of natural resources until it finally produces a collapse; or that technology alters social structures in such ways, like urban overcrowding, that poverty *increases* rather than diminishes (as in fact has happened in some places). It has been suggested that the power of technology strains beyond endurance the human capacity for responsibility and thus will inevitably be misused. To all these critics the technological society appears not as

---

[3] The absence of economists and political scientists from the study group precluded the exploration of the relation between technology and appropriate systems.

[4] See the distinction between technology as tool and as system in the report of the 1975 Mexico Consultation, *Anticipation,* No. 22, pp 14 ff.

promise but as fate. Others add to this list of woes that some experiments are also inherently, essentially, evil and should not be done (although, to be fair, it should be noted that societies are now monitoring this kind of experiment).

Against such a negative, fatalistic appraisal, this report has defended the positive evaluation of science-based technology, stressing its enlarging, humanistic possibilities. Of course, one cannot be sanguine. Nothing is guaranteed. But, to return to the pursuing theme of these pages, the Christian hope in the coming new being is also a present actuality, a transformation which allows us in some measure to transcend our selfish selves and employ God's gift in science and technology for all his children.

So there is hope for the future use of science and technology on behalf of humanity, and it is related to Christian hope. It is true that Christian hope, ultimate hope, does not need to be reinforced by the proximate hopes generated by science and technology. Ultimate hope stands despite everything, and that is its power. But scientific and technological possibilities can complement the encouragement we receive from our Christian faith, and show us some ways in which our ultimate hope can be active in this world. And among those ways is clearly the just sharing, even the sacrificial sharing, of technological benefits with all the human family. Those who are called into the body of Christ are empowered to lead the way.

3. A Statement of Hope from Youth

The following statement is the result of intensive discussion in one of the groups, composed of members of different age groups and confessional traditions, at the meeting of the Faith and Order Commission in Bangalore. The group discussed statements recently issued by different youth movements and groups throughout the world, each dealing in a different way with how to give account of the hope today.

The statement addresses not only all members of the Commission and the groups behind the texts, but more generally churches and church members who are young physically and mentally.

Youth should not be regarded as a special category — they are fully a part of the people of God; nor are they the "church of tomorrow" but members of today's Church. They are not confined to so-called youth issues, but as part of the universal community of faith confront all the problems facing humanity today.

Young Christians today, as part of humanity, find themselves confronted by massive problems, which govern the context in which they must live and work. We are conscious of the universal and social dimensions of sin, and that we must confront the forces of evil in a corporate effort as they manifest themselves in society.

Moved to Action by Problems at all Levels

We see these manifestations at different levels. At the global level we see such problems as disarmament and the increasing danger of proliferation of nuclear weapons; the persistence of endemic poverty; the complex problem of energy; new forms of imperialism and neo-colonialism; the whole spectrum of economic problems from unemployment to indebtedness. At the local and national levels we see the same problems, often appearing more sharply than at international levels. In addition there are many other problems such as violations of human rights and specific repressions within states.

As an example, in India 420 million people live below poverty line — not having 2.50 rupees to spend per day (US$1 = 8 rupees). And 40 million people are unemployed.

But the global, national and local manifestations are not separate. They are part of the same picture. For example, torture is carried out at local or national level, but there is a clear pattern of the same techniques appearing in many parts of the world, indicating collaboration between the security forces of different states. And the existence of poverty or starvation in a particular situation is not accidental — it is part of a broad picture with many factors, including national and transnational economic and political structures.

Many Christian youth and student groups have a deep concern for their societies, for the world, and for the Church. Yet many come close to despair.

Today, we are confronted by gross obscenity in human life. In the middle of the ocean of poverty, there are islets of affluence. There is a great contradiction between the wealth and the poverty. Here one person's hope of profit is another's despair of being condemned to a lifetime of poverty.

We should have no illusions about changing society easily. Yet there is great value in spiritual nourishment and preparation which raises consciousness, and in practical action which can be carried out at a local level. Simple actions, such as adopting a more modest life-style or sharing our resources, will not in themselves change structures. But they are a step towards changing society, especially if undertaken on a wide scale.

Among affluent youth in all parts of the world there are common problems. Many are inward-looking, concerned mainly with their own lives, and unaware of the injustices around them. An important factor contributing to this is inadequate Christian education, which fails to bring about a mature understanding of the Gospel and its call to justice.

There are major contradictions within societies as well as between societies. Christianity is heavily identified with a middleclass life-style and the status quo in society. Those who speak out prophetically are too easily labelled as revolutionaries or utopians, and thereby neutralized.

Christian youth often start towards action out of guilt feelings and/or a genuine desire to help others. But the response is too often purely charitable. Even if we give a percentage of our income to the poor, or contribute to aid programmes, we leave untouched the structures which contribute to or directly cause the problem we wish to solve. If we do this, we are still at the level of compassion and sympathy. These qualities will continue to be needed. But only if we move through empathy and anger will we come to the commitment which leads to risk and resolute action.

Whatever form it takes, it must be informed action, and it must be courageous. In witnessing prophetically, we do not seek martyrdom, but we must be ready to make the sacrifice of true discipleship.

In the midst of the problems which the world crisis has put before us today, we make the central affirmation that God in Christ has assumed our humanity and redeemed it, calling us to participate in his liberation of all persons and all things in the hope for the final manifestation of his kingdom.

Participation in Liberation

Objectively, we see the need for withdrawing from identification with the social and cultural status quo and participating in the suffering and hopes of those involved in the struggle for human liberation. The style of this participation will take various forms in different contexts in Church and society. It may include civil disobedience, mobilizing people to claim their rights, participation in political organizations and it will always include campaigns of education and awareness building; it will aim at transcending all barriers of separation and contribute to discovering new dimensions in human life for a just and participatory society; it will include the clear awareness that the difficult but not utopian struggle for human liberation cannot be confined to structural changes. A vast area of social and political work is connected with consideration of the daily problems of people. We consider that Christian youth can take part in that important sphere on which the future of a new society depends.

We also see the need for new styles of spirituality – the traditional Christian spirituality of adaptation to society should change into one of spirituality, of contemplation and struggle – completely open to God and not alienated from but closely related to political actions. Thus, for example, while prayer, liturgy have the purpose of glorifying God, they cannot exist without a deep awareness of the needs and problems of the world.

As Christian youth we affirm our responsibility *vis-à-vis* the Church and its spiritual renewal. There is a tension in our thinking about the Church – a tension between what the Church actually is and what the Church is called to become. The focus of our involvement in the life of the Church is precisely at such points of tension. We affirm that in order to be credible the Church must be endowed with a great spiritual independence. The Church can be credible only if its internal and external life is prepared to carry the Cross of Jesus rather than merely preaching it; if in the big battles of life it is prepared to renounce success and dwell on service; if it will embody Christian hope by showing freedom of judgment and courage to go against the tide. Finally, we believe that the concept of communion is fundamental to the life of the Church. Jesus Christ is the giver of this living communion and he is alive, even if the Church does not manifest it.

Today's youth are trying to explore new ways of expressing the Christian faith in the context of struggles for human liberation:

— One of the experiences which has marked today's youth is the formation of "confessing communities". These communities are characterized by a strong desire to live out more just and amicable relations both among their members and in society. The advantages of these "confessing communities" are evident: a gradual change of lifestyle among their members, and an always open frontier *vis-à-vis* society. But we are aware that in spite of the extraordinary outpouring of new experiences, they remain a valid model mostly for middleclass people, difficult to apply at the mass level.

— Others profess a new type of Christian community which is no longer constituted according to the inherited historical synthesis of Church and state. This community is constituted on the basis of common recognition on the part of the participant. It is based on relation by vocation which includes an essential element of corporate responsibility in relation to the people's movement.

In the course of these experiences, together with all people of good will who wish to bring about a more just and humane society, we have become aware that the liberation process today presents us more with problems than with certainties. We see in this century only the dawn of a new society and a new humanity. There is no guarantee that the "laws of history" will score an easy triumph over darkness. Indeed, the possibility of the entire human race destroying itself is not remote. But we feel also that the Christian community presents unrivalled opportunities to be the crucible in which men and women can be moulded who, by faith and in hope, are willing to make an incredible wager about God, man and the future; people who are willing to stake their lives today and tomorrow on the wager that the future does not rest with those powerful structures of death that surround us, but with the weakness of those who, in the power of the cross, dare to create what does not yet exist.

4. Witness Unto Death

Introduction

"Hope does not disappoint us, because God's love has been poured into our hearts through the Holy Spirit which has been given to us" (Rom. 5 : 5). Giving account of our hope is an integral part of our Christianity. We have not only to speak our hope in words but also to testify to it by deeds. The whole of the Christian life must be witness, but in certain circumstances, this witness may go to the point of surrender of life in a martyr's death. The Greek word *marturia* means precisely witness.

Christ is both the supreme witness to hope and also its source. It is to him therefore that we must first look. As himself "the faithful witness" (Rev. 1:5). He sums up in his own person the testimony borne by all the prophets of the Old Testament and by all God's messengers. During his life, He "made the good confession before Pontius Pilate" (I Tim. 6:13). He placed his life in the hands of God, who saved him out of death and exalted him in glory. He is thus able to communicate to humanity the gift of the Spirit, which founds the Church, and to entrust the Church with bearing witness before the world.

I. The Firstborn of a Crowd of Witnesses

A. *The earthly life of Jesus as a model for believers*

a) Jesus the Messiah, consecrated by God and anointed with the Holy Spirit, is the witness to the Father. He does not act of himself (John 5 : 19). By deeds as well as words He translates the Father to humanity and reveals who the Father is for us. He comes for the sake of sinners, like a doctor for the sick. He brings God's pardon (Mark 2 : 17; John 4, the story of the Samaritan woman). He performs acts of liberation in the healings which defeat the powers of evil and set people free from sin. In this way He makes salvation manifest and causes hope to spring out of despair.

195

b) Jesus is the servant whose life was lived in obedience to the Father. He humbled himself and took the form of a slave, expressing for us the humility of God himself. He is God in the service of men, come not to be served but to serve (Mark 10:45; Luke 22:27; John 13:5). Thus, in showing the humble face of God, he does not crush human beings but gives them their dignity. They are then able to flourish and to open themselves to the love which, by bestowing on them their complete identity, is a source of hope. Jesus' own attitude is the foundation for mutual service and the love of neighbour.

c) The message enacted by Jesus is the cause of scandal: "Whoever would save his life will lose it". What picture of God is presented by an untriumphant Messiah? Confrontation with the Jewish religious authorities was inevitable. Nor, at the same time, could He avoid political implications. He will be accused of rising against Caesar. He must answer Israel's expectations and give concrete signs of hope (cf. the feeding of the crowds). His aim thereby is to make people look towards the final reality; the bread of life, the word which lasts for ever.

So Jesus knows the ambiguity of human situations, the ambiguity amidst which believers also live. He had to be discerning; sometimes He had to hide, sometimes He had to give messianic signs which were divisive.

d) The divisions which Jesus provoked led him to the cross, which is the ultimate surrender of a life totally dedicated to God and to humanity. This very cross will become the ground of hope. The relationship between cross and resurrection is fundamental to the whole New Testament. The Lamb is given glory because he has been slain (Rev. 5:9). It is precisely in the shame that the eschatological glory of Christ breaks through (John: the crown of thorns and the inscription on the cross). This transfigures the condition of every disciple of Christ who drinks the cup of the cross, whether drop by drop or at a single draught.

B. *The glory of the cross and the gift of the Spirit*

It is by being "lifted up" that Christ draws all people to himself (cf. John 12:32). He gives the Spirit, who is the advocate, the witness who convicts "the world" through the conscience of those whom he brings to believe that Christ is ultimately victorious over the world which condemned him (John 16:8-11). The Spirit is the great teacher, who leads believers into all truth (John 14:26; 16:13-15) and anoints the hearts of Christians with his teaching (I John 2:27). The gift of the Spirit is the foundation of the Church, which at Pentecost bears witness to the resurrection of Christ. The Church is the community of those who look to this fundamental hope and testify to it in their lives.

Already Christians have received the Spirit of the Son and are able to cry "Abba, Father" (Rom. 8:14f; Gal. 4:6). It is their assurance and their joy to be invited to abide in the communion of the Father and the Son.

Thus Christ's disciples will be enabled, by the power of the Spirit, to bear witness before the courts (Mark 13:11; John 15:26f.). Christ himself will be present in the martyr's combat.

In the energy of the Spirit, Christ gathers his Church through the efficacious sign of the eucharist, by which believers are united to his cross and resurrection. They are thus invited to look towards the Messiah's wedding feast and to make manifest in the world the love and the mutual service which are both the condition and the fruit of eucharistic communion.

The translation of these elements concerning Christ and the Spirit into the life of the Church will have the following five dimensions: eucharistic; apostolic or missionary; catholic or ecumenical; eschatological; diaconal.

II. "We Cannot do Without the Lord's Supper"

1. The Apostle Paul tells the Corinthians that their celebration of the eucharist is a proclamation of the Lord's death until He comes (I Cor. 11:26). In this perspective, the Christian eucharist is a perpetual sacrament of Christ's martyrdom in the time before his final return in glory. Already in this interval, the risen Christ makes himself present, in the Holy Spirit and by the sacramental sign, in order to conform us to himself, to make us into witnesses of the same God to whom he bore witness in his life, death and resurrection. Our sacramental configuration to Christ in the Spirit means that we put our deepest hope in God alone, in the One who raised his chief witness from the dead and will be able to do the same for those who faithfully follow Christ in a testimony of which He himself is the pattern, the inspiration and the strength.

2. Sometimes historical circumstances will demand that the Christian witness to the God of Jesus Christ take the form of a *marturia* in the strongest sense of the term. In these extreme cases, where Jesus has already passed because of the opposition which his testimony provoked, the Christian is called on to persevere even to the point of death. The history of the Church affords many examples to show that God's grace will not fail his elect, even in the extremity of their suffering. Often it has been very explicitly from the eucharist that Christians under trial have drawn the divine strength with gives them courage and keeps them faithful. *Sine dominico, non possumus*, said the martyrs of Abitinae in the early fourth century: "We cannot do without the Lord's supper".

But with the grace of the eucharist nothing proved impossible to the Christian martyrs. Already at the beginning of the second century, St. Ignatius of Antioch foresees that his martyrdom will "grind" him into one bread with Christ. Fifty years later, the martyr Polycarp will give to his parting prayer the form of an *eucharistia.*

3. In the early Church there were martyrs who looked forward to meeting again, "that very evening", around the table of the Lord in God's eternal kingdom. So it is not surprising that there should be a long tradition of building the sacramental altar over the "temples of the Spirit" which the bodies of the martyrs had been. There can be a very strong sense of the martyrs' continuing participation in the eucharistic celebration of the Church on earth, and every celebration of the eucharist gives earthly form to the urgent cry of the faithful souls beneath the heavenly altar: "Lord, how long?" (Rev. 6:9-11). To hasten the attainment of God's kingdom, in which the true hope of humanity will be satisfied by the One who is its source and goal, the Alpha and the Omega (Rev. 1:8), Christians will seek in the eucharist the strength needeed for bearing faithful witness in conformity with Christ and after the pattern of all who have already followed in the steps of their Lord to the point of death. They will know that the sufferings of this present time are not worthy to be compared with the weight of glory which awaits them in God's kingdom and which is already theirs *in spe,* "in the dimension of hope" (Rom. 8:17-25). They hear the promise of Jesus in John's gospel: "He who eats my flesh and drinks my blood has eternal life, and I will raise him up at the last day" (John 6:51-58). The eucharist anticipates the heavenly banquet to which God is inviting all nations, when death has been abolished (Isa. 25:6-9).

4. Especially in difficult circumstances, the very celebration of the eucharist can constitute an act of witness. In "impossible" situations, it proclaims that God alone creates a saving future. When it cries "Maranatha", the eucharistic community is calling for the overthrow of all that is opposed to God; it is praying for the final coming of God's kingdom: "Let grace come: let this world pass away" (Didache, 10). This hoped-for future is already prefigured in the fact that the eucharistic community itself includes pardoned sinners, reconciled adversaries, and the desperate restored to life: all are welcomed by the Lord at his table of justice, peace and joy in the Holy Spirit (cf. Rom. 14:17).

III. "The Blood of the Martyrs is the Seed of the Church"

1. An apostle is an envoy representing the one who sent him. Sent by the Father, Christ is his personal representative on earth and bears witness to the One whose mandate he accepts. When his own testimony, which is definitive, is coming to an end, Christ promises and gives to

his disciples the same Holy Spirit with which he himself was anointed, in order that they too may bear witness to him, and therefore to his Father, to the ends of the earth, beginning from the very place where his own witness reached its summit in martyrdom (Acts 1:8). The witness of the apostles may lead them, as it did Jesus, into situations of opposition and even of persecution; and indeed the universal tradition of the Church holds most of the apostles to have been martyred. Before hostile religious and political authorities, it is the Holy Spirit who will inspire their testimony to the gospel which is intended for every nation. (Mark 13:9-11; cf. John 15:27f.).

2. It is by the power of the Holy Spirit that Christians will be enabled, in a context of suffering, to "give an account of the hope which is in them" (I Pet. 3:15). By their very suffering they bear in their bodies the marks of Jesus (cf. Gal. 6:17), becoming one body and one blood with the One who, in them, suffers persecution: "Saul, Saul, why persecutest thou me?" (Acts 9:4). Martyrdom may be the climax of a freely given commitment, of a whole life dedicated to the spread of the gospel: as He approaches his own martyrdom, Paul, having meanwhile become an apostle, will speak of the gift of himself as a sacrificial libation offered to God (II Tim. 4:6).

3. Often in history, the flourishing of new local churches, if not their foundation, has followed the martyrdom of the first evangelists or disciples in those places. "The blood of the martyrs is the seed of the Christians" (Tertullian). Manifestly the converting grace of God works with particular power through the witness of martyrs. First on the purely human level, but then more theologically, the impressive and persuasive force of the martyrs can be ascribed to the following factors:

a) To commit one's very life to the service of a cause is powerful testimony to one's conviction of the truth of that cause.

b) Precisely in the service of his cause, the martyr is the absolutely *free* person, liberated from all created goods. Such liberty is contagious.

c) Trusting in God as the One who is able to raise from the dead, the Christian martyr is a strong witness to hope in the final and complete victory of the God who is preparing for men and women an everlasting life in his kingdom.

d) The forgiveness which Christian martyrs often display towards their executioners, following the example of Jesus Luke 23:24) and of St Stephen, the first martyr (Acts 7:60): this forgiveness testifies to the mercy of God who is seeking to bring people from their failures, faults, refusals, revolts, from their egoism and their sin, to a life of love which shares in the self-giving life of God.

4. The reading of the acts of the martyrs and their presence in preaching serve to strengthen the churches in their witness today. It is desirable

that an ecumenical anthology of both early and modern accounts of martyrdom should be published for the use of the churches, since the recognition of martyrs already transcends confessional boundaries and brings us all back to the centre of the faith, the source of hope, and the example of love for God and fellow human beings. The use of such a book would also strengthen the solidarity of all Christians in prayer and action with those who are in difficult or dangerous situations.

IV. Reconciled Through Sacrifice

1. The martyr is configured to Christ. The Christians of Lyons, in the letter of 177 A.D., recognize in the stake to which Blandina is attached the very cross of Christ, and Blandina herself is said to "have been clothed with Christ".

Now Christ died to restore the unity of God's scattered children. "He is our peace, who has made us both one, and has broken down the dividing wall of hostility" (Eph. 2:14).

In the witness of the martyrs we may rediscover the effective work of Christ who breaks down the barriers erected by sin and human weakness.

2. In the martyrs the Church discerns Christ himself, the very heart of its faith, beyond all interpretations and divisions. That is why the martyrs of the early Church and some great witnesses in the later history of the Church are the common property of all Christians. In the tapestry of Christian history, the ever-renewed succession of martyrs is the golden thread. This also explains why, in some countries, the churches are engaged in the process of a mutual recognition of the saints, even if they were killed in the course of inter-confessional struggles: beyond the inevitable cultural and ecclesiological limitations of their confession of faith it is possible to recognize the absoluteness of the Christ to whom they desired to bear witness.

This makes it possible, too, to recognize with joy and appreciation the ultimate witness of non-Christians whose love was great enough to lay down their lives for their friends.

V. For a Transfigured World

1. The martyr bears witness to the living God and to the coming of his kingdom. By his death he contests all attitudes which would absolutize the present state of affairs, and he affirms his faith in eternal life. Yet Christian hope does not demobilize us with regard to engagement in history. On the contrary, it supplies reasons for such involvement and the courage to undertake it. The Christian knows that he is sharing in the work of God which aims to bring about a new creation.

2. Hope inspires acts or attitudes which announce the definitive kingdom of God. These "prophetic" acts and attitudes must not themselves be absolutized, for account must be taken of the permanent ambiguity of human situations and of the resistance shown by men and women to the coming of the kingdom.

3. That is why the concrete choices can be, and are in fact, diverse. Some Christians are called on to bear witness to the Absolute: such is the case of martyrs clearly put to death for their confession of faith in Jesus Christ. Other Christians bear their witness through their active involvement in history. The diversity of concrete choices is the source of tensions and crises in society and in the churches. Yet the diversity can be valuable if it is lucidly lived as between partners in a dialogue, and with an effort to transcend mutual excommunications and rather look for the things which unite in spite of the differences in the choices.

4. Still in our days there are relatively clear situations in which the witness's choice is simple, even if it needs courage: this happens when he or she is faced with *either* confessing Christ and being killed *or* denying Christ and escaping alive. But it may also happen that Christians have neither the means not the capacity nor the opportunity to build by themselves a world according to the Gospel. From a rather broad range of possibilities they must then choose to bear witness with others to human values such as they discern them in the light of the Gospel and under the guidance of the Spirit.

VI. By This will You be Known

1. An integral part of Christ's witness is his solidarity with the hopeless, his self-identification on the cross with those who feel themselves abandoned by God. Yet it is precisely there that his divine Sonship becomes manifest. He proclaims his Father's reign in this way: "The Spirit of the Lord is upon me, for he has anointed me to preach good news to the poor. He has sent me to proclaim release to the captives and recovering of sight to the blind, to set at liberty those who are oppressed, and to proclaim the Lord's year of favour" (Luke 4:18f.).

2. Following its Lord, the Church will testify to its hope in the kingdom by acts, signs, gestures which prefigure, indeed in a creative way, the final salvation of humanity.

Where oppression seethes, the Church will testify to liberty. Where injustice reigns, the Church will work for justice. Where fears abound, the Church will show the love of God which leaves no room for fear. Where oppositions occur between races, classes, sexes or generations, the Church will seek a reconciliation which preserves diversity in unity.

Against torture and all dehumanizing practices, the Church will commit itself on behalf of human beings created in God's image and destined for his glory.

3. In some situations, the gospel choice will be clear. But elsewhere, the ambiguity of a sinful world will make discernment difficult and witness risky. Invoking the Spirit, Christians will dare to take a courageous path to which they will be pointed by their experience of the grace which has oriented and nourished their life ever since their baptism.

Questions

Having being asked to reflect on martyrdom as ultimate hope, we cannot tackle, let alone resolve, so many questions which yet are urgent for the lifestyle of Christians. We would, however, simply point out that Christians cannot escape the concrete problems put to their consciences. We are now thinking of such burning issues as the following, among many others:

a) The manufacture and trade in armaments put questions to Christians who are engaged in them at various levels: What concrete choices are they called on to make?

b) In countries under dictatorial régimes, what are the ways to fight the situation: engage in guerrilla warfare? Leave the country in order to continue the struggle from outside? Respond to violence by violence?

c) In a democratic country, Christian witness can be expressed by taking stands at the national level: What pressures are to be exerted on a government to stop a war and restore peace? to ensure a better distribution of the national income and of the world's riches?

VII. Prayer

Lord, we give you thanks for the many witnesses who, in the footsteps of your Son, have sealed with the gift of their life their fidelity to the hope sown in their hearts by your Spirit.

They have been the glory of your people, whose courage and perseverance they have sustained throughout the trials of our pilgrimage towards you.

Sustain and strengthen those of us who today are obliged to sacrifice their health, their position, their liberty or even their life for love of their fellows and the service of your kingdom.

Forgive us our weakness, our cowardice, our surrenders, our counter-testimonies. Forgive us also the blood we have shed.

Keep us, we pray, in the communion of the martyrs and the saints who, having borne witness to you on earth, now rejoice before your face, eternally. Amen.

Growing Together
in Unity

1. Koinonia and Consensus
Towards Communion in One Faith

ANTON HOUTEPEN

Communion and consensus are keywords of hope for Faith and Order. In dealing with many divisive issues in order to reach consensus and to bring the churches into closer communion, the meaning of these two keywords of hope was explicitly reflected upon on several occasions. We find examples of such reflection in both the report from Crêt-Bérard[1] and from the Odessa consultation on "The Teaching Authority of the Church". But what exactly is the relation between this search for consensus and the real communion (koinonia) of the churches? What kind of consensus is needed and would be sufficient to bring us together into one communion?

I hope the following theses might be helpful to launch our debate on unity.

The communion

The first thesis is that our concept of "communion" suffers from a deficient understanding of christology, even if it is related to the trinitarian perspective, as was the case in Nairobi (Section II, part II). Even there, it is one-sidedly described as "participation in the divine nature" (II Peter 1:4). It is related to the meeting of the apostles with the risen Christ, his cross and living presence today through the Holy Spirit. But according to the New Testament, koinonia means the participation in the total event of Jesus Christ: his life, death, resurrection and parousia. In fact, we are tending to forget that the living communion of the disciples during the lifetime of Jesus is as basic for our understanding of koinonia as the post-paschal encounter with the risen Christ. This means, among other things, the following:

● Dr Houtepen is Ecumenical Officer of the Roman Catholic Diocese of Breda, The Netherlands.

[1] *Towards an Ecumenical Consensus — Baptism, Eucharist, Ministry, Faith and Order Paper No. 84.* Geneva: WCC, 1977, p. 4.

— participation in the koinonia is regulated by a discipline of behaviour and by the criteria for discipleship, rather than by adherence to common interpretations of Scripture or by common expressions of worship. These criteria for discipleship imply the radical commitment to the kingdom of God, the readiness to share in the fate and destiny of Jesus, a life in the hope of the resurrection, a community life, ruled by the demand for continuous reconciliation, admonition and the possibility of repentance. The disciples share with Jesus the baptism of metanoia, the bread of life, and the cup of judgment (Mark 10:38; John 6). The post-paschal community of disciples — which is the Church — is living through the Holy Spirit according to the same spirituality (Acts 2:42-47). It is a communion of common fate and destiny, not a "school of thought".

— the limits of the Christian community — or rather its openness — are measured by the liberating and redeeming "memoria" of an excommunicated man. Communion as participation in the event of Jesus Christ means communion with a man who was extremely open and free to mix with people who were not qualified for participation in the Jewish religious community and who was, for that reason, himself excommunicated and cursed by crucifixion. But through resurrection, he was rehabilitated by God. Such a participation in the Christ-event means that the disciples are in a similar situation. Therefore, it can be said that they are anointed by the Spirit, like Jesus himself (I John 2:20).

The consensus

The consensus in this original community was a *consentire,* rooted in the common fate and destiny, rooted in sharing with Jesus, rather than a doctrinal consensus. The New Testament tells us little about the "technique" of consensus in one faith. Paul summarizes the early Christian attitude in Philippians 2:

> If then our common life in Christ yields anything to stir the heart, any loving consolation, any sharing of the Spirit, any warmth of affection and compassion, fill up my cup of happiness by thinking and feeling alike, with the same love for one another, the same turn of mind and a common care for unity... (Phil. 2:1-2).

The consensus is built on the confession of the same Gospel, the praise of Jesus, true man, true Lord. Here the New Testament uses the word *homologia/homologein.* (We find this term, for example, in I John 2:23; 4:2-3; II John 7, but also in Romans 10:10 and Philemon 2:11, and even in Matthew 10:32). It is one of the oldest technical terms for the consensus in one faith. The object is always the reality of Jesus, the choice for or against him (cf. I Cor. 12:3). Another New Testament term, translated by consensus or *consentire* is *sumphonia/sumphonein.* In Matthew 18:19, we find this term in the well-known text, which could be called the shortest ecclesiology of the New Testament:

I tell you this: if two of you agree on earth *(sumphonesosin)* about any request you have to make, that request will be granted by my heavenly Father. For where two or three have met together in my name, I am there among them (Matt. 18: 19).

So "consensus in one faith" as *homologia* and *sumphonia* is characterized by praise and prayer, based on the intimate relation with Jesus, with the Father, through the Spirit. Consensus is the *result* of an already existing communion. The object of faith is that communion itself. Texts, doctrines, agreements and forms of worship may make it explicit, but they are not conditions for the koinonia.

The conditions

In the course of centuries, the emphasis shifted considerably. The limits of the community became marked in a growing juridical way by "conditions for communion" and "requirements for membership", by regulations for excommunication and penance, by measures protecting the identity of the "true Church", against all kinds of "heresies", by the forming of a binding "deposit of faith", by a ministry deciding on questions of determination of faith, by sacramental forms and rules of conduct.

We shall not condemn such a development: most churches say that the inspiration and the guidance of the Spirit were behind it. It helped the Church to survive throughout the centuries. But at the same time, it caused many splits and divisions. Now, in the ecumenical movement, we try to reevaluate the original idea of communion and consensus and to find out what the real "structures" of our communion are. How do we participate in the fate and destiny of Jesus and by what main "structures" can we express that koinonia? Several attempts have already been made to describe the main areas of existing dissensus, and consensus required for unity (for example, the famous Lambeth Quadrilateral, the New Delhi and Nairobi statements on unity). Three "main conditions for unity" have been mentioned in Faith and Order discussions. I shall not try to add another list. But I have four remarks:

a) If we call these areas of consensus only "conditions" for unity, we might create the impression of trying to measure the possibility of communion between churches by the yardstick of a parliament-like ratification of the credentials of churches. These credentials of a church, however, are its life in faith, its sharing in Jesus Christ by Word and sacrament, its discipline of being true disciples, its readiness for reconciliation, its care for unity, its longing for catholicity. We cannot measure this reality of communion in Christ on the basis of agreements about minimum conditions.

b) The communion is already existing. We repeat that again and again. So we agree that all of us share in the event of Jesus Christ. But in the meantime, we refuse to share that supreme sign of our common fate and destiny — the eucharistic communion. We are now tempted to produce communion on the basis of negotiations, denying implicitly that the reality of communion must be received again and again in the dynamic relations into which God himself has called us (I Cor. 1:9). Before all consensus work should come this humble recognition of each other as part of the communion of Jesus Christ.

c) But who is the subject of all those "conditions for unity" upon which we are working so hard? If it is the churches, how can we relate to the people in the churches: the mixed marriage couples, the children sharing religious education, the many church members who can only partially identify themselves with the official church doctrines from the past, the multitude of ministers already sharing pastoral responsibilities, the theologians agreeing on many weighty points already? Where are the people in the younger churches, who would like to share full communion with their fellow Christians in the diaspora, but who are forbidden to do so in the name of the universal Church or of their confessional family? Should we not take more seriously this process of convergence at the grass-roots level, based on the actual *consentire* of Christians in matters of life, work and communication?

d) If we cannot avoid listing the "structures" of communion, then we should not forget one structure, which is essential to the New Testament idea of communion: the element of the "discipline of our communion". Discipline but not in the sense of "discipleship". The "praxis" of Christians should be a serious structure of their communion. Of course, we may say that this is implied in the confession of the one faith. But even our common ancient creeds do not refer to such a praxis of the kingdom. For our time, a common Christian "praxis" would help us a lot in giving account of our hope and in growing together into unity.

2. The Indian Experience In and Towards Unity

SAMUEL AMIRTHAM

I have been asked to share with you the Indian experience in church unity as my contribution to the panel discussion. I am grateful for this opportunity. I am a member of the Church of South India (CSI), a united church which came into being about 30 years ago by the union of churches that belonged to the Anglican, Methodist, Presbyterian and Congregational traditions. These 30 years of life of the united church have not been smooth sailing in any sense, and have had their joys and agonies. I would like to say, first of all, something about the experience within the united church and then, secondly, something about the experience on the road to wider unity of the churches in India, hoping that this will have some significance for our discussions here on the theme of "Growing Together into Unity". The particularity of one experience has, surely, implication for the universality of the concern.

Reflecting on the experience of unity in the Church of South India, the very first thing I would like to affirm is that this unity came as a gift of Christ. It is still a marvel. in our eyes, how this was ever made possible. The conviction has grown stronger over the years, not least because of the lurking dangers to unity, that it was something much more than a human achievement. The power of the Holy Spirit was manifest in creating this wider fellowship in the Spirit. It was the empowering of the Spirit that made the churches take this step of "adventure in obedience". Obedience, as Bishop Newbigin once said, is not a favourite word in our times. But it is our conviction that, at a decisive moment after about 30 years of union negotiations, the step of obedient action had to be taken and the uniting churches were given grace to do so.

● Prof. Amirtham is principal of the Tamil Nadu Theological Seminary at Arasaradi, Madurai, India.

Fears proved wrong

Secondly, we in the united church realize now that certain fears entertained at the time of union have been proved wrong. One of the fears was that of the loss of identity, the loss of cherished traditions and relationships. The accepted principles of union at that time included those of "unity in diversity" and "the preservation of all that was precious to each tradition" in the united church. But still one had to be prepared to die to the old identity. But to our surprise, we have now discovered a new identity, more wholesome and richer, more promising and more authentic than the old one. Richer, because union has resulted in an enrichment of liturgical and congregational life; more wholesome, because of the availability of a wider and more diverse fellowship; more promising because this new identity rather looks forward to the future in faith and hope than back to the past; and more authentic because, while being rooted and related to the same Lord as before, the churches are now more related to each other in the context in which they are set and to the mission of the Church in India.

One of the problems then for some members of the uniting churches was breaking their relationship with their "historical identity", ties with fathers and mothers, brothers and sisters in the so-called "mother churches". I remember a sermon in those days in which the preacher reminded a church council in this context how, if one was willing to forsake his father and mother and brother and sister for the sake of Christ, Christ will give them hundredfold in this life. An interesting interpretation! And yet, how true it has been in the experience of the wider fellowship of the united church. In the Nairobi document on unity, we read as follows:

> Organic union of separate denominations to form one body does mean a kind of death which threatens the denominational identity of its members, but it is dying in order to receive a fuller life. That is literally the "crux of the matter".

The Church of South India can witness to the fact of gaining a new identity through the loss of an old one. It must be added, however, that the CSI has written in its constitution that it would be prepared to die any time for the sake of wider unity of the Church in India. No newly found identity can be final.

Unity and community not identical

A point must be made also about the quality of the inner life of the CSI. In spite of the initial enthusiasm, we soon learned the sad lesson that formal union of churches in itself does not change the quality of fellowship inside the churches. Unity of churches is no guarantee for community of persons. Congregations and dioceses continue to be divided because of language, caste, lust for power, disparities of economic wealth, and insensitivity to the need for recognition and participation of minority groups. In fact, even some of the joint endeavours for mission in the sphere of development programmes have become additional factors for fights and rivalries. The church finds itself unable to be delivered from those problems that plague the society at large. The powers that divide the society are equally strong in the church. So we now learn that the task of building up a community, community of love, of mutual caring and sharing and suffering is not identical with that of achieving visible unity of the Church. This fact, among others, was highlighted by a study carried out in the CSI after 20 years of its life. The report was published under the title, "Renewal and Advance". The study made it clear that a united church has to be continually renewed for mission in the power of the Spirit, for the sake of community. Renewal for community is necessary if church unity is to be meaningful.

This aspect of the life of the united church should not, however, underestimate the positive benefits of union. The united church has gained a greater confidence to bear witness to the world; union has enhanced, to some extent at least, the credibility of the Church's claim as reconciler of divisions and to be a sign for God's promise of unity of all humankind. The sharing of resources has strengthened the life and witness of the churches, and their service to society and action for justice.

I would now like to make some remarks about the attempts for wider unity in India. A similar union of churches as that of CSI took place in North India, and the Church of North India (CNI) came into existence in 1970.

Union negotiations began between the CSI and the Lutheran churches in South India soon after 1947. Visible unity between these churches has not become a fact yet, but full fellowship has been achieved. One of the fruitful results of these conversations has been the greater theological clarity that has come in matters like historical episcopate, sacraments, authority of the Scriptures and creeds, law and Gospel, on which agreed statements were declared as early as 1958. Since then, there has been a slackening of enthusiasm in negotiation talks, a reluctance to face structural issues. Some time ago, a two-phased programme of four years each was agreed by the joint theological commission of the churches, to be consummated in organic unity. But action has not yet been taken for the implementation of this proposal.

Towards wider union

The union talks among the CSI, CNI and the Mar Thoma Church have been more fruitful. Both the CSI and the CNI had affirmed at the time of their union that they had not attained the goal of unity, which is nothing short of the visible unity of all Christ's people in India. The path of unity is always and everywhere a pilgrimage in faith to the promised land, yet unknown. A milestone in this pilgrimage was reached when, on 4 July 1978, the three churches established a joint council.

211

This is definitely a great step forward in manifesting the unity of Christ's people in the whole of India. These three churches have been in a unique situation as far as their mutual relationship was concerned among all groups of churches negotiating for union in different parts of the world. They have been in full communion with one another for some time. They have doctrinal unity, accept the same creeds, have the same approach to authority of the Scriptures, accept one another's baptism and eucharist. They all possess historic episcopate for their ministry and mutually recognize each other's ministry. They remain different in organization. But this was no sufficient reason to remain separate. It is the recognition of this fact, the desire to offer obedience to Christ in unity, and the conviction that the Holy Spirit is guiding them into the next step, that led these churches to the setting up of the joint council. The council will have advisory functions with regard to the internal life of the churches and authoritative function to act on matters relating to joint action. The heads of the three churches are the co-presidents of the joint council.

Some have described this union as "conciliar unity". It is questionable if it is proper to describe this union as conciliar unity. In any case, the joint council has rejected both terms of organic unity and conciliar unity to signify the nature of this unity. Some members of these churches feel that this is an easy alternative to organic unity and that the churches have not faced the issues of organic unity. The council, however, made it clear that it is not a kind of compromise formula for satisfying the sentiments of those who were not prepared to pay the price for a deeper unity. On the contrary, the uniting churches see this as an important act of obedience to Christ, recognizing the realities which have shaped the present life and the present context in mission of these churches. It is also an act of commitment to each other and to Christ, to discover more meaningful and comprehensive levels of unity.

New models for new situations

In a sense, these three churches are still divided. They have their own separate historical, cultural, ecclesiastical, liturgical and linguistic and other backgrounds. The CSI and CNI have in them some of the traditions of the churches which started modern Protestant missions. The Mar Thoma Church traces its history to the beginning of the church founded by St Thomas in India and has preserved the early liturgy of St James and celibate episcopacy. The CSI and CNI have clear geographical boundaries; the Mar Thoma Church is spread all over the country, though concentrated in Kerala. But in spite of this, they have an inner unity. To express this unity, a new model had to be found. The models of CSI and CNI unions, however useful a few decades ago, were not found to be adequate. New situations call for new models.

This is an important insight that the enthusiasts of earlier models had to learn. No one model of unity is adequate for all times and all situations. The main basis of unity is the living presence of Christ in his Body, the Church. It is in sharing this body of Christ that unity is manifested. No one model, therefore, can have exclusive claim for validity.

However, creating new models for unity is not the most important thing. The main concern of the Indian Church ought to be the fulfilment of God's mission in India. This implies a commitment of the churches to be involved in the struggles of the Indian people for realizing their hopes and aspirations, taking initative to unite with the forces that strive for liberation of the poor masses of India from everything that dehumanizes and oppresses them, a commitment to national integration and solidarity, and a commitment to the proclamation of the Good News in all spheres of Indian life, so that all may have abundant life. Models of unity must be created with this vision in mind. In a sense, therefore, the urgency for mission gains priority over concern for church unity. A Hindu friend of mine once said that he found our unity discussions very amusing, to say the least. He thought that Christians should be spending their energy on matters that are important to the world and not on matters that are important only to the Church. Though I tried to defend the importance of church unity for the world, I felt that he had a point.

A word may be said in conclusion about the outcome of the national consultation of all churches in India, including the Roman Catholic Church, on conciliar unity, held early this year. There were deep questionings about the divided state of the churches in the context of their mission. Indeed, the first two papers presented were, "Mission in the Context of India's Heritage" and "Mission in the Context of India's Socio-Economic and Political Situation". There was questioning about the sin of pride that still divides the churches. One of the participating bishops said in his closing sermon: "When we analyse the cause of division in Christendom, ultimately we come to the conclusion that pride of man is the primary cause of division." A Roman Catholic participant has asked in a review of the consultation why the Roman Catholic Church and the Orthodox churches are not even willing to join the National Council of Churches of India. While many theological issues were squarely faced, the possibilities of moving from "theological ecumenism" to "practical ecumenism" in this "pre-conciliar unity period" were also discussed. Some recommendations to the churches for action were made: that Christian festivals must be celebrated in joint worship; that joint action be taken in matters of of human rights and development; that exchange of pulpits be arranged and that regular intercession in eucharist be offered for one another. These recommendations are significant, because shared celebration, shared service, shared listening to God's Word and shared prayer surely point the way to a more fully shared life in the one Body of Christ.

213

3. The Eucharistic Life

The Church as a Eucharistic Community at the Local Level

NICOLAS LOSSKY

I shall not dwell here on the concept of the local church, but assume the standpoint expounded by Jean Zizioulas in *In Each Place*.[1]

To summarize the main points: The local church is the eucharistic community assembled together around its president, whom we call the bishop. It brings together all in that place who belong to the Church, irrespective of race, sex, class, social, ethnic, political or economic status. This local eucharistic community confessing the catholic faith is in communion with all local churches confessing the same faith. Jean Zizioulas's article provides an excellent discussion of the various terms employed here.

Communion

The eucharistic life is life in communion; communion is "sharing together a common bond — this participating together establishes a new relationship between the participants. They constitute a community... The common bond is the very life of the God of love. They are in communion with the Father, through the Son, in the Holy Spirit. This establishes a new relationship between the participants, one which is as real and as mysterious as their relationship with God. This is the deepest and most ultimate level of their communion, since it is the beginning of the ultimate reality."[2]

Communion is therefore an eschatological reality. In the eucharist, we offer our gifts, we offer ourselves, for the Holy Spirit to incorporate us in the Body of Christ. In a mysterious (sacramental) way we already share, therefore, in the divine life of the Holy Trinity.

The new relationships disclosed to us in this participation are also kenotic relationships (self-giving sometimes to the point of death itself). They

---

● Prof. Nicolas Lossky teaches at the University of Nanterre, Paris.

[1] Geneva: WCC, 1977, pp. 50-61.

[2] P. P. Duprey in an unpublished paper.

are in the truest sense personal relationships (since the *person* is understood to be life in communion, on the pattern of the divine Trinity, existence with its impetus towards the other, with its solicitude for the other...).

In practice, this relationship in communion means, among other things, a refusal to identify others by their labels (male, female, English, French, Indian) or by their problems (as young people, old people, rich, poor, unemployed). He or she is essentially a creature of God.

This refusal to identify others by their labels or their problems does not mean that we deny, obliterate or forget their reality. Just because the other is Peter or Paul or Mary, a creature of God, bound to me (and me to him or her) by the bonds of Christ's Body, his/her problems become in a sense *my* problems (even if I find myself in conflict with these problems). *All* those in whose midst God has set my life are God's creatures (even my torturer).

History

Hence, though communion is an eschatological reality, it is in no sense a negation or obliteration of the realities of history. The gifts we bring, the persons we are (and therefore the network of relationships this implies), the whole of the reality which we bring with us is the history of our time. We bring it as an offering and the eschatological reality of communion gives it a new colour, a new dimension which is different from that of simple linear evolution. It is this new colour, this new dimension, which makes it possible to transform the character of our relationships in the concrete realities of history.

Communion is not confined to one moment in the week, but embraces all the time of our life and every aspect of our life. Communion therefore necessarily entails sharing at all levels. Of course, at the local level, according to what each of us brings with him/her as an offering, it also embraces a much wider range of levels (for example, the Indian textile industry, and the international trade of the European Economic Community). Precisely because it is eschatological in character, communion requires a full involvement in history (each according to his or her gifts).

Self-questioning

In communion, all who live in our locality are our concern. This applies especially to the problem of confessional pluralism. It is impossible to settle down comfortably in schism. The new relationship, life in communion, should have consequences above all for this situation. The ecumenical dimension (that is, keen sense of the scandal of Christian disunity and, perhaps causally related to it, the disunity of the whole human family) is clearly part and parcel of the eucharistic life, the life of communion, in one place.

It is impossible for a local church to have a good conscience about its reality as the Church if it is not constantly, sincerely and untiringly preoccupied with the fact of disunity, in a spirit of communion and not in an imperialist empire-building spirit.

Fidelity to the apostolic faith is not the fierce defence of some entrenched fortress. It is rather a listening posture, an "attentive affirmation" and exchange in the light of the Gospel of Christ. It implies a constant self-questioning in the Holy Spirit, enabling us constantly to distinguish between the tradition as the breath of the Holy Spirit and everything that is "cultural". It is not a matter of suppressing, but of ensuring that culture is not imposed under the label of tradition. By its very nature, the life in communion is not domineering but liberating, permitting each to live fully the life God has given him or her.

Dialogue

We are not at liberty, therefore, to sleep peacefully meanwhile. We must work as hard as possible to reestablish communion with all in the Body of Christ. Certainly, this is not easy. It presupposes that we recognize that this communion is the expression, the seal, of the confession of the one apostolic faith.

Moreover, it is God himself who will establish communion when it seems good to him to do so. But He will not do this as some *deus ex machina*. He will not do this without our persistent endeavours in this direction. To pray for unity requires of us that we should be extremely vigilant and attentive to the movements of history, to the changes and developments in our situation (what our brother actually says is not necessarily what we believe he *ought* to say, consistently with his past history).

If our eucharistic ecclesiology (the notion of the local church with all that it implies) deepens to the point of real consensus, we must not then be afraid to enter into a new dialogue.

Meanwhile, the pain remains. Our consensus is still far from complete, far from ripe; the communities to which we shall bring it are not of one mind, not ready for it; they have to be made ready. This should be an act of the Church, unanimous, and not merely of a "representative" group. As we bear the pain, we should also share the joy of our brothers and sisters as they receive God's Word and communicate in the body and blood of Christ. Let us rejoice together that our friends are celebrating the feast!

This joy is tinged with pain. But the joy of Easter does not obliterate the cross. Good Friday is already a day of joy, too. As one of the great spiritual guides of the Church of England said at the beginning of the 17th century, it is not for nothing that we call this Friday *Good* Friday. It is a day of joy and victory, of victory over death.

4. A Lived Community

JEANNE HENDRICKSE

I am a black woman from the Republic of South Africa — Azania. These two facts influence who I am, and consequently my theology as well. It is through the eyes of blackness and woman that I perceive the world and out of this context I speak to you today, as a black woman from a third world country. But, you will say, technologically South Africa is an industrialized country. Yes, it is. When you take the GNP of white people, it falls into the First World. But if you take the GNP of the blacks alone, it falls into the Third World. Three out of five of our black children die of kwashiorkor (a protein deficiency disease) before the age of five.

Our struggle is a common struggle, a struggle for humanness; our hope is to become our fullest human potential that God has created us to be. Our hope is that white people and affluent people will recognize that we too, like themselves, have been created in *imago dei*. If you defile me as a black woman, are you not also defiling the image of God? I ask you beloved sisters and brothers in the words of Camus: "Don't walk in front of me, for I may not follow; don't walk behind me, I may not lead; walk beside me and be my friend."

I ask you to walk with me, and see through my black woman's eyes what our hope is, and what for us growing together into unity means and requires.

I ask you brilliant scholarly theologians to bear with me the cross of simplicity of the local black church, that is, the people at the grass-roots level. What I have to say may not be theologically profound. In fact, some may even wonder whether it is theology. But what I have to say is relevant to life, involving situations. It is out of the grass-roots understanding of our experience of pain, suffering, hate, forgiveness,

---

• Ms Hendrickse, South African, is presently doing doctoral studies in the USA.

acceptance, love, that I speak. It is in this context that we experience the reality of life, death, resurrection, hope, love, unity. We believe that the Holy Spirit still teaches us and calls and summons us to listen. I have seen and experienced the dehumanizing atrocities of apartheid: apartheid which paralyzes minds which are not allowed to grow, and punishes those who dare to think of themselves as created in God's image and entitled as God's heirs to enjoy the common heritage of God's creation.

How can the Church in South Africa, divided by apartheid, begin to be reconciled? How can we enter into an experience of unity, when not only theologically but racially we are divided? First and foremost, we have to be free; we have to be free to be human, free to become our fullest God-created potential. In anger we pray: "Dear God, when will you let us go and be free? For centuries, we have turned the other cheek — our cheeks have become bloody and raw and still our white brothers and sisters go on slapping. They do not even realize that we are human. They do not see that we belong to your family and that you are our divine parent. We pray for patience; we pray that we may forgive seventy times seven. We pray for acceptance; we pray for understanding; we pray for love; we pray for unity."

Yet we cannot speak of unity and oneness until we experience forgiveness, old-fashioned conversion and transformation, love and understanding. Jesus taught us to leave our gift at the altar and go and make our peace with our brother, our sister first, then to come back and offer our gift. How can we offer the gift of ourselves while we have hatred and division in our hearts? First, we must come to an agreement; we must die to the old and be resurrected anew, free, as equals. Then we can talk of unity.

What does it take, therefore, to grow together towards and into unity? Let us look at the theme: "Growing Together into Unity".

Growing (synonyms: maturing, developing, expanding, enlarging, nurturing)

Growing is painful. It necessitates death to the old, and becoming new, different, changing. The seed must die to become a plant; the caterpillar dies to become a butterfly. This change, this transformation is painful, challenging, risky, but there is ultimately joy.

Our theme says **"together"** we must do this changing, dying — black, white, woman, man, Catholic, Orthodox, Protestant. It means becoming a community of Christ-centred people. But there is the stage of the pupa, dormancy, when seemingly nothing is happening. Here patience is required, so that internal changes can mature, and the death of static, stagnant myths, so that the new in Christ can emerge. In this way, I hope that our community of women and men in the Church can grow together. Then the shared joy. A symbiotic relationship is implied, a feeding of each other, both deriving benefits from the other, together forming a new creation.

The growing transformation is painful. The winds of change enable the man to share his apples with the woman and the woman to share her bread with the man. Together they experience joy. Is this communion?

Then the hurt, misunderstanding, separation, anger, walls built. How many walls have we built around us? Walls of denominationalism, walls of racism, walls of sexism, walls of issues of all shades and hues. We need to grow and break down the walls of ego which divide us. Each I-ego, each collective ego, each denominational ego, each doctrinal castle becomes a prison. The "Church Multinational Cooperative Structure", our castle, becomes a prison which separates. I recall that some ministers of religion in the USA, when asked to support disinvestment in South Africa, objected because they were concerned about their pension fund when they retired. Clergy separating themselves, partaking and prepared to retire on the blood and sweat of their black brothers and sisters.

We need to go back to Jesus of Nazareth and the Bible. Yes, it may mean crucifixion; but is not being Christian accepting to be crucified?; to sell all for the kingdom?; to lose life that we may gain life? Are we prepared to die so utterly, completely, totally as Jesus died for God's kingdom? If we are co-creators with God, can we not, through grace, form and be part of the New Creation in Jesus Christ?

I think of South Africa where the various Congregationalists and the Disciples of Christ have united (the union formed has a black majority). The Tjonga Presbyterian Church was prepared to join with this body, but not with their white counterpart. Now, by coming into union with the already united churches, the white and black Presbyterians will be united. We pray that this union will materialize.

Unity (synonyms: singleness, oneness, harmony, completeness, solidarity)

I shall deal briefly with only three factors which I see as essential to unity.

1) *Consciousness* — *awareness* of that which separates and divides us:

a) Language: In seminary education, most women run into a battle with languages. This is, however, only a superficial problem indicative of a deeper underlying oppressive structure of exclusiveness, as when theologians speak of a "doctrine of man", etc. If we are growing into unity, we need to be aware of our language usage to be inclusive of all humankind. It is so easy to exclude fifty percent of the world's population by the language we use!

b) Interpretation and theology: In *Theology Today*[1], Catherine Gonzalez has said:

> Theology does not have its source within our own experience. It has its source in the revelation given by God, but our interpretation of that revelation has everything to do with our situation. Men have the tendency to forget the second part of this statement, and assume the theology they create is "undefiled" by such non-intellectual factors. At the present time, some women who have been alienated from the Church because of its failure to recognize the masculine bias present in its theology may have the tendency to forget the first half.

It is important, therefore, for us to be involved in, and to be part of a study such as "The Community of Women and Men in the Church", so that we may learn to share our gifts.

c) Actions: We must be conscious and aware of our attitudes, actions, life-styles as they affect others in the Body. For example, our attitudes and actions *vis-à-vis* the ordination of women, investments in South Africa, baptism and eucharist, the gay community, the disabled, children, the aged, the mentally ill, the counter-culture, and so on. Another example: five of us eat one kilo of meat at one sitting. How many families in Bangalore have one kilo of protein for the whole week? Let us try to take up the challenge of Mr Fernandes and try to get a world market for home industry. What we eat, wear and use affects the whole world.

2) *Confession — forgiveness:* We must forgive oppressors for oppressing and forgive ourselves for allowing ourselves to be oppressed. "Forgive as Christ forgives."

3) *Love:* "Now abideth faith, hope, love, these three; but the greatest of these is love. " "Love one another as I have loved You." Such love will ensure a humane life-style for the whole of humanity.

Some practical questions

I have some practical thoughts and questions I should like to leave with the committees discussing unity:

Committee I — "The Meaning of 'Conciliar Fellowship' ":

- Could we talk of "conciliar community" rather than of "fellowship". Community seems to be more inclusive and indicates a common position and body of persons, joint ownership, companionship, koinonia.

Committee II — "Towards Communion in One Faith":

- What is communion?
- What is faith?
- Is our faith in Christ Jesus, or in human, maybe divinely-inspired creeds?

---

[1] Vol. 34, No. 4. Princeton, N.J., January, 1978.

- Consider the challenge from Dr Siddharta that Christianity is one religion that could be relevant to the new age. Do we not need to be involved and be this new Creation in Christ Jesus?
- Jesus' teachings are relevant to all times and places, but they must be seen in the context of the community.
- Do we teach by the authority of Christ Jesus, or by the authority dictated by a hierarchy?

Committee III — "Growing into One Eucharistic Fellowship: One Baptism, One Eucharist and a Mutually Recognized Ministry":

- Here again the possible use of the word "community" rather than of "fellowship".
- I borrow from a sermon by John Bennet on "Foot Washing" — how ludicrous it would be to our discussion if our Christianity were based on foot-washing rather than on the eucharist: *(a)* do we sprinkle or immerse the feet? *(b)* do we wash the right or the left foot first, or both at once? *(c)* who can wash whose feet? *(d)* can women's feet be washed? *(e)* can women wash feet? *(f)* what is the ecumenical consensus on foot-washing? *(g)* what about the liturgy of foot-washing?

Committee IV — "The Discipline of Communion in a Divided World":

- Will women's presence in the ministry make a difference in the socio-political-cultural realm?
- How can the study of community, of women and men, ministers and laity, co-workers, co-creators help in understanding?
- Is there justice in the Church? Will the Church make a difference?
- Christ Jesus came for the salvation of all persons. Do we by our pietistic views and Christology exclude others? — "the kingdom of God for the special, elect Christians"?
- What is an integrated community of women and men in the Church?
- What is the meaning of servanthood? Men serving God, women serving men, so men can serve God?
- What is communion?

Committee V — "New Ecumenical Experiences and Existing Ecumenical Structures":

- In dialogues, can we listen with a third ear and see with a third eye? Through grace, then, maybe we shall hear and understand one another.
- Let us put praxis into operation.

I would like to end with a challenge to us all. Don't get involved with growing together into unity unless your bones, heart, soul, your whole being, cries for unity:

- don't get involved with human cries of pain, separation, agony, suffering, loneliness, the turmoil of torture, and travail of an earth raped naked of resources, humanity groaning as a woman in labour giving birth;
- don't get involved with injustice, liberation, human rights, hunger, oppression, dignity, unity of churches, understanding, reconciliation, peace;

- don't get involved, unless your whole being cries with Christ for justice, love, humanness, unity, peace;
- *but if you dare, dare to get involved!*

You *will* be involved, you will never rest again. You will be misunderstood. You will be crucified. If you dare to hope; if you dare to hope for justice, love, reconciliation, peace, unity; if you dare to act with consciousness; if you dare to die for Christ; *if you dare to be involved, God will strengthen you.*

If you dare to risk, to love, to fight, for full humanness for all people, you will not have lived in vain. If you dare, you will live the joy of the resurrected life of Christ.

If you dare, *we shall be one.*

5. Towards a Common Profession of Faith

J. M. R. TILLARD

In our discussions and studies on baptism, eucharist and the ministry, we have registered a number of important convergences and even some substantial agreements. This undoubtedly represents a major advance along the road to the "conciliar fellowship" to which the Nairobi Assembly devoted its attention. Yet all of us realize that this advance is not only insufficient, but will also continue to be insecure so long as other more fundamental agreements have not been reached.

The fact is that sacraments and ministry only derive meaning and truth from the faith itself. All our traditions insist that this faith is no extra ingredient added to the basic elements of ecclesial communion nor even an element which is in every respect identical with the rest. It is the faith which gives to the whole its Christian authenticity. Ecclesial *koinonia* is the communion of *believers,* the sacraments are sacraments *of the faith*, the "authoritative" teaching of the ministers is the teaching of the faith, and its credibility is proportionate to its fidelity to this faith. The further we get in refining and (already!) discussing our consensus texts, therefore, the more we realize that the sincerity of our endorsement of them will depend in the last analysis on our clarifying certain fundamental questions of faith which have not yet been tackled directly. In the absence of such clarification, the considerable advances already made would lack the support needed if progress is not to be illusory.

Unity in faith essential for conciliar fellowship

The fact that the close connection which exists between fidelity to Christ and service of people has been so much in the forefront of our concerns in recent times, and especially in the last decade, lends fresh

---

● Fr J. M. R. Tillard teaches at the Faculté Dominicaine de Théologie, Ottawa, Canada.

urgency to this inquiry into the character of our common faith. It is in the very midst of our wrestling with the world's problems that we must "give account of the hope that is in us" and give it *together*. Our ecumenical task and our mission are, we repeat, inseparable. This world of ours puts radical questions to our faith, questions which go farther than those dealt with in the agreements so far drawn up or in process of being approved. They are concerned with God himself, with his relationship to human freedom, with the real nature of salvation, with the existence of the kingdom of God of which the sacraments are the sign and pledge. How are we in these circumstances to give an account *together* of our hope and of the faith on which it rests if we are not consciously agreed on at least the central points of this faith? Moreover, it is no longer enough to repeat the old formulas and to rest content with a vague assent. Without blunting their edge, we must re-read and reinterpret them in the light of new contexts and situations. Since the credibility of our witness depends on our being one in the confession of Christ, we must all join together to work out the form in which the Christian faith should be confessed today.

We have thus reached a decisive point in our journey towards "conciliar fellowship". We are waking up to the fact that, in this fellowship, the *truth* of the faith professed counts just as much as the fact of being *together*. In other words, we are becoming acutely aware that our churches must become one *in* the faith and *through* the faith, if they want their *koinonia* to be directly continuous with the Gospel. Conciliar fellowship can only be an authentically *Christian communion* if it rests on a measure of agreement sufficient for all to be able to consider themselves in truth as one in faith and in mission. Any unity in mission not so linked with unity in faith would signalize an appalling schizophrenia.

But a question arises here which is an extraordinarily difficult one. When are we able to declare ourselves one in faith, in this way, in utter truthfulness? Although the divided situation in which we find ourselves may not always be the result of doctrinal differences, it nevertheless embraces today a far-ranging confessional diversity. But both the history of the Church and our ecumenical experience show that it is impossible to equate unanimity in faith with uniformity in expressing or even understanding this faith. Being transcendent and catholic, this faith can remain the same in a variety of embodiments and in different explanations which derive in part from the plurality of cultures and situations. And we agree that the development of an ecumenical consensus goes hand in hand with a recognition of fairly wide margins of differences. The required unanimity is compatible with an accepted diversity. Our quest for a common profession of faith can therefore be focused in the following question: What are the points on which we should be agreed in order to be able to achieve the measure of unanimity in the faith *quod requiritur et sufficit* for the establishment of conciliar fellowship? Put still more concretely, what is the required but sufficient (*quod requiritur et sufficit*) content of the confession of faith which our churches will proclaim together and with one accord at the beginning of the Council we are preparing for and hoping for?

Agreement needed on certain principles

To answer this question, we need first of all to have reached agreement on certain principles relative to both theology and methodology. To set us thinking here, it may be useful to suggest a number of such principles without claiming to be exhaustive or insisting on any scale of priorities.

Firstly, the meaning of the verb *sufficit* in the formula *quod requiritur et sufficit*. Its theological significance in this context is that by its very nature the common faith does not necessarily require all Christians to be unanimous on all the points handed down in the traditions of the churches. I have already referred to this. It should be added that this margin of difference is not simply an *a posteriori* concession, but also corresponds to the order of what is *a priori* desirable. In musical terms, the diversity of interpretations and emphases brings out the richness of the theme, provided it does not deviate into cacophony! Moreover, this call for diversity is intimately connected with the need for the faith to be embodied in the values of the created order, not so as to destroy them, but to lead them to their fulfilment.

In respect of method, however, the *sufficit* of the formula implies, above all, a call for realism, for it is clear that, allowing for the need to respect a healthy diversity, it is still possible to hope that the agreement between churches may be more complete than that permitted by circumstances. It is equally clear, however, that to start out by seeking to make reconciliation between churches conditional on their meeting the requirements of perfection would be to destroy any hope of seeing conciliar fellowship established one day. Unity can be restored only in stages. We need to find a confession of faith sufficient to make it possible, in spite of everything which continues to set the ecclesial traditions in opposition to each other, to proclaim and declare Christ together in an unequivocal way, one which does not suppress anything which needs to be said in order to be able to call ourselves truly Christian. In spite of everything, I must be able to recognize authentic Christian faith in the faith of the representative of another church, even of one fairly remote from my own, seated beside me at the conciliar table. This is the first step. Starting from here we shall then have to grow together towards the fullness of faith, letting ourselves be questioned and enriched by each other. We shall have to learn to "receive" one another.

New emphases in faith must be included

Secondly, since the expression of the common faith here is one which takes the form of verbal formulas, it is essential that we should be guided not only by the confessional documents, but also by the actual life of the churches, because an attitude, a custom, or a way of doing things may translate the faith more authentically than an official formula. The confessional documents should be interpreted in the light of ecclesial praxis. The faith being what it is, these documents are not sufficient in themselves. While this may tend to encourage severity, it may also help to produce greater receptivity and give greater flexibility to verbally formulated disagreements.

In this light we should identify existing convergences in the life of the churches, expressive in their way of a consensus in practice which precedes and influences the common confession of faith we are looking for. These convergences certainly have a bearing on the content of our faith which we are seeking to express together. They certainly have a bearing, too, on the content of the traditional faith inherited from the apostles, transmitted in baptism, proclaimed in the creeds common to all Christians (Apostles' Creed, Niceno-Constantinopolitan Creed) and in the confessions of faith peculiar to certain churches. But by entering into the quests and problems of the contemporary world and by seeking to fulfil their missionary calling together, the churches have been led to focus more sharply on certain aspects of the apostolic texts which in the past did not form part of the explicit content of the confessions of faith. Today the confession of Christ includes a special emphasis on the inseparable connection between salvation in Christ and the advent of conditions of justice and peace in our world and the elimination of all forms of discrimination. In the actual living of our faith, therefore, the *propter nos homines et propter nostram salutem* acquires new dimensions. The convergence of the churches in this respect undoubtedly impels us to give it the weight it deserves in the consensus we are preparing.

But to fail to integrate these new emphases, these new translations of traditional affirmations, these reinterpretations of the apostolic faith, and sometimes even these additions to the "truths of faith", into the total content of the articles of faith proclaimed in the classic symbols, and to judge them in the light of this total content, would result in serious inconsistencies and even in contradictions which would undermine the very basis of any effort to achieve consensus. It cannot, in fact, be a question of inventing anything. It can only be a question of confessing the content of the apostolic faith in a new way, one which is responsive to the present situation and influenced by it. This is supremely important in the matter of the relation between God and man. Sensitivity to human beings and their vocation must be placed within the context of the transcendence of God and of the Christian conviction that only under divine grace does a person find fulfilment.

226

The vital part of evangelical truth upheld and expressed by ecclesial practice, however, extends beyond the content which is made explicit in verbal confessions, and has always done so from the very beginning. Important elements of the Christian mystery do not appear in the most ancient and most authoritative confessions of faith. The eucharist is a case in point and the ministry another. In view of the history of our divisions and the part played in our polemics by some of these elements, it will be necessary, first of all, to agree on identifying which of these elements are vitally and inescapably related (*quod requiritur*) to ecclesial communion. This is all the more necessary since these elements are the ones which, more than the articles of the creeds read in abstraction and without reference to the institutions, enable us to see whether or not we have the same vision of the mystery of the Church. This point, therefore, will inevitably be at the heart of our discussions.

Differentiating between essentials and non-essentials

Thirdly, whatever form the confession of faith we shall have to prepare may take (and at this stage it is impossible to predict what this form will be), it will require us to reach agreement on the hierarchy of Christian truths. This will still be with a view to determining the essential core *quod requiritur et sufficit*. For the margin of admissible — and even desirable — diversity within the conciliar fellowship can only be assessed in terms of what is radically required if one is to be able to claim to hold the Christian faith. Hence the need to distinguish between what is essential and what is non-essential, not only in the formulas of faith, but also in ecclesial praxis (the faith as lived).

But what are the principles on which this difficult judgment is to be based? It is hardly necessary to recall that differentiation between essentials and non-essentials has always proved an arduous business, as the controversies preceding the Jerusalem Council demonstrate (Acts 15: 1-29).

We must firstly distinguish clearly between the actual object of the faith as lived and the forms in which it finds expression. The scholastics would speak here of a strict distinction between the *res*, on the one hand, and the *verba* or *sacramenta* employed by the Church to reveal it or to translate it. The faith is focused on the *res*, not on the formulas. But the latter do not all have the same connection with the truth they claim to serve. The fact is that we must not equate the dogmatic formulas in which the object of faith is offered to the Christian conscience in a manner which claims to be authoritative and normative, the bodies of doctrine in which these formulas are embedded, and the great theological systems which attempt to explain their meaning. These three levels of expression and explanation of the faith are not watertight compartments, of course. But it is still essential not to turn their mutual interplay into an undifferentiated uniform mass. A theological system, even if officially adopted by a church, does not have as strict a connection with the object of faith as a dogmatic formula, even if the latter turns out to have been influenced by a specific theology. The bodies of doctrine themselves have a looser connection with the object of faith than do the dogmatic formulas.

This distinction makes it possible to recognize that there can be genuine communion in respect of the deep grasp of the object of faith, but at the same time a difference in the way this object is expressed. For example, in the Act of Union in 433, Cyril of Alexandria acknowledged that the different theological formulas which set Alexandria and Antioch in opposition concealed an implicit unity on the essentials of the faith. It could very well be that today, in spite of the doctrine of consubstantiation and that of transubstantiation (which really are two different doctrines), the Lutheran tradition and the Roman Catholic tradition are in agreement on the essence of the faith in the eucharistic presence of our Lord. Everything, then, which does not in itself contradict the essence of the given faith should be recognized as compatible with the degree of communion in the faith *quod requiritur*. In other words, wherever this essence is preserved, even if there is a wide doctrinal diversity, the degree of faith *quod sufficit* also exists.

But how are we to know with sufficient certitude – at the conclusion of a hermeneutical process which has made clear its purpose and meaning – that a dogmatic affirmation (at least regarded as such by a church or group of churches) belongs to the core of the given faith and therefore to *id quod requiritur ad unitatem?* For not even the dogmatic formulas are all of equal importance. Thus, the ecclesial traditions, while agreed on the special authority of the Scriptures as transmitting the testimony of the apostolic community, also know that the evangelical truth can only be fully grasped within the setting of the life of the Christian community. After the apostolic period – which is the normative one – the Church, the bearer of the Spirit, but also involved in history, was led to bring out the full meaning of this faith handed down from the apostles. It had to translate that which it experienced in its liturgy and bore testimony to – sometimes to the point of martyrdom – into terms which made it possible for it both to maintain its unity and to give an account of its hope. It was thus led by the Spirit to work out all the elements necessary (*id quod requiritur*) for a secure communion with the apostolic faith. Most of our traditions agree in acknowledging that this period – of the creeds, of the birth of the great liturgies, of the great councils – in which the Church worked out the basic points in its understanding of the faith, particularly by the conciliar definitions of the divine trinity and the person of Christ, is the great formative period which identifies precisely the essential kernel of the faith. It must therefore give us our bearings in our search for *quod requiritur et sufficit* and it provides the basis on which we can build together the conciliar fellowship. But when does this special period end?

Without assuming the answer which has been given to this last question, it is possible to indicate already two points which will prevent us from going round in circles in our search for a common confession of faith. The presence of the Roman Catholic Church as one of the partners in the ecumenical dialogue obliges us, moreover, to be clear in this area.

Place of general councils' declarations

The first of these two points concerns the authority of the dogmatic formulas produced by the "general councils held in the West", even prior to the Reformation. This authority is not identical with that of the decisions of the councils of the early centuries, whatever their degree of representativeness. This is because of the absence of a considerable group of bishops, of the Orthodox bishops at least, whose episcopal character was recognized by the Catholic Church, that is, its connection with an authentic ecclesial responsibility bestowed by the Spirit. The dogmatic decisions of the general councils of the Roman Catholic Church cannot and do not claim to add anything essential to the fundamental truths affirmed by the Scriptures and by the Christian community of the special period just described. Moreover, Vatican I explicitly declared that its declarations were in harmony with "the constant usage of the Church and the declarations of the ecumenical councils, especially of those in which the East and the West met together in the union of faith and love" (DS 3065). Besides, Vatican II sought to bridge the centuries of division. This reference to the faith of the early centuries applies equally to the appreciation of the dogmatic value of the "confessions of faith" of churches issuing from the Reformation.

The second point concerns the declarations of the Roman magisterium, even those *ex cathedra*. In the situation of division in which we find ourselves, what we have said about the "general councils" of the Roman Catholic Church applies also to these declarations of the Roman magisterium. These, too, have a secondary status in the hierarchy of truths. Is anyone in the Roman Catholic Church prepared to claim to place the trinitarian or christological dogmas on the same level as the two Marian dogmas defined *ex cathedra*? The dogma of Ephesus concerning the divine maternity is more important than the definitions of the immaculate conception and the assumption. The weight of these two latter definitions must be judged in relation to the former.

Two-fold task for the Church

If the principles I have just indicated are accepted, the churches face a two-fold task: one which they all share together, and another which each of them must face in its own conscience and with its own ecumenical courage.

The common task is obvious. Without cheating and without lapsing into cheap compromises but rather endeavouring to listen seriously to one another, they must together decide the content of faith *quod requiritur et sufficit*, if they are to be able to share in a council which would be really ecumenical in the sense that the early councils were ecumenical and not just a ramshackle assembly of delegates who are unable to recognize each other as sharing the same faith, the same eucharist, the same ministry. For in this context, the term "council" is not in fact a synonym for an "assembly" pure and simple. It denotes an assembly of Christians who are already reconciled with one another despite continuing differences and even conflicts. And the common profession of faith is an essential element in this reconciliation. The drafting of agreements on baptism, eucharist and the ministry has already provided us with a working method, even if we realize that the work of specialists slowly learning to appreciate and to understand each other is not a very adequate representation of the totality of the churches involved, and that the bulk of the membership of our Christian communities does not always follow suit. It is therefore up to each church to find ways and means of assimilating the work of the official commissions without rupturing its internal unity.

This last remark already points to the important part to be played by each church separately in the development of a common profession of faith. But there is more to it even than this and something even more difficult. Each church must apply to its own doctrinal tradition the distinction between essentials and non-essentials so as to be in a position not to require of others more than is really required, while still being convinced that by consenting to the *quod sufficit* it is not selling the faith short. This is something which it can only do for itself, something moreover which could have considerable consequences for its own internal life. The Disciples of Christ, for example, have to ask themselves whether their position on the creeds counts among the essentials; the same question arises for the Baptists in respect of their view of baptism. Can the Roman Catholic Church acknowledge that the fundamental articles of faith are fewer in number than the Catholic dogmas, and that by not insisting on acceptance of the last two Marian definitions as a condition of entry into a "communion of faith" with itself, it would not be playing fast and loose with the will of Christ? As you can see, these are delicate questions to which it is not easy to reply without certain qualifications; a good deal of finesse is called for. But how are we to avoid putting these questions if ecumenism is to have any future and if the conciliar fellowship expounded at the Nairobi Assembly is to be more than just a dream?

For a church to ask itself such fundamental and radical questions does not mean any renunciation of its identity. And it need not imagine that its "confessional" riches are destined to disappear, to the detriment of its own members, once this initial hurdle has been cleared. The authentic conciliar fellowship requires that, after centuries of isolation and frequent opposition, we should let ourselves be questioned and enriched by each other. It really is not just a matter of gluing broken fragments together. The Roman Catholic Church, for example, can hope that the conciliar fellowship will gradually (in the process of fraternal dialogue) come to recognize the truth contained in the last two Marian dogmas and the light which they shed on the mystery of salvation in Jesus Christ. It can also hope that the difficulties which other traditions have with this point will help it to a deeper understanding of its own doctrine. Similarly, the Orthodox churches should hope for an understanding of the spiritual and dogmatic riches which underlie their veneration of icons. The *id quod requiritur et sufficit* does not condemn the *id quod non requiritur* to obscurity, oblivion and to the limbo of the "henceforth useless". It assigns it its true place.

But this is not a problem peculiar to those churches which have in their heritage a doctrinal richness which they must in some sense classify by introducing an order of priority. It also arises for those churches which up to now have not adhered to this or that point which the quest for a consensus on the common confession of faith will recognize as essential (*requiritur*). In certain cases, this situation could be a serious one. For failure to meet the requirements of *id quod requiritur* is in fact tantamount to placing oneself — at least in the eyes of other ecclesial groups — outside the true faith in Christ and his Father: in other words, to excommunicate oneself in the most radical sense of the word. We must be clear-sighted here. It could be that the number of member churches of the World Council of Churches, despite the official description of the Council and its reference to the confession of Christ, is greater than the number of those which will be able to identify themselves with the confession of faith which we must now seek to draw up. This will have the force of a test. What are we to do if we find ourselves in the situation indicated, especially if the explicit rejection or the mere omission of the point in question is intimately bound up with the "confessional" position of the church in question? Logically, one can see only two solutions: either "conversion" (at the risk of losing its "confessional" colour) or retreat into its traditional position (and by losing "communion", also losing the label of "Christian").

Receiving old truths in a new way

Each church — in whichever of the two categories just mentioned it belongs — can in the end be led to "receive" in a new way certain of the truths which it has always held. A serious ecumenical dialogue, conducted on the basis of a profound mutual respect, in fact frequently leads the partners to a much richer reading of the points which divide them, precisely because each of them has previously been seeing them only in a partisan way. Think, for example, of the idea of "memorial", emphasized in the consensus on the eucharist, and what it has done to help us to re-read the sacrificial character of the Lord's Supper, to the benefit of the Catholic tradition as well as others. But this "re-reception", if it is really to be exploited to the benefit of each church and not to create in it uncomprehending divisions gradually shattering its inner consensus, demands a sustained pastoral effort directed towards all categories of members. The experience of certain bilateral conversations is very instructive here.

In conclusion, a simple observation: the step we are preparing to take will probably be a very difficult one. The difficulty stems from its object, but also from the present situation in theological research. It is at a moment when, in most churches, extremely radical positions on the christological dogma and the trinitarian faith are being propagated, that we are being required to produce a confession of faith which, without swerving from fidelity to the traditional faith, will nevertheless be sensitive to the questions of our time, precisely those which often explain the endeavours of leading theologians. But the very difficulty of the task enables us perhaps to measure its urgency. How can churches divided among themselves, suspicious of one another, discern in their duty to respond to the needs of men and the requests of our time, the pathway of fidelity to the evangelical truth? This formidable task will only be adequately performed by all the churches together; it exceeds the capacities of each church taken separately. This is what gives ecumenical work its true purpose: the service of Christ and of his Gospel.

Reports on
Growing Together
in Unity

Reflections on the Common Goal

Introduction

During the second week of the meeting in Bangalore, the Faith and Order Commission devoted its attention to issues related to the search for the visible unity of the Church. The starting point of all the deliberations was the report of the Fifth Assembly of the World Council of Churches from Nairobi "What Unity Requires".[1] The primary purpose of the discussion was to develop further the directions given by the Assembly. After a brief plenary debate, the Commission divided into five committees, each dealing with one particular aspect of the search for visible unity. Special emphasis was placed on the implications of the report of the Assembly for further work in the coming three years until the next meeting of the Commission on Faith and Order scheduled for summer 1981.

The reports of the five committees were discussed by the full Commission and transmitted to the Standing Commission for final editing and appropriate action. The material elaborated by the committees has been grouped under the following headings:

1. Reflections on the common goal (Committee I)

2. The common expression of the apostolic faith (Committee II)

3. Towards an ecumenical consensus on baptism, the eucharist and the ministry (Committee III)

4. Towards common ways of teaching and decision-making (Committee II)

5. Mutual intercession (Committee V)

6. The unity of the Church and the community of women and men in the Church (Committee IV)

---

[1] *Breaking Barriers*, Nairobi 1975, ed. David M. Paton. London: SPCK and Grand Rapids: Wm. B. Eerdmans, 1976, p. 57 ff.;

7. The unity of the Church — two examples of interdisciplinary work (Committee IV)

8. New ecumenical experiences and existing ecumenical structures (Committee V)

9. Conclusion.

The whole discussion about the present state of the search for visible unity and the next steps required was permeated by the conviction that in the future the work of the Faith and Order Commission needs to be carried out in closer consultation with the churches. Theological agreements have now reached the point where further progress can be made only by a determined process of reception. It is essential, therefore, that both the plans and the findings in the coming years should be more deliberately shared with the churches associated with the work of the Faith and Order Commission.

Clarifying conciliar fellowship

The report "What Unity Requires" of the Fifth Assembly underlined the need for at least a general agreement on "the unity we seek". On the basis of their understanding of the nature of the Church, the various traditions hold and promote different concepts of the unity of the Church. If the churches are to advance towards unity, they need to develop a common vision of their goal. In the course of the last decades, several attempts have been made to offer at least in outline a common description. The most notable are the statements of the Assemblies of New Delhi and Uppsala. The Fifth Assembly in Nairobi made two important contributions to this debate. It introduced into the constitution of the World Council of Churches a list of aims and purposes and, after considerable debate, adopted the following formulations concerning the search for the unity of the Church:

> "The World Council of Churches is constituted for the following functions and purposes:
>
> (i) to call the churches to the goal of visible unity in one faith and in one eucharistic fellowship expressed in worship and in common life in Christ, and to advance towards that unity in order that the world may believe
> ... "

Further, the Fifth Assembly gave a fuller explanation of the goal of visible unity through the following statement in the report of Section II "What Unity Requires":

> "The one Church is to be envisioned as a conciliar fellowship of local churches which are themselves truly united. In this conciliar fellowship, each local church possesses, in communion with the others, the fullness of catholicity, witnesses to the same apostolic

236

faith, and therefore, recognizes the others as belonging to the same Church of Christ and guided by the same Spirit. As the New Delhi Assembly pointed out, they are bound together because they have received the same baptism and share in the same eucharist; they recognize each other's members and ministries. They are one in their common commitment to confess the gospel of Christ by proclamation and service to the world. To this end, each church aims at maintaining sustained and sustaining relationships with her sister churches, expressed in conciliar gatherings whenever required for the fulfilment of their common calling."

Since the Assembly, this statement has created widespread positive interest as a thrust forward, urging all churches to make visible and to manifest in history the unity of all for whom Jesus interceded in his high-priestly prayer. The statement also raised questions which indicate the need for further clarification. At Bangalore, Committee I had the task of clarifying the concept of "conciliar fellowship" and of indicating the ways in which further work on "the unity we seek" needs to be done.

The Committee came to the following conclusions:

A re-affirmation of the goal of visible unity

The Faith and Order Commission is committed to keep before the churches this vision and goal. It is its constitutional task to contribute to the creation of conditions which will make it possible for the churches to enter into full communion. They will then recognize each other's ministries; they will share the bread and the cup of their Lord; they will acknowledge each other as belonging to the body of Christ in all places and at all times; they will proclaim together the Gospel to the world; they will serve the needs of humankind in mutual trust and dedication; and for these ends they will plan and take decisions together in assemblies constituted by authorized representatives whenever this is required.

We are fully aware of the sad and scandalous fact that this goal of visible unity is still far away. But we wish to affirm that the vision of unity in such a "conciliar fellowship", sharing the one apostolic faith as well as the gifts of baptism and the eucharist, is alive in us. Although it may seem to be only a distant possibility, the vision provides inspiration and guidance already in the present as we envisage the way ahead. Christ himself summons us to pursue the goal. Since He is the centre of our lives, the realization of the unity for which He prayed is a central task for us. The Gospel to be proclaimed to the world includes as an essential part the communion (koinonia) of the Church with Christ and of Christians with one another. Therefore, division must not be regarded as a secondary issue. Those whom Christ has brought together in his body through his suffering and death on the cross, and through his resurrection, must not be put asunder by anybody. The love which is in Jesus Christ holds us together. Therefore, it is a matter of grateful and obedient discipleship not to acquiesce in the divisions but to engage constantly anew in the struggle to break old and new barriers which separate us from one another.

Why repeat what has been stated many times ? Simply because the striving for visible unity is slackening in many quarters. Some who have set out on this road have become victims of frustration. Others declare themselves content with the measure of good will and cooperation which has developed among the churches over the last decades, and cease to reach out to new stages of unity.

This is not to say that no efforts at promoting unity are being undertaken. In fact, the search for unity goes on at all levels of the churches' life. Congregations and groups within congregations are seeking new ways of cooperation. They pray for each other, they seek a deeper mutual understanding. Barriers of distrust are being removed. Joint action expands. Theological commissions are at work, at national, regional and universal levels, to articulate the consensus among the churches. Common understanding is being reached on many issues which, in the past, have caused alienation, division and enmity.

All these efforts are to be welcomed and need to be continued. The search for unity must proceed at many levels and involve more and more Christians. There is no uniform strategy in moving towards unity. According to different situations and conditions, different methods must be employed. The multiplicity of efforts is not without problems, however. We are concerned that instead of being complementary, they might counteract and neutralize each other. There is need to work in concert. The vision of full visible unity in conciliar fellowship provides the frame for working in concert. The agreements which have emerged or are emerging from multilateral and bilateral dialogues must be taken seriously by all churches and, as far as they are acceptable to each church, translated into practical decisions which affect the relations with other churches. The far-reaching results of dialogues present the churches with the challenge to give new expression to the oneness in Christ for the sake of the Gospel and to the glory of God.

a) Visible unity and conciliar fellowship

"... The one Church is to be envisioned as a conciliar fellowship of local churches which are themselves truly united." What does this mean ? "Conciliar fellowship" refers to a communion of local churches which is capable of holding assemblies or synods of authorized representatives of the various local churches.

Unity is the presupposition for such assemblies and synods. The primary task of all ecumenical endeavours is therefore the promotion of that unity. Representative conciliar gatherings will be one expression and manifestation of that unity. The World Council of Churches cannot call a universal council. This will be the prerogative of the churches as they unite. But the churches through their common life and work in councils (*conseils*) at the local, national, regional and universal levels, as well as through other ecumenical efforts, can seek to bring about a situation in which unity can be established and a representative conciliar gathering can be held. To achieve this they need to engage in a movement of ecumenical life based on Christian prayer, repentance, love, dialogue, growth in understanding and actions which open the doors to deeper communion.

The main value of statements such as those of the Assemblies in New Delhi and Nairobi is to provide a framework for the search for unity. It would be simplistic to regard them as solutions of the ecclesiological differences. They rather present a programme for further common studies. They are a challenge to the churches to use the findings of multilateral and bilateral dialogues and whatever other means are available to move forward towards the full rediscovery of the unity in Christ.

They also provide a frame for living, witnessing and serving together. The Church is a sign and instrument of Christ's mission to all humankind. The sign is obscured by the present divisions. Will the churches continue to be a misguiding sign by remaining a divided and fragmented people ? Or will they seek to be a reliable, trustworthy sign as a people constantly uniting in mutual forgiveness and reconciliation ?

The notion of the Church as sign and instrument has already been discussed by Faith and Order on previous occasions.[2] At Bangalore special mention was made of two aspects. In affirming the sign-character of the Church, two dangers can be avoided. The one would be to imagine that the Church could be called to bring about the Kingdom of Christ and to take into its own hands what Christ alone can fulfil. The other would be to be oblivious to the calling visibly and tangibly to manifest our oneness in faith and hope in history. To be a sign and instrument is one way of expressing that Christians are called to be faithful stewards of God's gifts, "in full accord and of one mind" (Phil. 2:2).

The concept of "conciliar fellowship" presents a challenge to all churches. Churches which regard themselves as representing in historical continuity the one, holy, catholic and apostolic Church need to find ways of transcending the canonical boundaries whereby they identify the Church; they must reflect on the possibility of recognizing other churches as holding the same apostolic faith and sharing the same eucharistic fellow-

---

[2] See: *What Unity Requires*, Faith and Order Paper No. 77, pp. 3 ff. Geiko Müller-Fahrenholz : *Unity in Today's World*, The Faith and Order Studies on Unity of the Church – Unity of Humankind, WCC, 1978, pp. 78 ff.

ship; they need to discover ways of associating with them and moving together with them to full conciliar fellowship. Churches which consider the one, holy, catholic and apostolic Church to be a reality far greater than the historical reality of any church tradition need to reflect on the ways in which the sense of community can be developed which is the presupposition of true conciliar life.

b) ... local churches which are themselves truly united

The report "What Unity Requires" drew attention to the ambiguity of the term "local church". Since the Assembly, the issue has been carefully studied.[3] Clearly, the meaning of the term "local" varies from tradition to tradition.[4] The different uses reflect different ecclesiologies not yet reconciled with one another.

The formula "local churches which are themselves truly united" brings also into the open different approaches to the realization of unity. Many say that true unity requires the gathering of all in each place into one eucharistic community; there would be no room for a continuing life of the confessional traditions. Others say that unity according to Christ's will does not necessarily require the disappearance but rather the transformation of confessional identities to such a degree that unity in full sacramental fellowship, common witness and service, together with some common structural/institutional expression becomes possible. While the first view is rather connected with the concept of "organic unity", the second is held by those proposing the concept "unity in reconciled diversity". The two concepts are not to be seen as alternatives. They may be two different ways of reacting to the ecumenical necessities and possibilities of different situations and of different church traditions.

c) "Council", "councils" and "pre-conciliar"

In English, the term "council" and its derivatives are capable of two different interpretations:

i) The term can refer to a gathering or *assembly of official representatives* of local churches within a fully united sacramental fellowship.

ii) The term can also refer to the *associations of churches* at local, national, regional and universal levels which have come into existence as a fruit of the ecumenical movement. They are not bound together in full sacramental fellowship. They have, however, some features of conciliar life and are instruments for creating closer relationships between churches separated from one another both confessionally and geographically.

---

[3] See *In Each Place*, Towards a Fellowship of Local Churches Truly United, WCC, 1977.

[4] See *In Each Place*, pp. 6 ff.

Other languages do not suffer from the same terminological difficulty. They use different terms for the two meanings. The Greek language uses the terms *synodos* and *symboulion*; the Latin *concilium* and *consilium*; the French *concile* and *conseil*; the German *Konzil* and *Rat*; the Russian *sobor* and *sowiet*.

The double meaning in English has sometimes led to misunderstandings. Those who understand the term "conciliar fellowship" in the sense of (ii) are either discontent because it seems to suggest less than the organic unity for which they hope and work, or they rest content because it seems to give support to the view that the associations which exist today are a sufficient expression of the unity we seek.

The report "What Unity Requires" of the Fifth Assembly makes it clear that the term is to be used in the meaning given under (i). Conciliar fellowship means a communion capable of holding representative councils.

How then is the present stage of the ecumenical movement to be described ? The report "What Unity Requires" and other documents refer to it as *pre-conciliar*. It is important to agree on the precise meaning of this term. In the Orthodox church the term is used to refer to the period in which a council (*synodos, sobor*) is being directly prepared. The Orthodox churches are today in a pre-conciliar period because they have agreed to prepare for the celebration of a pan-orthodox council. The usage of the term in this particular meaning only makes sense within the context of a fully united sacramental communion. Christians of all traditions, however, are able to use the word "pre-conciliar" in a more general sense in order to refer to the various efforts and developments which prepare for and herald the future conciliar fellowship.

Recommendations

1. The vision of the common goal articulated by the Fifth Assembly needs to be further clarified and explained. This effort should not be seen as a verbal ballet between concepts like "conciliar fellowship", "organic unity" and "unity in reconciled diversity", but rather as a struggle to find a way of presenting the vision that will give real hope to ordinary members of the churches that the vision is, by God's will, both desirable and achievable. It is recommended that the Standing Commission work on a communication to the churches on the common goal.

2. The description of the unity we seek offered by the Fifth Assembly does not overcome the differences in the understanding of the nature of the Church; it provides a common setting and a fresh approach for discussing them. Therefore, it may be advisable to return in future to a study of the fundamental ecclesiological issues which separate the churches. Special attention should be given to a) the Church as effective

sign and instrument; b) the ecclesiological implications of the various concepts of unity at present under discussion, for example "organic unity", "unity in reconciled diversity"; c) the ecclesiological implications of the term "local churches which are themselves truly united"; d) ecclesiological aspects of the ecumenical discussion on baptism, the eucharist and the ministry.

3. Fresh attention should be given to intermediary steps between the present stage of the ecumenical movement and the final goal of visible unity.

4. In particular, the Commission should seek to offer guidelines and practical help in finding ways relating the different levels of ecumenical experiences and dialogue to each other so as to facilitate the process of reception and common growth into unity.

5. The debate on the vision of conciliar fellowship should be continued on as many levels and in as many settings as possible. Special attention should be drawn to two consultations which may be regarded as models: the consultation organized by the Conference of European Churches in Sofia (1977) on "Churches in conciliar fellowship", and the Indian National Consultation on "conciliar Unity" (1978). Churches and families of churches engaged in bilateral conversations should reflect on the concepts of unity underlying their efforts and consider ways in which they can contribute to the clarification of the common goal.

The Common Expression
of the Apostolic Faith

Though the Commission regarded further clarification of the common goal to be necessary, there was general agreement that this study should not receive primary attention. Efforts should rather concentrate on the actual requirements for the unity of the Church. Again and again three requirements were mentioned : a) consensus in the apostolic faith; b) mutual recognition of baptism, the eucharist and the ministry; c) structures making possible common teaching and decision-making. It was felt that the study of more general ecclesiological issues should not defer the exploration of these three requirements nor the drawing of practical consequences from the findings already obtained.

Various terms were used to refer to these three requirements. Some spoke of "conditions for unity", others of "fundamental structures of communion". Both terms have their disadvantages. Perhaps Paul's analogies from the relations of foot and hand, ear and eye in the body may be extended to the point of saying that there is need for a "vertebrate communion", a communion given a strong spine by these elements of common confession of the apostolic faith, achieved mutual recognition and means whereby the churches may teach, speak and act together.

The report "What Unity Requires" speaks of the "conciliar fellowship" as witnessing to the one apostolic faith. It contains the following recommendation : "We ask the churches to undertake a common effort to receive, re-appropriate and confess together, as contemporary occasion requires, the Christian truth and faith delivered through the Apostles and handed down through the centuries. Such common action, arising from free and inclusive discussion under the commonly acknowledged authority of God's word, must aim both to clarify and to embody the unity and the diversity which are proper to the Church's life and mission.

243

Committee II reflected on the way in which the one Church is based on the confession of the one apostolic faith. Instead of proposing a set of general considerations about a possible confession of faith, the committee immediately tried to formulate a common statement of faith. Not surprisingly this attempt met with many problems. But the committee felt that the problems to be worked on in future could be brought out much more sharply by offering an actual statement.

The report of the committee reads as follows:

We have not been working on a better edition of the creeds nor on a comprehensive statement of the Gospel, but rather we have tried to express what binds our churches together in the present situation. What we have produced is an expression of our common faith and is not meant to replace the ancient creeds; indeed, we are offering a description of where we are as regards our common faith — we have not written a statement that is full and adequate in the mind of everyone.

We are agreed that we must distinguish between faith as commitment and the doctrinal formulation of faith. Faith as the human response to the grace of God, as commitment with love and hope, is essential. The attempt to give it a doctrinal formulation is secondary to it. Therefore, every statement of faith must be recognized as limited in scope, expression and relevance. It cannot itself become the object of our faith.

We recommend to the Faith and Order Commission to receive this statement as a first attempt to state our faith knowing full well that it represents nothing more than a proposal to be worked on.

A COMMON STATEMENT OF OUR FAITH

PREAMBLE

As we seek to give a common statement of our faith, we are mindful of the existing fellowship of churches which is marked by a common confession of "the Lord Jesus Christ as God and Saviour according to the Scriptures". Already we have joined hands seeking to fulfil together our "common calling to the glory of the one God, Father, Son and Holy Spirit".

Because we have travelled together on the road of faith, experiencing, in spite of our historical divisions, the unifying power of Jesus Christ and his salvation and growing together in his service, we desire to express more fully our common faith in the triune God who has called us to himself and wants us to share in his mission for the salvation of all humankind.

As we seek to confess our faith together, we want to be faithful to the apostolic faith according to the Scriptures, handed down to us through the centuries. At the same time we want to face the new situation and the challenge for mission today. Furthermore, we are aware that a common confession of faith should be the sign of our reconciliation.

PART I

As Christians we confess Jesus Christ, the only source of salvation for humankind and for each individual human person. He is the one Lord of his Church, the cornerstone of its unity. The Church is based on his ministry, remembers in her worship his incarnation, his suffering, crucifixion and death, proclaims with joy his resurrection and eagerly awaits his second coming. As our Saviour he is truly God and truly man. He has authority to grant us communion with God in the presence of his reign, which overcomes the power of death and sin and every misery, division and separation among us; but he also shares in our sufferings and temptations so that in spite of them we may have confidence in him and in the promise of his kingdom. He is the new Adam, in whom we recognize the destiny of human beings and into whose image our lives shall be transformed.

In Jesus' ministry we encounter the one God and creator of all things, whose eternal love is concerned for every single human person and thus constitutes the dignity of each human being. God, the Holy Spirit, is the eternal link of love, between God the Father, and God the Son, and spreads abroad God's love to all his creatures to overcome their miseries and separations. In the ministry of the Spirit we receive life and are transfigured, inspired and liberated by the divine presence among his creatures and are sealed in hope. God, the Father, Son and Holy Spirit extends love and judgment to all creation to overcome its separations and calls the Church into the unity of one body, in order to be more fully the sign of a new humanity.

The one faith is confessed and lived in the community of the faithful who have been called through the preaching of the Gospel and gather around the Lord in the Spirit. We enter into this community through baptism which is our participation in the death and resurrection of Jesus Christ. We are incorporated into the eucharistic community in which the Word is proclaimed and the sacrament duly celebrated.

The one faith is the full responsibility of each member of the community, not, however, separately one from the other, but in communion. The presence of the Lord in the midst of his people expresses itself in a variety of charisms and services, which equip them for their mission among men. Such charisms and services are the instruments of the Holy Spirit in the building up of the Church, enabling its community to persevere in the apostolic teaching, in fraternal communion, in the breaking of bread, and in prayer (cf. Acts 2 : 42). The one(s) who presides over the community has the particular responsibility of being, in the Holy Spirit, the servant of the unity of the Church by the proclamation of the Word in the eucharistic community. His (their) service aims at reinforcing the communication in the community, with a vision of fuller communion.

The confession of the one faith is not a question of majority, but rather, it is a confession in one Spirit. Such a confession naturally implies a total commitment of life on the part of all members of the community.

The community experiences a communion in one Spirit which is not limited to one period in time or to one given place (*hic et nunc*); it is the communion with all witnesses to the apostolic faith in all places and at all times. It is a confession in the communion of saints.

PART II

Growing together in one faith, the divided Christian communities are prepared to share already now a doxology, taken from our common heritage, the Scriptures. One passage which condenses many aspects of our common confession is to be found in Ephesians 1 : 3-15.

Together with this doxology:

We confess God's involvement in the history of humankind, revealed through Israel, fulfilled in Jesus Christ, communicated to us by the Holy Spirit, into which fulfilment all humanity is called;

we confess the destiny and dignity of all *human beings*, rooted in God's initiative and design;

we confess our dependence upon *God's redeeming and liberating grace,* because we are caught up in the ambiguities of our history and because we live in sin;

we confess the reality of the *Event of Jesus Christ* — his life, his death, his resurrection — and the reality of our answer of faith, given to that Event, that brings us, through the Spirit, to the incorporation into Christ, which means our salvation;

we confess the reality of *the Church*, being the Body of Christ, called to be the nucleus and servant of the unity of humankind and of the universe. We confess our responsibility as Christians to have the mind of Christ and to live and act accordingly in the community of humankind; faith without work is dead;

we confess the presence and the working of *the Spirit*, the pledge and seal of the kingdom, into which we are confirmed.

Towards an Ecumenical Consensus on Baptism, the Eucharist and the Ministry

Mutual recognition of baptism, the eucharist and the ministry has already been mentioned as the second requirement for the unity of the Church.

The Commission on Faith and Order has already done considerable work in this area. At its meeting in Accra (1974), the Commission issued three "agreed statements" under the title *One Baptism, One Eucharist and a Mutually Recognized Ministry* (Faith and Order Paper No. 73). The Fifth Assembly decided to send them to all member churches with the request to respond by the end of 1976. A large number of official replies were received. They were carefully reviewed at a special consultation in May 1977. The Standing Commission addressed to the Central Committee of the World Council of Churches (1977) a report on the assessment which was later forwarded to the member churches.[1]

The question was before the Commission at Bangalore as to the best ways of proceeding further. The Standing Commission had appointed a small group to propose further steps. It met twice in early 1978 and prepared the following discussion paper for the meeting of the Commission in Bangalore:

Proposals for Further Work

The Central Committee of the World Council has urged the Faith and Order Commission to prepare a revision of the Accra statements on

---

[1] *Towards an Ecumenical Consensus: Baptism, Eucharist, Ministry*, Faith and Order paper No. 84.

baptism, eucharist and ministry in time for the Sixth Assembly of the World Council of Churches. The following questions arise:

i) What are the purposes of these revised statements?

ii) What form should the revised statements take?

iii) What is the relation between the emerging consensus on these matters and the liturgical forms of the churches?

iv) By what procedures can the revision take place?

i) The Purposes of the Revised Statements

The question must be faced: What is the place of these three statements in the movement "towards communion in one faith"? Committee III at the Bangalore meeting will be examining the question of the nature and extent of the doctrinal consensus required for churchly communion and unity. Committee II and Committee III should each ask: Could agreement on baptism, eucharist and ministry be seen as expressing in a focal way all the doctrinal agreement that is necessary for "communion in one faith"? Or are baptism, eucharist and ministry simply three areas of doctrine among many others? What are the relationships between baptism, eucharist and ministry, on the one hand, and other possible focal expressions of corporate faith, such as creeds, on the other? How important is the prospect of churchly "communion in one faith" to the different churches? The responses of the churches show that they attach differing degrees of importance to sacraments: how important are these differences of emphasis among the churches?

Then the question arises also of the status given by the churches to such agreements as may be achieved in the revised statements on baptism, eucharist and ministry. Would the churches be willing to include the agreed affirmations in their own catechetical teaching? Might acceptance of the agreed texts be considered to establish sufficient community in teaching among the churches, at least in matters of baptism, eucharist and ministry? What could be the practical results for inter-church relations among churches which agreed on these matters, and to this degree?

The revision of the statements must serve to encourage progress towards a more all-embracing communion at all levels of the Church's life: global, regional, local.

ii) The Form of the Revised Statements

The statements on *baptism and eucharist* should be carefully revised, paragraph by paragraph, taking into account the responses which the churches have already made to them in the form which they received at Accra.

The responses indicate that it would probably be valuable to make a distinction between fundamental affirmations for common teaching and a commentary which could perform several functions:

— the commentary could bring out more fully the ecumenical importance of the affirmations in the agreed text concerning such matters as anamnesis, epiclesis, or the relations between baptism and faith;

— it could make clear not only the positions which were being excluded on hitherto controversial questions but also the central areas in which variety of expression might be acceptable;

— it could give examples of the effect of contexts on the way the matters are viewed, and might thus encourage the preparation of regional and local commentaries in which the affirmations of the text were applied to particular circumstances;

— it could emphasize the lines of convergence which were already leading towards a more complete consensus, showing also how progress might be made on difficult questions which so far remained open;

— it could explore some practical implications of the fundamental affirmations for the life of the churches.

The Accra statement on *ministry* is of rather a different character to those on baptism and eucharist. It is more in the style of a commentary. Hence it would be important to formulate a statement on ministry of the same dimensions and kind as those on baptism and eucharist. A commentary would bring out the ecumenical importance of the degree of agreement thereby reached. The commentary could also discuss the practical and sociological questions concerning the varied styles and exercice of ordained ministry. The question of the ordination of women arises, and it would be helpful if the Commission would indicate ways in which this question should be included in the revised statements. Throughout, ordination and the ministry of the ordained would need to be set in the context of the total ministry of the whole Church.

iii) The Emerging Consensus and Liturgical Forms

The Accra statements, particularly those on baptism and eucharist, already list the elements that properly belong to liturgies of baptism and eucharist which would now or in the future match the affirmations of agreed teaching. Has the time now come to take further steps to express and foster — in the doxological mode — the emerging doctrinal consensus?

There is no question of seeking a uniformity of liturgy. On the other hand, there is need to grow together as a worshipping community as well as a community of faith and teaching. How can the churches help each other in this area ? The churches should re-examine their own liturgies in the perspective of the agreed fundamental affirmations on baptism, eucharist and ministry. An exchange of worship materials might be useful. It might also be possible to formulate in common some liturgical structures and prayers which the churches could recognize as embodying the common teaching in doxological form.

Several recent developments give courage for proposing this last step. For one thing, liturgical revision in many churches has produced rites which display a remarkable convergence in structure, substance, and even wording. For another, inter-church texts have been produced, for example by COCU and by the Committee for an Ecumenical Eucharistic Prayer in the USA, for use at baptism and the Lord's Supper. Yet again, the various churches have gladly used ecumenical orders of service formulated for such occasions as the Week of Prayer for Christian Unity.

Could the following moves now be made, therefore ? The affirmations and commentaries on baptism, eucharist and ministry might be supported by worship material that would give added liturgical concreteness to the emerging consensus. This material could be of three kinds:

— first, an anthology of official worship texts from the different churches, illustrating how they were growing together in liturgical forms;
— second, a collection of materials prepared for earlier ecumenical gatherings;
— third, some model liturgical structures and prayers which the churches would be free to adopt, if they so wished, for their own use as "alternate texts" or on ecumenical occasions.

These materials could be of service to the churches which were in the process of revising their own liturgies of baptism, eucharist and ordination.

Most of these materials might be included in a separate publication. But it could be important to include, for example, some model eucharistic structures and prayers in an appendix to the agreed statements themselves. The Commission's opinion is sought on this question.

iv) The Procedures for Revision

As requested by the Nairobi Assembly, many churches made first responses to the Accra statements by the end of 1976, and this material is available, of course, to help the revision. On particular questions, further responses have been solicited from the churches by the Faith and Order Secretariat and the small group appointed by the Standing Commission of Faith and Order.

The group considers that an outline draft of the revised statements needs to be made ready by Easter 1979. Throughout, there will be need for consultations on specific issues. At present, discussion appears necessary at the following levels:

— with appropriate groups, where particularly sensitive issues are at stake, for example with representatives of the Baptist and Pentecostal churches;

— on the question of *episcope* and episcopacy;

— in bodies engaged in bilateral conversations and in union negotiations;

— by studies undertaken at the initiative of churches at local, national or regional levels, so that "contextual" contributions may be fed into the very process of revising the statements that are intended to have universal scope;

— at a specially called larger meeting or meetings of theologians from the whole confessional spectrum.

The revised drafts would be subject to further work by the Standing Commission and then would be presented to the next meeting of the Faith and Order Plenary Commission in 1981. With the Standing Commission of 1982 overseeing final revision, the revised statements would be put before the WCC Assembly of 1983.

Throughout the process of revision it is important that there should be interaction between the more official bodies and groups of people who have special experience and interest in the matters under discussion. For instance, groups of persons in inter-church marriages and locally united parishes are vitally concerned in many of the questions. Neighbouring local churches might discuss the issues together, and a place might be found for exploration of the question in Christian education programmes. In these ways, the fundamental fact will be kept present that Christian communion is a communion among living persons.

* *
*

At the meeting in Bangalore, Committee III dealt with these proposals. It came to the following conclusions:[2]

A. The Purposes of the Revised Statements

The purposes may be stated thus:

a) To stimulate all churches to share further in the process initiated by BEM and continued by FO84.

---

[2] Note: The following abbreviations are used in the text:
BEM: *One Baptism, One Eucharist and a Mutually Recognized Ministry*, Faith and Order Paper 73, Geneva 1975.
FO84: *Towards an Ecumenical Consensus: Baptism, Eucharist and Ministry*, A Reply to the Replies of the Churches, Faith and Order Paper 84, Geneva 1978.
DP: Discussion paper prepared for the meeting of the Commission in Bangalore.

b) To educate members of all churches particularly through catechetical teaching and ministerial preparation (see page 248).

c) To help further in the process of churches growing together whether formally in union schemes and in bilateral conversations or less formally in relating side by side in a particular context.

The revised statements should seek to say clearly what can be said together. They should also uncover the characteristic differences that remain but should do so in such a way as to enable the churches to understand and appreciate the views of others. For within the differences that still remain lie the seeds of further progress towards consensus. The statements should seek indeed to challenge the churches on specific issues as for example is done in BEM, p. 17 para. 24 where those practising the two different forms of baptism are each challenged by insights from the other's position.

The statements should not be seen in isolation in the process of growing together. In many other ways, the churches grow closer together as, for example, in common service and witness to the world and in together giving an account of the hope that is within them. There are also other areas of convergence and divergence, such as political and economic factors which unite or divide churches.

The statements should be seen as aids to growing together into unity although they will not always be used as a basis for union. They presuppose, in any case, a sufficient agreement on basic Christian doctrine. They are not credal statements. So they do not of *themselves* necessarily express in a focal way all that is required for communion in one faith, but they could, if accepted by relating churches, lead to mutual acceptance of members and ministries and so to eucharistic sharing. Every effort, therefore, must continue to be made to ensure maximum participation in the process and adequate reception by the churches at all levels, for within each church there is a living and lively diversity which needs to be incorporated into the process.

B.   The Revision of the Agreed Statements

a) An adequate introduction

It is evident both from the replies of the churches and from the group discussions that the statements must be preceded by an adequate introduction explaining the consensus process. On the whole, the committee judged that the material contained in FO84 moved very much in the right direction. In order to avoid misunderstanding, it may be wise to speak of the process as *convergence towards consensus*. The process is that of churches converging towards the goal of consensus. Beyond consensus could lie unity itself. Clearly, in the process of convergence a point may well be reached by some churches where there was judged to be sufficient consensus among them for certain definite actions to be taken, such as mutual acceptance of membership and ministries leading to eucharistic sharing. It cannot be too strongly stated that sufficient consensus for some will be insufficient consensus for others. This is to be expected and accepted by all churches as part of the process of convergence. Inevitably this will call for mutual understanding and patience.

Within this introduction also, something needs to be said about the subtitle of BEM, namely "Three Agreed Statements". Discussion has revealed that the word "statement", which is neutral in meaning in English, is difficult to translate accurately into French and German. The word *Erklärung* carries much more formality and a sense of being of an official nature than does the word "statement" in English, for example.

b) The form of the revised text

It is possible that in the revised text it may be necessary to include a brief preface to each of the three statements. Some of the material relevant to such prefaces is in the Note at the end of BEM (pp. 58-61). Being at the end, it has tended to be overlooked and possibly in the revision the relevant parts of that material, somewhat developed, could come before each text.

The committee took note of the suggestion (see (ii) p. 248) of a commentary to the text. It was aware also of the importance of the text being used in catechetical teaching. After considerable discussion, the following suggestions are made:

i) The three texts should appear in statement form as in BEM.

ii) There should indeed be a commentary but much briefer than envisaged in DP. The commentary should be limited to explanations of words and concepts. This briefer commentary is suggested because the group felt real danger in an extended commentary which would not only lengthen the document but could also complicate reception in the churches.

iii) At the end of the three statements questions should be appended, addressed both to national churches and to local churches, asking for reaction to the statements, whether acceptable or not, and seeking response on points of disagreement and reasons for them.

iv) The committee hopes that the statement on ministry in the revised text will be of the same length as those on baptism and eucharist but recognizes that this shortening will depend on progress being made in future discussions.

v) A workbook should be compiled as a teaching aid for church leaders, parish ministers, theological students and others, which would explain further words and concepts and contain other material which in DP, is suggested for a commentary. In addition, the workbook might contain examples cited of churches which have reached consensus and examples also of liturgical material relating to baptism, eucharist and ministry. Such liturgical material might helpfully contain explanations of the structure of the liturgies. The book might be designed so as to allow churches to add material of their own relevant to their particular context.

c) The content of the revised text

It was not the task of the committee to attempt a revision of the texts. The committee was encouraged to hear of the number of replies thus far received and recognized that FO84 had already begun the process of revision. However, in the course of discussion, certain subjects were raised of which note should be taken in the revision process. Some of them are already in FO84 but their importance is here underlined.

i) The relationship between baptism and confirmation and the activity of the Holy Spirit in these two actions.

ii) The practice of what is sometimes called "child communion".

iii) The sacramental efficacy of the signs and symbols used, particularly in baptism.

iv) The relationship of ministry to baptism, confirmation and eucharist.

v) The need for revision of BEM, para. 34 which seeks to speak of Christ's eucharistic presence.

vi) The question of episcope and episcopacy (BEM, pp. 35 ff. para. 33; FO84, p. 11 (3a)) clearly needs continuing consideration. In the group it raised immediately the question of authority and the relationship of the Bible to the traditions of the early Christian centuries. The fact that for many churches the question of episcopacy cannot be settled direct from the New Testament has led to placing the episcopate within the realm of purely human law as distinct from the realm of divine law. Earlier Faith and Order studies in scripture and tradition have shown that this simple distinction between divine law (found in scripture) and human law (later tradition) can no longer be maintained. This may provide a framework for further discussion of the question of episcopacy between episcopal and non-episcopal churches.

The group supports the suggestions made (on page 251) that the Plenary Commission should encourage the setting up of a study group (or groups) on the issue of episcope and episcopacy.

vii) BEM, p. 36, on the functions of ministry has been open both to misunderstanding and to challenge. For example, the description of the presbyteral functions given in this paragraph is unacceptable to some. In the Catholic tradition, the preaching of the Word and the administration of the sacraments is the common apostolic task of both bishops and presbyters.

viii) The statement on ministry appears to treat separately two matters, the relationship of which to each other needs to be clarified. On the one hand, there are the structures and orders of ministry (for example bishops, priest, deacon or pastor, elder, teacher, deacon) whereas, on the other hand, there are the practical functions or exercice of ministry in its sociological form and style, all of which have been extremely variable in the course of church history.

ix) The group gave considerable time to discussing what the best way might be to deal with the subject of the ordination of women in the revised statements. Members of the group recognized that the matter was for many a matter of inescapable importance and relevance and that discussion must go on. All were agreed that women have a vital and proper role in the ministry of the Church and some support was expressed for the ordination of women to the diaconate. The chapter in BEM (section D, p. 45) was felt by some to be too short to be able to deal with the matter as the subject deserves and too long for its present purpose of simply making a comment on the question. The passage, it was suggested, sat somewhat uneasily in its present context. Two possibilities were put forward : one was to shorten the section and the other was to make it section (9) under Section C "Conditions of Ordination" in the statement.

Members agreed that there should be a working group to consider the subject of the ordination of women in collaboration with those engaged in the study on The Community of Women and Men in the Church. Attention was drawn to the working paper on the subject in FO84, pp. 17-19. Particular attention was drawn to FO84, p. 19 where questions are raised on the issue and it was hoped that the churches could be encouraged to respond to them. The committee felt also that it would be particularly important to investigate the precise content of the tradition on the ordination of women and to evaluate its significance. Importance was attached to the preparation of material on this issue to be fed into the International Consultation on the Community of Women and Men in the Church planned for 1980.

C. Liturgical Forms and the Convergence towards Consensus

The suggestion has already been made for the inclusion of some liturgical material in the proposed workbook. In addition, the group supports the suggestion made (on page 250) that an anthology of worship texts should be compiled from different churches, illustrating the liturgy for baptism, eucharist and ordination and how the churches are growing closer together in liturgical forms. In addition, examples of services of mutual recognition should be included. It was noted that some churches do not have official worship texts and it was stressed that some examples should be obtained, if at all possible, of their forms of worship in baptism, eucharist and ordination.

It was recognized that such a collection might not be ready by 1981 and its compilation should not hinder the work of publication of the text revision of the statements.

D. The Procedure for Revision (see page 250)

a) The group welcomed the information that a consultation with Baptists to explore the issues involved in the debate on infant and believers' baptism will be held in March 1979.

b) As already suggested above, working groups on episcopacy and on the ordination of women should be set up.

c) The group strongly urges the maintenance of contacts with churches engaged in bilateral conversations and in union negotiations. It believes such contacts to be vital to the process of convergence towards consensus and to be mutually helpful.

d) On the whole, the time-table outlined was acceptable although certain voices said that the time was too short. The committee was not convinced of the value of calling specially a larger meeting of theologians from the whole confessional spectrum. Nevertheless, the group accepted that Faith and Order was bound by the request that the revised texts be ready for the Sixth Assembly of the World Council of Churches. This means that the Commission meeting of 1981 should have the preparation of the final texts as one of its more important agenda items and that necessary steps must be taken to provide the 1981 Commission with draft texts.

e) Finally, the committee would wish to impress upon all Commission members the responsibility of each to seek to further the work on the statements in his or her church context. The staff in Geneva and the small group appointed by the Standing Commission can only work on revision on the texts if reactions are received from the churches both to BEM and to FO84. After Bangalore, the maintenance of momentum in the "process towards consensus on baptism, eucharist and ministry" rests largely with each one of us.

Towards Common Ways
of Teaching and Decision-making

The Commission also spent considerable time on the third requirement for the unity of the Church, "Structures making possible common teaching and decision-making". Some work on this subject had been done in the years before the meeting in Bangalore. In 1974, the Commission decided to initiate a study with the title, "How does the Church teach authoritatively today?" An initial study paper was drafted[1] and several study groups agreed to participate in the effort. On the basis of their findings, a consultation was held in order to get a clearer understanding of the issues which are at stake (Odessa 1977). The report of this consultation was brought to the attention of the Commission in Bangalore.

Obviously, this third requirement for the unity of the Church is closely connected with the first two. Without agreement on the ways of common teaching and decision-making, it will not be possible to arrive at the necessary consensus on the apostolic faith and the sacramental order. Agreement on "authority in the Church" is in particular required to facilitate the process of reception.

Committee II dealt with these issues and submitted the following report.

A Statement on "Authority in the Church"

The Church comes into existence through the proclamation of the Gospel; she manifests and communicates its power. Authoritative teaching in the Church aims at nothing less and nothing more than to allow the power of the Gospel to have its full effect among those who believe in it as well as among those who resist it.

---

[1] See *One in Christ*, 1976, Nos 3 and 4.

Before the Church performs acts of teaching, she exists and lives. Her existence and her life are the work of the triune God who calls her into being and sustains her as his people, the Body of Christ, the fellowship of the faithful in the Spirit. The authority of the Church has its ground in this *datum* of her being. The whole Church teaches by what she is, when she is living according to the Gospel.

The Gospel we proclaim is the Gospel of God's free grace. He calls us into his grace which sets us free. Therefore, the authoritative teaching of the Church assumes the form of a joyful witness to God's liberating truth. This truth is its own criterion as it leads us into the glorious liberty of the children of God. We obey the truth because we have been persuaded by it.

All members of the Church are called upon to manifest the truth of the Gospel in their own lives and to share their faith with all people. Thus, authoritative teaching is a responsibility of the whole Christian community.

The communal authority is actualized by the diverse charisms of the Holy Spirit. Among them the ministry bears a major responsibility of serving as a unifying factor of all of them and becomes the instrument of expressing the common witness of truth according to the Word of God received in the community. There is a dialectical relationship between the ministry and the other charisms which is reconciled by the Spirit operating when the community is gathered as a whole invoking him from the Father. Authority is, therefore, a conciliar event at all levels and is especially expressed through the synods.

The ultimate authority is that of the Holy Spirit who makes Christ present and who shall guide us into all truth. He is at work in all other manifestations of authority in the life of the Church and prevents them from being opposed to each other. The Spirit-given authority of the Church, the Scriptures, the teaching ministry of the Church and the confessional statements are authoritative on the basis of the truth of the Gospel as received by the whole Church. Although conflicts happen, there should be no false alternatives between the Scriptures and the Tradition, the ordained ministry and the laity, the truth of the past and the truth of the present, and the faith of the corporate body of the Church and of the individual person as these dimensions are constitutive elements of the revealed truth of the whole Church.

Recommendations

i) We recommend a study on the New Testament concepts of doctrine and authority with regard to the unity of the Church.

— A more solid scriptural basis is needed for an ecumenical view on the function of both doctrine and authority; for example what is the exact meaning of concepts like didache, homologia, exousia, parrhesia, apostolos, didaskalos, prophetes; what are the implications of texts such as Matt. 7:29; Matt. 16 and 18; Matt. 23:5 and 8; Matt. 28:19-20; Luke 10:16 for the kind of authority which is needed in the Church; how are we to deal with the dialectical relation between the assembly and its ministers (as in Acts 6 and I Cor. 12)?

ii) We recommend a consultation on the relation between the authority of the Scriptures and the authority of the ongoing tradition process and its crystallizations, especially the function of the ancient creeds, for the unity of the Church.

– Ever since the Fourth World Conference on Faith and Order in Montreal (1963), (Scripture, Tradition and Traditions, No. 45), uncertainty about this relation has caused problems. The exact interpretation of the phrase "the apostolic faith according to the Scriptures handed down to us through the centuries" (see the third paragraph of the Preamble of "A Common Statement of our Faith") was an important point of debate in our committee. For some of us this implies the affirmation of the binding authority of at least some elements in the ongoing transmission process, like the creeds of the Ancient Church. For others, according to Montreal, there is no dichotomy or duality; the living Tradition is the life of the Gospel and of the Spirit in the Church through the centuries, interpreting the Word of God again and again in new situations and cultures: this produces an inheritance which is important for us as the faith of our fathers, but the Tradition is also actual as the present proclamation of the Word of God in the Church.

There were attempts at clarification at the Faith and Order Commission meetings in Bristol (1967) "The significance of the hermeneutical problem", and Louvain (1971) "The Council of Chalcedon" study, and the study on "The Authority of the Bible". The report "How does the Church Teach Authoritatively Today?" made an attempt to overcome the earlier comparative descriptions but did not yet reach a sufficient consensus. Is a consensus possible, for instance, on the basis of the report of the Venice consultation on the one apostolic faith, organized upon the request of the Joint Working Group, by the Faith and Order Secretariat and the Secretariat for Promoting Christian Unity of the Roman Catholic Church?

iii) We recommend undertaking a special study – within the framework of the ministry study – on the function of a local and translocal form of "episcope", serving the communion of the Church and protecting both the content of our faith and the quality of the act of faith within the community.

    – Several bilateral conversations have made specific contributions to this theme (Anglican/Roman Catholic International Commission, Venice statement on the Authority of the Church, USA Roman Catholic/Lutheran dialogue; Groupe de Dombes, and so on).

    – All churches accept a form of pastoral oversight. The question whether the historic episcopate is the only legitimate form of such a ministry of "episcope" deserves intense consideration and study in the coming years.

iv) We recommend to continue the study on the teaching authority of the Church, taking into account the results of the study thus far and the outcomings of the consultations and studies mentioned in recommendations 1-3, paying special attention to contemporary problems of the Church's credibility mentioned in the report "How Does the Church Teach Authoritatively Today ?", like the following:

    – the question of a legitimate plurality over against illegitimate pluralism;

    – the need for a greater participation of the whole people of God in the teaching authority of the Church, including the necessity of "reception";

    – the need for a dialogue with people of other faiths and ideologies.

v) We commend to the churches the practical proposals of the Odessa consultation regarding the creative use of possibilities for the common teaching of the churches given in Appendix V of Bangalore preparatory volume "Growing Together into Unity", pp. 16-17.

vi) We recommend to reflect further on the following points of debate:

    a) the distinction between "confession" (homologia) and "teaching" (didache);

    b) the distinction between *official* teaching (on the basis of a legitimate office) and *authoritative* teaching that proves itself in the conscience of the faithful as authentically apostolic;

    c) the relation between the self-authenticating truth of the teaching and the process of its reception;

    d) the distinction and relation between the historical (and thus also relative and provisional) forms the teaching of the Church takes and the eschatological truth expressed in it;

    e) the interrelation of the various criteria of reliability and verification;

    f) the role of prophecy in the Church;

    g) the Christian praxis as an important factor of credibility and as part of the teaching itself.

Mutual Intercession

For many years, the Faith and Order Commission has been responsible for the preparation of the Week of Prayer for Christian Unity. Since 1965, the material for the Week of Prayer has been worked out jointly with Roman Catholics appointed by the Secretariat for Promoting Christian Unity.

Both at the meeting of the Commission in Accra and at the Fifth Assembly of the World Council of Churches in Nairobi, strong emphasis was laid on the need for regular mutual intercession among the churches. The proposal was made to offer to the churches an "Ecumenical Prayer Cycle". At its meetings in 1976 and 1977, the Standing Commission discussed the proposal in some detail. The Cycle has been published in English and is available for use in the congregations. Editions in other languages will appear in the course of 1979.

At Bangalore, the Commission commended the Prayer Cycle in the following statement:

The Ecumenical Prayer Cycle

The theme of "Growing Together into Unity" has its own integrity. That integrity is nowhere more evident than when thoughts are turned into prayers. During the Bangalore meeting, the new Ecumenical Prayer Cycle was used in daily intercessions. This use showed clearly that the Cycle is not simply a calendar of names of churches, a useful instrument and nothing more. Rather, it offers the opportunity to keep the relations between churches, their growing together into unity, firmly and clearly on the spiritual level, deeply rooted in the life of prayer to the Father in the name of the Son through the Holy Spirit. Intercession is a form of prayer which arises from the work of Christ on our behalf, that perpetual intercession which He ever lives to make for us (Heb. 7:25).

Yet intercession is not spiritual in a sense which renders it only other-worldly. To intercede for other churches requires that those who pray

261

should know them in their concrete, historical actuality, with their problems and their opportunities, their fears and hopes, their particularities of life and worship and witness. This is where the Ecumenical Prayer Cycle will so significantly supplement the existing materials for intercessory prayer, enabling churches to pray for *all* other churches with at least some knowledge of them.

This general prayer does not of course preclude particularization. Most churches already have some special links with other churches, which give fuller content and sometimes poignancy to their intercessory prayers for them. Moreover, when particular trials beset a church or a Christian group, other churches may feel called to intensified prayer for those who suffer. But to pray regularly for *all* other churches will keep before every Christian something of the catholicity of the Church of Christ.

Intercession of this kind is no easy substitute for theological conversation, diaconal service or cooperation in mission. To pray for another church requires an energy of will and imagination, a deliberate enterprise, first of thankfulness and then of care and compassion. To pray for another church is to open oneself before God and therefore to open oneself not only to give but also to receive within the fellowship of prayer and service. So in all that follows, discussion and recommendations, agenda for Faith and Order work, especially difficult tasks in which the limitations of human abilities are evident, the Ecumenical Prayer Cycle has a vitally important part.

Such a practice of continued intercession for one another will enable the churches to see one another not with the eyes of theological appraisal or historical assessment but as joint petitioners before the throne of him who said, "Behold, I make all things new", who in Jesus Christ our Lord frees and unites us — the God of hope who fills us with all joy and peace in believing so that by the power of the Holy Spirit we may abound in hope (Rom. 15:13).

The Unity of the Church
and the Community of Women and Men in the Church

The Community of Women and Men in the Church study was initiated at the Faith and Order Commission meeting in Accra, August 1974 (Faith and Order Paper No. 71, Appendix D, pp. 107 ff.). At the Fifth Assembly in Nairobi, 1975, it was recommended as a new WCC programme (*Breaking Barriers*, p. 69 and p. 309) and it was established as such by the 1976 Central Committee, located in the Faith and Order Commission in cooperation with the Sub-Unit on Women. Plans for the study were discussed at the Standing Commission in Loccum (Faith and Order Paper 83, p. 28 f.) and the first presentation of the programme to the Faith and Order Commission was given at the Bangalore meeting.

The group on the Community Study was one of the three groups which reflected on unity and human divisions within the general theme "Growing Together into Unity". Representing eight countries and a diversity of churches, the group worked to advance in the Faith and Order Commission and in the churches concrete plans for furthering the understanding of the nature of community between women and men.

The thinking of the committee was stimulated by the document "An Account of Hope from Women" (FO/78:6, Appendix VIII) and also the response to this by the Working Group on Community of Women and Men at the Bangalore meeting, both included in this volume under "Accounts of Hope". Among the discussion papers for this meeting was a "Study Guide" to the study *The Community of Women and Men in the Church* (FO/78:7, item B10).

The committee began by examining the nature of community and discussing examples of work already done at regional and local levels on this theme (Section II below). It then gave attention to evolving certain

263

strategies and recommendations for further implementation of this programme, encouraging local initiative but suggesting that the WCC act as a reference point and stimulus (Section III below).

I. Dimensions of Community

It is possible to find a common meaning that applies to the wide variety of situations for which the term "community" is used ? Many groups, small and large, become communities. Marriage is a community of two persons. "A Christian community" in a certain place may number thousands, or even millions. And that community has many diverse aspects. The committee limited its approach to the issue of the nature of community through an examination of the dimensions of community life.

Our appreciation of community is influenced by our experience of Christian tradition. Persons of other faiths and viewpoints may not necessarily share our understanding. We also recognized that communities are far from perfect, with the result that some dimensions which are mentioned become obscured by such human failings as self-interest, despair and misunderstanding. We also realized that some of the dimensions we pointed out apply more fully to some communities than to others. Nevertheless, in our week of study we did identify certain common elements:

A. *Acceptance of each member as a valuable person.* This fundamental valuation integrates the community yet does not smother the great diversity among persons.

B. *Humility.* This is a willingness to receive : the opposite of pride. It is founded on knowledge of personal limitations and social shortcomings.

C. *Belonging despite...* The community is not broken by the imperfection of its members. In one's community, wherever it happens to be at a given moment, one is "at home".

D. *Sharing of assets.* Whether visible or invisible, assets or resources are essential to community. More than the sharing of excess or the superficial is needed.

E. *Close proximity.* Closeness, physically or, more important, of inner selves and intentions, is essential. Community meets a severe test here, seen most clearly perhaps in the family.

F. *Appreciation of what makes continued community impossible.* Communities can reach a point of no return without this fact being realized by those involved. A true community knows when it must divide, and it is able to divide without recrimination.

264

G. *Forgiveness of sin.* To err is human, and personal sin is writ large in the community setting. The erring member needs to be absolved by the other members. Impossible demands make community impossible.

H. *Ability to resist pressure, or even persecution, which fragments the community.* Communities seek to live. The testing of this will to live in times of threat from outside shows the strength or otherwise of the community.

I. *The community affirms and renews the same promises and traditions.* Without a common foundation, agreed expectations and adherance to a common history, community cannot exist. Community is much more than merely "being together".

J. *The eucharist is a model of the style and discipline of community.* The eucharist nourishes, gives purpose and vision, and empowers for the future. All communities have a eucharistic quality in that the members are nourished, given purpose, vision and power from a common source.

K. *Community reflects the unity-in-diversity of the Holy Trinity.* God is One and unbroken; yet in distinction, identity, and equality, there is relationship between the three persons or hypostases. God relates inwardly and outwardly. Likewise, communities have unity, yet they must encompass diversity.

L. *Christian community has Christ as its centre.* A unique feature of a Christian community is that it gathers around Jesus Christ. Christ welcomes all. Christian communities are therefore never self-enclosed but exist for the acceptance and service of others. We note, too, that community in the Christian sense is never "spiritual union" alone. The material and the spiritual enrich each other. In the early Christian tradition this question occurs (paraphrased): How can we share what is imperishable unless we are prepared to share what is perishable ?

II. Examples of Study Being Carried Out

The group reported several ways in which the issues of the community study are already underway in various parts of the world through theological study programmes, consultations, various ecumenical and educational programmes. Many of the concrete examples are already becoming "signs" of new community between women and men. They include:

1. Theological courses in which aspects of the Study are already being taught in the following places: India, Finland, Holland, USA.

2. Small groups are examining the relation between sexism and racism, sexism and classism, sexism and socialism.

3. Consultations have been sponsored by universities, seminaries and church organizations, for example in Nigeria, Australia, Sweden, United Kingdom, Belgium, Eire, Germany.

4. Courses for pastors and seminary students exist on building partnership and team ministry among women and men in the Church.

5. Consultations are being arranged around issues in church and society, such as abortion, marriage, family life, male and female sexuality, care of children.

6. Pastoral opportunities for counselling are developing in relation to such rites of the Church as baptism and marriage, and in relation to marriage and divorce.

7. Consultations of theologians and theological students are planned on topics related to our study, like the June 1978 Faith and Order consultation on "Ministry, Mariology and Biblical Hermeneutics"; Sub-Unit on Women meeting of women theological students at Cartigny, July 1978.

8. Educational materials for children and youth are being written, including new curricula for teaching roles of men and women today.

9. Study programmes through church bodies and women's organizations are being published at local and other levels; example : the American Lutheran Church Women Study, "Take a New Look : The Role of Women and Men in the World Today".

10. Ecumenical consultations, international and regional, have already been held such as the conference on "Sexism in the 70s", Berlin (June 1974); the conference on "Women and Men as Partners in Christian Communities" in Louvain, Belgium (August 1975); and the "Asian Women's Forum" in Penang (May 1977).

11. Regional consultations on the Community Study itself such as the Asian consultation on the Community of Women and Men in the Church Study held in Bangalore, India, August 1978.

III. Strategies and Recommendations for the WCC Study

A. TENTATIVE TIME-LINE

The time-line of the Study was discussed. The focus for 1979 will be on the regionalization of the study, facilitating through communication and fundraising local and regional studies and regional consultations. By January 1980, all reports from local groups are to be sent to the Study Desk as part of the preparation of materials and invitations to the August 1980 international consultation on the Study. A working group will meet to prepare a full report on the Study and its implications for the Central Committee of the WCC and for the Faith and Order Commission, both meeting in 1981. It is anticipated that local and regional groups will develop and continue during this period. In 1981 and 1982, the Study Desk will be devoted to implementing the study in relation to the planning for the Sixth Assembly of the World Council of Churches in 1983.

B. STRATEGIES FOR COORDINATION WITH GROUPS OF SIMILAR CONCERN

Where appropriate, coordinate with groups of similar concerns; making use of the Community of Women and Men in the Church *Newsletter* which contains information on groups, bibliographies, and other items, relating to issues of men and women and children in families, the International Year of the Child and so on; collaborate with persons working with the poor in rural and urban development, and, wherever possible, using the study as a means of bringing together long-established separate groupings in the churches.

C. STRATEGIES FOR INITIATING REGIONAL AND LOCAL STUDY

1. Given the contextual nature of the Study, it will have a diversity of approaches in the regions, cultures and churches. In most regions, however, certain common guidelines for organization and communication could be used:

a) Identify groups already working on issues of the Community Study in church and society.

b) Give attention to the design of local studies so that they address the specific needs of women and men at all levels of society.

c) Make materials available in the language and style of each region.

d) Work with publishers and magazine editors so that materials will reach more local groups.

e) Give special attention to working with existing clergy groups and church bodies.

f) Contact ecumenical and confessional organizations with a view to promotion of the study (while at the same time encouraging local groups to begin when they are ready).

g) Give attention to regional and national funding needs.

2. *Regional Planning.*
On the basis of discussion with persons from the regions, the following approaches were suggested for regional planning:

i) *Africa*. Though the time is short, a Community of Women and Men Study may be possible in 1979. The All Africa Conference of Churches should be the main communication channel, in close collaboration with SECAM (Symposium of Episcopal Conferences of Africa and Madagascar), the National Conference of Catholic Bishops, the National Councils of Churches, and WCC member churches. The participants in the initial consultation should be theologians (women and men). The theme should be on the theological implications of these new sociological realities. This would be a first step in developing a diversity of strategies to get the study penetrating churches and groups at local levels.

ii) *Asia and Australia*. Work is underway in many places, including the first regional consultation on the Community Study which took place in Bangalore, August 1978. Contact with the Christian Conference of Asia was stressed. On national levels, NCCs could be very helpful. It was suggested that a person might be found to work through the CCA to coordinate the Study and facilitate the process and the contributions from this area.

iii) *The Caribbean*. In relation to the meeting of the Central Committee in Jamaica, it was suggested that a meeting on the study be arranged, bringing together various groups interested in the study. Representation from Cuba and Central America was discussed.

iv) *Eastern Europe*. Channels of communication already exist with women's organizations, some lay academies, the Christian Peace Conference and official ongoing CWMC studies in some churches. It was suggested that a different strategy might have to be worked out in relation to the Orthodox contribution.

v) *Latin America*. For Latin America, a major issue was that of finding structures through which the Study would operate. Main channels seem to be women's organizations, Protestant and Roman Catholic, theological seminaries, and centres for religious education. It was suggested that key contact points for the Study be established in the North, South and Central areas.

vi) *North America*. Country-based studies were suggested. For Canada, the first step is to identify major centres where work is already underway. For the USA, it was recommended that a steering committee be established and that a seconded staff person be found to coordinate the Study, locating that person in the NCC Faith and Order Commission. No one from Mexico was present. Major groups to work with the Study are theological seminaries, denominational women's groups, Church Women United, and official CWMC studies within denominational groups.

vii) *Western Europe*. The issues of the Study are being raised in all countries. Because the stages of discussion and perspectives vary greatly from place to place, a "country" strategy was suggested, with cross-country consultations on special issues and discussion with the Conference of European Churches regarding the Study in relation to its programme. The major groups taking initiative are women's organizations, women theologians and theological student groups, organizations of women pastors, and official CWMC studies in church bodies.

viii) *South Pacific*. The Pacific Council of Churches was suggested as the contact point where there is already a related study on Marriage and the Family.

IV. Recommendations to the World Council of Churches

1. Request the Programme for Theological Education to make available to theological libraries (which are now being assisted) sets of 10 books on subjects related to this Study, in consultation with the libraries involved.

2. Plan a consultation of theologians on biblical, historical and doctrinal issues related to the topic.

3. Where possible, establish regional committees to coordinate the Study.

4. Examine the possibility of relating to a meeting of the women participants prior to the Commission on World Mission and Evangelism conference on the theme "Thy Kingdom Come" to be held in May 1980 in Melbourne.

5. In the light of the fact that presently needed funds are in hand, fund-raising efforts in 1979 are recommended to be, first for regional purposes and second for the 1980 world consultation.

6. Add to the further study on baptism, eucharist and ministry, a consultation on "Women in Ministry".

7. We recommend the recently published *Study Guide on The Community of Women and Men in The Church* for widespread use in all of our churches and other Christian groups, believing that its methodology is helpful, open-ended, theologically responsible, and ecumenical. We do suggest, however, that in any future editions of this study guide, the members of the Advisory Committee be identified by name and background so that its composition may be clearly perceived.

8. We recommend that the Faith and Order Commission bring together a group of scholars representative of Orthodox, Roman Catholic and Protestant traditions to examine the evidence of Scripture and Tradition as it relates to the role and participation of women and men in the Church.

9. We recommend that a document be prepared on the stated positions regarding ordination of women in the various church bodies over the

past few years. The document would print the actual texts and compare the texts, so that these may be more clearly understood, openly discussed, and readily available.

10. We recommend the investigation of the implications of Marian doctrines as part of the hope of Christian women and men in the community of the Church, within a particular question as to whether Protestant, Anglican, Orthodox and Roman Catholic teachings may in fact be converging in this area.

11. We recommend that a collaborative study be initiated between the Community of Women and Men in the Church study and the sub-units on Church and Society and Dialogue to examine the relationship of women and men in the Church as it compares with those found in other religions and in non-religious cultures.

12. We recommend that all churches begin now to consider seriously the elimination of all exclusively masculine language in biblical, liturgical, and other official texts where the inclusion of both sexes is clearly intended and no doctrinal point is involved inasmuch as such exclusive use of masculine terminology, even if unintentional, may hinder the full participation of the community.

13. We recommend to the Faith and Order Commission that a consultation be held in order to clarify the nature and marks of the community we seek, and that equal numbers of men and women be present.

The Unity of the Church:
Two Examples of Interdisciplinary
Work

The Section II Report of the Nairobi Assembly established the fundamental link between the trinitarian basis of unity and the calling of the
churches to manifest their unity in service to a world which is torn apart
by injustice, inequality, misunderstanding and hatred. It was not possible
for the Commission to investigate and address all of the different sources
of division confronting the human community. Rather, attention was
focused on two issues and their impact on the unity of the Church and
the unity of humankind.

A. The Unity of the Church and Dialogue with People of Other Faiths and Ideologies

BACKGROUND

1. Since the Fourth Assembly of the World Council of Churches in
Uppsala (1968), the Faith and Order Commission has been engaged in
the study on "Unity of the Church and the Unity of Mankind".[1] The
study paper on the subject begins by asking: In what sense can we speak
of the 'unity of mankind'? What has the Church to say about the solidarity of the human race? How is the unity of the Church related to
the unity of mankind?"

To set the unity of the Church in relation to the unity of humankind
has many important implications. Certainly it makes the churches aware
of the need to pursue the unity of the Church in a wider context which

---

[1] *Unity in Today's World* – the Faith and Order Studies on "Unity of the Church –
Unity of Humankind", by Geiko Müller-Fahrenholz and others, Faith and Order
Paper No. 88, Geneva: WCC, 1978.

includes the people outside the Church and the problems and issues they pose for Christianity. On account of this, we need to take into account implications of dialogue with people of other faiths and ideologies for the Faith and Order quest for the unity of the Church.

2. In 1977 the sub-unit on Dialogue with People of other Faiths and Ideologies of the World Council of Churches held a meeting in Chiang Mai (Thailand) on the theme "Dialogue in Community". The Faith and Order Commission was represented in that meeting by a staff member and five Commission members. At one point in the Report of the meeting in Chiang Mai, we find these words: "In the consultation we experienced both the possibility for common confession of the faith and worship together and also some of the obstacles to Christian unity. We were agreed in giving a vital place in our thinking to Bible study and worship... We were however also aware of problems concerning the authority of the Bible remaining unsolved amongst us and of the need for a much closer attention..."

3. The paper "The Significance of the Old Testament in its Relation to the New", the outcome of a study done by a small group from the Faith and Order Commission in July 1977, based on previous study on the authority of Scriptures, further raised the need for the Faith and Order Commission to take seriously the lessons of dialogue with other religions and ideologies. The paper does not restrict itself to the question of the relation of the Old Testament to the New. It raises the issue directed to the relation of the Old Testament to other religions and ideologies. This expanded interest of the Faith and Order Commission, although requiring careful approach, must nonetheless be welcomed.

This was the basic background against which the sub-committee on the unity of the Church and dialogue with people of other faiths and ideologies in Committee IV was asked to explore the relationships between the search for unity with the Church and experience of dialogue.

VARIED CONCERNS

The term "dialogue with people of living faiths and ideologies" covers a wide range of varied, complex realities. Varied, both because national and social settings are so different (compare Christian-Muslim contacts in Indonesia and Britain, or Christian-Hindu discussions in India and the United States), but also because there are so many levels and intensities of contact, from say neighbourly relations in everyday life in a city to the strains of an inter-religious marriage in a traditional village, to academic discussions between teachers of two or more faiths. Complex because in thinking of the interaction of two or more religious traditions almost any human realities — marriage patterns, literature, political priorities, education, let alone distinctly "religious" acts or teachings — can throw up important questions. This applies not only to religions with long written traditions, but also to religions in Africa which put emphasis on oral traditions. Furthermore, when political ideologies, especially Marxist-Leninist ideology, are taken into consideration, the varied and complex character of dialogue is even more deeply felt. In dialogue we thus deal with a delicate matter which requires great sensitivity. This should be kept in mind as Christians engage themselves in dialogue in order to search for ways to enhance unity in human community as well as in Christian community.

TWO CONCLUSIONS

1. For the sake of its own unity, the Church needs to continue a worldwide debate in order to reach a deeper understanding and take constructive actions with regard to dialogue. Dialogue is in reality a fact of daily life, especially in the Asian and African countries as far as religions are concerned, and also in socialist countries insofar as socio-political situations become the focus of attention. The current emphasis on dialogue is basically an invitation to accept it as our normal way of living and through it to build a human community in which integrity and welfare of persons may be enhanced. At the same time, through dialogue Christians may discover afresh God's ways of working with the nations and thus gain an understanding of the Gospel at a deeper level and obtain new insights to give witness to it. Thus the Church should encourage responsible involvement in dialogue with the hope that new horizons may emerge as the Church goes about the task of witnessing to the saving love of God.

Therefore the concern for dialogue is a vital part of the longterm growth of the churches into effective mutual accountability across cultures and continents. Dialogue is also a necessity because it may help churches and Christians to rediscover the dynamic of the Christian faith and renew their commitment to unity as a service to the unity of humankind.

2. It is vital that, as the churches become engaged in dialogue, they find ways of sharing and supporting the efforts of Christians in each place so that they may help one another to grow into maturity of faith. This is important because each actual step of dialogue tends to reflect the historical, social and cultural situation of Christians (and their partners) in the particular area concerned. In India, for example, there are conscious attempts on the part of some churches to use indigenous cultural expressions, religious scriptures and forms of worship in Christian liturgy, homily, and even in building a community which seeks to include Hindus. Efforts along this line are also attempted by some African Christian communities. It is easy to be critical about these attempts and efforts on the part of those Christians who do not have to live in the religiously pluralistic situations. There is also a danger of these efforts and attempts becoming isolated and thus losing the opportunity of contacts with other Christian communities for either critical evaluation or

mutual enrichment. There is therefore an urgent need to find much fuller ways of sharing and bearing each other's burdens and of being encouraged by each other's joys.

RECOMMENDATIONS

In the light of discussions the sub-committee on dialogue makes the following recommendations:

1. that whenever possible collaboration with the sub-unit on Dialogue with People of Living Faiths and Ideologies be encouraged;

2. that the paper on "The Significance of the Old Testament in its Relation to the New" be commended, particularly its section on "The Old Testament and People of Other Faiths", for study and elaboration;

3. that "Recommendations 50 and 51" in the above mentioned paper be altered as follows:

   a) the significance of the Old Testament for Judaism and Christianity be pursued;

   b) studies of the value to Christians of the sacred writings of the various faiths and ideologies be carried out in each area, with a view eventually to relating the findings to the authority of the Bible.

These studies should be carried out with the unity of the Church in the context of the unity of humankind in view.

B. The Unity of the Church and Inter-Church Aid

PRESUPPOSITIONS

The Nairobi Assembly of the World Council of Churches offered a vision of Christian unity as a "fellowship of local churches which are themselves truly united". In describing the quality of the fellowship, the report went on to say: "They are one in their commitment to confess the Gospel of Christ by proclamation and service to the world. To this end each church aims at maintaining sustained and sustaining relationships with her sister churches...". In fellowship, the churches will share their resources in order to strengthen their witness and their service in the world.

The relationship between inter-church aid and the unity of the Church has been the subject of conversations between the staffs of the Commission on Inter-Church Aid, Refugee and World Service (CICARWS) and the Faith and Order Commission. At its Commission meeting in Strasbourg (France), in July 1978, CICARWS considered the theme "Service and Unity". The report of the meeting was made available to the Faith and Order Commission and served as a resource in our discussion.

As we shared our reflections together, it became apparent that aid can strengthen the movement towards unity. Indeed, inter-church aid, as it exists among the churches today, is a sign of the growing unity of the Church. It is in our time an anticipation of the conciliar community of the future. However, we have also shared stories which make it clear that aid can disrupt the fellowship within and between churches.

The imperative for us as Christians to offer service in the world is evident in the incarnation, ministry, teaching, death and resurrection of our Lord, whom we profess to follow and obey. Particularly in the eucharist we recognize our common commitment and shared responsibility for service. In the eucharist we have a share in the life of Christ offered for the whole world, and we are drawn into the sphere of Christ's ministry for the world. The holy communion is a sharing in the body and blood of Christ. This sharing is meaningful and real only if we share in the material goods and the blessings God has provided for all humankind. The Lord whom we meet in the bread and the wine is the Lord whom we meet in the oppressed, the needy and the poor. The service offered to the hungry, the homeless, the imprisoned, the naked and the sick is service offered to Christ himself (Matt. 25-40). Aid makes visible and tangible what is prayed for in intercession.

As churches seek to be faithful to this call to service, they will share many things in many ways. Inter-church aid includes more than material resources. Equally important are mutual prayers of intercession, acts of solidarity in moment of crisis, and mutual exchange of theological resources. Regular visits between persons of different churches help to build a sense of shared community in one faith. Insights grounded in special experiences may be shared with others. "Sustained and sustaining" relationships must embrace the fullness of life in Christ.

ISSUES

In our discussions we have discovered many issues for which we have not found adequate solutions. We recognize that our reflection is only the beginning of a process, and perhaps it is sufficient at this stage to raise issues with a new clarity and sharpness and to point towards a process which may enable the churches to grow towards a fuller unity. The following topics have commanded most of our attention:

1. *The Structures of Aid*. In countries where resources are available for material aid, churches and their auxiliaries often find it necessary to create special agencies for the collection and distribution of aid. These administrative units are inclined to become centres of power and influence independent from the community life of the church.

Techniques for the promotion of giving often seem to put agencies in competition with one another, presenting a confusing picture to those who would support aid work. On the other hand, churches seeking aid

275

are also confused by the different interests and criteria used by various agencies in allocating funds.

The structures of aid tend to become bureaucracies with a vested interest in their own self-preservation, even when they have become outmoded. Their struggle for continued existence may work against unity.

Aid given exclusively through bilateral or confessional channels will inevitably tend to preserve the division of the Church. Denominational pride or confessional prestige are not appropriate criteria for inter-church aid. Churches engaged in union conversations may be influenced by the fact that entering into fuller unity in the local situation will jeopardize bilateral aid relationships.

Aid tends to create patterns of dependency and to prevent local churches from taking responsible decisions on their own mission priorities. When their programmes are determined by the availability of aid for specific projects, the churches are denied the opportunity to develop a full sense of responsibility for mission in their situation and are not encouraged to grow together in unity.

2. *The Politics of Aid*. The giving of aid often requires that the giving and receiving churches take a particular side in a conflict situation. In some instances, the appropriate side for Christians to support is clear; more often, however, the churches themselves are divided. Aid may encourage reconciliation and assist in a just resolution of the conflict, but it is also possible for aid to be a divisive factor. Decisions in these situations will not be made easily and must be seriously considered with full reference to the context. We believe that the impact of aid on the unity of the church must be one of the important criteria for decisions concerning the giving and receiving of aid.

When governments contribute to the funds used in inter-church aid, special problems may arise. Suspicions about the motivations behind such gifts and the causes they support may be disruptive in the recipient community and may result in strained relations with the civil authorities.

3. *The Unity of the Human Community*. Aid can have an integrative value, encouraging all people to work in community, to develop new styles of sharing, and to discover new dimensions of trust. Unfortunately, it is also true that patterns of aid within the Christian community may disrupt the harmony of the larger community. For example, where Christians are a small minority, the concentration of financial resources in the Christian community exclusively may be seen as a threat to the others, therefore resulting in alienation and mistrust. Therefore, concern for the unity of humankind must be a criteria in aid relationships.

RECOMMENDATIONS

i) *World Council of Churches Projects*

When the World Council of Churches responds to appeals for inter-church aid, certain values and priorities should be operative in their evaluation of the appeal. Favourable attention should be given to projects which are jointly conceived by the churches in a given area and planned with the participation of the people, including people of other faiths or ideologies, whose welfare will be affected. Emphasis should be placed on the sharing of locally available resources before aid from other sources is sought. Consideration should be given to projects which are specifically aimed at the realization of local unity and the inner renewal of the Church.

ii) *The Role of the World Council of Churches in Inter-Church Aid*

We recognize that most aid does not flow through WCC channels but is given through bilateral or confessional relationships. Even though the World Council of Churches does not exercise control over the churches and has no coordinating authority, we believe that the World Council of Churches can help the churches to become sensitive to the issues of church unity and inter-church aid and their interaction. The World Council of Churches is a forum where the churches can discuss the implications of inter-church aid and can encourage one another in mutual accountability.

We have been encouraged by the description we have heard of the "country programme" as an evolving model of collective action. The programme calls for the churches in a local setting to take counsel together, to establish their own priorities for mission; and to share their available resources together before receiving jointly any material aid from outside. An equally important aspect of the programme will be the effort to assemble the "giving churches" to encourage a united response to the appeal.

Because the country programme promises to be an important step towards the elimination of many of the church divisive aspects of inter-church aid, we would encourage its further development as a priority in the WCC's programme.

iii) *Suggestions to the Faith and Order Commission*

We suggest that the staff of the Faith and Order Commission initiate a dialogue with the staff of the Commission on Inter-Church Aid, Refugee and World Service on these issues, perhaps under the Ecumenical Sharing of Resources study, and that a new emphasis be placed on the unity of the Church.

We suggest that the commissioners of these sub-units of the World Council of Churches be given an opportunity to share in a dialogue on inter-church aid and church unity.

We suggest that the Faith and Order Commission develop models for sharing beyond material resources. The development of a calendar of intercessory prayer is a good example of how churches may be encouraged to share their spiritual lives. A regular programme of inter-church exchange and pastoral visitation would be helpful.

New Ecumenical Experiences and Existing Ecumenical Structures

As the churches have engaged in the ecumenical movement, they have grown in communion with one another. Today this communion finds expression in many forms. The purpose of the following report is to reflect on the interplay between new ecumenical experiences and existing ecumenical structures as they both seek to contribute to "visible unity in one faith and one eucharistic fellowship expressed in worship and in common life in Christ". What are these experiences ? What do they mean for the churches ? What challenge to they constitute to the existing structures of ecumenical sharing and collaboration ?

This reflection is of great importance today. The new experiences point to the growth of unity among Christians and churches. They may have something to say about the future unity which the churches are to achieve in and through the ecumenical movement. They may be signs of anticipation. At the same time, the reflection needs to be a task of discernment. While many of these experiences point the way forward, others may contain the seed of new division. Not all movements which transcend the barriers between the confessions necessarily promote the unity of the Church. They may be forces for the revitalization of the Church but, in some cases, they may become strange forms of "sectarian ecumenism" without regard for the fuller dimensions of the Christian tradition. As in all churches, so also in the ecumenical movement, the "gift of discerning the spirits" is required.

The principal criterion is whether new experiences contribute to communion in Jesus Christ as God and Saviour and to the visible unity of the Church as a sign of the future unity of humankind.

279

1. New Ecumenical Experiences

Obviously, it is impossible to give an exhaustive picture of the innumerable new ecumenical experiences. Only a few illustrations can be given. In our discussion we have been led to distinguish different categories.

a) *Formal efforts undertaken by the churches*

Communion among the churches has come into existence, in many cases, as a result of conscious efforts by the churches. Expressions of such communion include:
- common prayer, especially during the Week of Prayer for Christian Unity;
- common programmes of humanitarian service;
- development of interdenominational theological faculties;
- formation of Councils of Churches at all levels;
- union of different churches, such as the Church of South India and the Church of North India and many others.

b) *Communion in theological work*

Obviously, the developments in theological thinking transcend the boundaries of the churches. Theologians and educators find themselves in communion established by discussion and dialogue. Their common work often exceeds what is experienced in the churches. Some examples are:
- Bible translation and distribution;
- commentaries on the Bible written by scholars of different traditions;
- the field of catechesis, such as the common curricula in East Africa;
- associations of theologians, church historians, and so on.

c) *Inter-church marriages*

The mixed marriage movement, as it exists for instance in France and in Switzerland, constitutes the potential for a growing communion between the churches. The pastoral need involved in these families has led the churches to provide a ministry and sacramental life which go beyond what they have known until today. This "dialogue within love" serves as a microcosm of the Church's search for a fuller life in Christ.

d) *More spontaneous movements and communities*

While the forms of communion so far described have a clear relationship to the church traditions today, there are more and more movements and communities which owe their existence primarily to a spontaneous impulse. They are the expression of the desire to find forms of relevant community and action in today's world. They usually centre around spiritual communal values or result from the need for common action. For example:

- the present charismatic movement springing from within and outside the churches;
- action groups committed to economic and political change including liberation movements;
- small communities, especially in cities, experimenting with new life-styles;
- youth movements, like the Council of Taizé, festivals and celebrations.

e) *New church movements in Africa*

The Committee gave special attention to the significant growth of new church communities in many African countries. They are to be seen primarily as an expression of the longing for more appropriate cultural forms of worship and community life. In many respects, they constitute a new tradition, not represented among the historical traditions which participate in the ecumenical movement. The same could be said of certain Pentecostal communities. Some of these have begun to make their entry into the ecumenical movement.

In most parts of the world, new forms of communion can be found which not only add diversity to the Christian tradition but at times intersect with other living faiths.

2. Questions to the Churches Participating in the Ecumenical Movement

These developments and experiences constitute a challenge to the churches.

How do the churches evaluate the degree of communion which has come into existence through their conscious efforts? Do they regard it simply as an improvement of relationships or do they consider it as initial steps on the way towards the actualization of the oneness of the Church? How are they prepared to build on this communion further steps towards unity?

There is an incongruity between the separation of the churches and the actual experiences of reconciliation among Christian persons and groups in many places. Communities of mutual love and common witness continue to come into existence as a result of the churches' failure to be themselves that kind of community. How do the churches relate to this search for new forms of relevant communion and action? Do they regard these movements and communities as "exceptions" and "anomalies" or are they prepared to accept them as calling into question their customary structures and life-style ? Can they make room for the experiences of their life and ministry ? Do they recognize the fact that the enormous wealth of new forms of community might be a fresh blossoming of the Tradition as new gifts which the Spirit gives to the churches ?

On the other hand, questions must be asked of these new developments and communities. How can they stay in the continuity of the Christian tradition ? How can they avoid exclusivism and further division ? How can they maintain the sense of the catholicity of the Church ?

Because of the ambiguity which may accompany a number of these new experiences and movements, the churches are challenged to "test the spirits". Positively, this would involve a sympathetic understanding of the felt need for a sense of belonging in a community of spirituality, mutual love and common action. At times, however, some of these movements confront the churches with serious departures from the basic affirmations of Christian faith. The churches then are called to give an account of the faith that is within them. This means not only "telling the truth in love" but also acknowledging the opportunity for the churches to make a fresh statement of the faiths that holds them together.

3. Questions to Existing Ecumenical Structures

The ecumenical movement has led to the formation of ecumenical structures at many levels of the churches' life. They vary in form and purpose from country to country. The main forms of ecumenical collaboration are the councils of churches. In many countries they have come into existence before the foundation of the World Council of Churches; in other countries they have been founded as parallels to the World Council. Fulfilling an indispensable role in the life of the churches, these structures have brought the churches together to share in prayer and dialogue, in practical collaboration and projects of human development. They have helped the churches to go beyond encounter and cooperation and to form a provisional fellowship on the way to unity.

But questions arise. Do councils continue to serve the cause of unity or do they rather institutionalize a limited degree of unity and perpetuate division ? Do they serve to go on to the next step on the road or do they give the churches a good conscience by leaving them at a stage where they are not quite divided but not yet united ? Without self-correction on the basis of the ultimate goal, could councils become monuments to an outdated stage of the ecumenical movement ? How do existing ecumenical structures relate to the growing fellowship among Christians and the emerging theological consensus among the churches ? How do they relate to the growth of new movements and communities ? People engaged in new developments and experiences often see the ecumenical structures as being mere organizational or bureaucratic instruments. Ecumenical structures are, therefore, often bypassed and ignored by those for whom they should, in fact, constitute a hope for deepened communion and greater relevancy of witness.

A few observations:

— Where councils exist, they are not inclusive in membership, for only a limited number of Christian traditions in a country are represented. In only about 20 countries is the Roman Catholic Church within the membership of national councils. In many countries, the evangelical movements and the Orthodox Churches do not belong to the councils. In some countries, no council exists at all. New ecumenical experiences draw as a rule on the heritage of all Christian traditions. They are "more ecumenical" than most councils and since they are not in themselves ecclesial entities, they have no natural way to relate to the "existing ecumenical structures".

— Often, councils have been established with limited purposes. By their constitutions they are confined to project oriented collaboration. They are not asked to deal with issues of doctrine, ecclesiology, worship, spirituality etc. Through their social and political action, they succeed in creating a manner of Christian association — often indispensible — which is not sufficiently undergirded by spirituality, worship, and theological reflection. Often, the tasks to which they are committed are not long-lasting because of that very insufficiency.

— In some cases, councils have run into the danger of becoming a divisive factor. Instead of gathering the churches together on their way to unity, they have simply added new institutional factors which complicate the interaction of the churches.

Further questions for exploration:

— As councils become more inclusive, how do they avoid the tendency towards theological minimalism and a more hesitant common action ?

— Could there be more deliberate work in councils on issues of faith, worship and spirituality ? Could the councils become places for the common affirmation of the Christian faith, for the discovery of new forms of worship, and for a new sense of tradition ?

— Could a deliberate effort be made to place in mutually beneficial relationship new ecumenical experiences and conciliar structures ? Can councils serve as an instrument for the interplay of the constituent churches and the new movements and groups so they may discover their need for one another ?

— Can councils become the means for making possible events by which the "unity we have" can be celebrated more inclusively and festively than our present ways of association permit ?

As we have seen in previous sections of this report, more and more Christians identify only partially with the tradition of their churches. They are accepting values and insights from other Christian traditions, often from other faiths, and incorporating them into their life. At the same time they find it difficult to articulate this new experience and to relate it to the established churches. The Faith and Order Commission may perhaps provide means for this articulation and interaction. The Commission should therefore increasingly direct its attention towards those engaged in new ecumenical experiences and movements.

To meet this need, the work of the Commission will have to acquire a style which is more deliberately pastoral. It will need to address as directly as possible the issues and problems which arise from new ecumenical experiences. A new language may need to be found.

Some important considerations:

1. A survey on a selected number of new ecumenical experiences and an analysis of their implications for the ecumenical movement might be prepared.

2. Ways should be explored in which groups, communities and movements which otherwise do not meet the criteria of membership may effectively relate to the World Council of Churches. Examples of such movements have been given in the first section of this report. The discussion of this issue will inevitably raise they issue of "testing the spirits". Obviously, the exploration must not lead to a change in the character of the Faith and Order Commission and its by-laws which state its main task to help and to serve the unity of the churches.

3. The resources of the Week of Prayer for Christian Unity and of the Prayer Cycle should be fully used to relate to new ecumenical experiences. Reports on the celebration of the week and the spirituality of intercession should be prepared from time to time.

4. A special effort should be undertaken to prepare documents and other material which respond to the needs of inter-church marriages. Attention is drawn to the French publication *Foyers Mixtes* and other literature concerning inter-church marriages. The Faith and Order Secretariat should try to be in touch with those persons in various countries who coordinate groups of inter-church marriages and reflect on their experiences. There is evidence that the work of the Faith and Order Commission on baptism, the eucharist and the ministry has been especially welcomed and used by persons living in mixed marriages and by the clergy who minister to them.

5. Given the growing importance of pilgrimages, the Commission might give some attention to the ecumenical significance of pilgrimages. How can they become a meaningful expression of Christian unity for the par-

ticipants ? In particular, how can pilgrimages to ancient sites marking the key events in the life of our Lord and the cradle cities of the first Christian communities become pointers to the unity in his name ?

6. An opportunity should be found to examine in more depth the questions which arise for the churches from new ecumenical experiences (see pages 279ff).

7. The role of existing ecumenical structures, especially of councils of churches, requires assessment. A self-assessment guide might be prepared for councils to evaluate the degree to which their programmes institutionalize the division of their member churches or contribute to the advance towards unity. A special concern would be the cooperation and understanding between councils and church union committees. The findings should be summarized and interpreted. Eventually, a consultation on the role of councils in the search for visible unity might be arranged.

Conclusion

Growing together unto unity! The movement towards the goal often seems almost imperceptible. Even reasonable hopes are not always fulfilled. Many efforts fail. Conversations which gave rise to high expectations can be disrupted. New beginnings are constantly required.

Bangalore: Yet another meeting on the unity of the Church. Let us use a parable. You run for a bus, scramble aboard — and then the conductor says "We are only going to the garage for an overhaul". Was this the feeling at Bangalore? Have we come only to discover that a set of concepts is being yet again overhauled in response to intellectual criticisms?

No, the study of various aspects of growing together into unity was taken up in the setting of an account of Christian hope. There was a strong feeling that the bus is going to a definite goal. That which is affirmed concerning the wholeness of God's purpose for humankind applies also to the fulfilment of Christ's will for his Church — to "present the Church to himself in splendour, without spot or wrinkle or any such thing, that she might be holy and without blemish" (Eph. 5:27).

All four words of the title "Growing together into unity" are important. The meeting was concerned with that *unity* which is both God's gift and his will; it recognized that the unity which is God's will is one *into* which men and women are brought as they become able to confess together the Christian truth and faith and are bound together by the same baptism and share the same eucharist under a ministry everywhere recognized; Christians must be *together* in this work because as the report "What Unity Requires" puts it: "Since Christ died and rose for all and his Church is to be the sign of the coming unity of humankind, it must be open to men and women of every nation and culture, of every time and place, of every sort of ability and disability; in its mission it must actively seek them wherever and whoever they are, and in its company they must find their true home" (*What Unity Requires*, p. 66). Finally, it is by a process of *growing* that the empirical churches as we know them today respond to God's invitation and summons to full fruition of that communion for which Christ prayed.

Participants

Voting Participants

The Rev. Samuel K. ADA (Evangelical Church of Togo), Republic of Benin
Archbishop Shahe AJAMIAN (Armenian Patriarchate of Jerusalem), Israel
The Rev. Dr. S. T. Ola AKANDE (Nigerian Baptist Convention), Nigeria
Archpriest Pavel ALES (Orthodox Church of Czechoslovakia), CSSR
The Rev. Dr. Samuel AMIRTHAM (Church of South India), India
Dr. Kamol ARAYAPRATEEP (Evangelical), Thailand
The Rev. Wesley ARIARAJAH (Methodist Church), Sri Lanka
Prof. Ivar ASHEIM (Church of Norway), Norway
Metropolitan BARTHOLOMEW (Archondonis) (Ecumenical Patriarchate of Constantinople), Turkey
Dr. Robert BERTRAM (Lutheran Church-Missouri Synod), USA
The Rev. Plutarco BONILLA (Methodist Church), Costa Rica
Protopresbyter Vitaly BOROVOY (Russian Orthodox Church), USSR
Fr. Frans BOUWEN (Roman Catholic Church), Belgium
Prof. Raymond E. BROWN (Roman Catholic Church), USA
Prof. Robert McAfee BROWN (United Presbyterian Church in the USA), USA
The Rev. Albert To BURUA (United Church of Papua New Guinea), Papua New Guinea
Mrs Pam CHINNIS (Episcopal Church), USA
The Rev. Martin CRESSEY (United Reformed Church), England
The Rev. Dr. Paul A. CROW Jr (Christian Church (Disciples of Christ), USA
The Rev. Herbert DAUGHTRY (Pentecostal Church), USA
Dr. Raoul DEDEREN (Seventh-Day Adventist Church), USA
Prof. John DESCHNER (United Methodist Church), USA
Dr. (Mrs) Ellen FLESSEMAN-VAN LEER (Netherlands Reformed Church), Holland
Bishop GREGORIOS (Coptic Orthodox Church), Egypt
Prof. Juan GUTIERREZ (Roman Catholic Church), Peru
Miss Seni HAAPIMAA (Orthodox Church in Finland), Finland
Dr. Adolfo HAM (Presbyterian-Reformed Church), Cuba
Fr. Edward HAMBYE (Roman Catholic Church), India
Ms Jeanne HENDRICKSE (United Congregational Church of Southern Africa), USA
Fr. Pierre HERVOUET (Roman Catholic Church), France
Prof. Glenn HINSON (Southern Baptist Convention), USA
Rektor Christoph HINZ (Federation of Evangelical Churches in the GDR: Lutheran), GDR

287

Fr. Thomas HOPKO (Orthodox Church in America), USA
The Rev. V. O. JATHANNA (Church of South India), Switzerland
Miss Annie JAUBERT (Roman Catholic Church), France
Dr. E. C. JOHN (Church of South India), India
Prof. Istvan JUHASZ (Reformed Church in Rumania), Rumania
Fr. Aram KESHISHIAN (Armenian Apostolic Church), USA
Dr. Nelson KIRST (Evangelical Church of the Lutheran Confession in Brazil), Brazil
Prof. Jean-Louis KLEIN (Evangelical Lutheran Church in France), France
Dozent Totu KOEV (Orthodox Church of Bulgaria), Bulgaria
Prof. Gerassimos KONIDARIS (Church of Greece), Greece
Prof. Kosuke KOYAMA (United Church of Christ in Japan), New Zealand
Dr. Ulrich KÜHN (Federation of Evangelical Churches in the GDR: Lutheran), GDR
The Rev. MacLean A..KUMI (Methodist Church), Ghana
Prof. William H. LAZARETH (Lutheran Church in America), USA
Dr. Béla LESKO (United Lutheran Church in Argentina), Argentina
Prof. Jan Milic LOCHMAN (Swiss Protestant Church Federation), Switzerland
Prof. Nicolas LOSSKY (Russian Orthodox Church), France
Mrs Florence MAHONEY (Church of the Province of West Africa), Republic of Congo
Dr. André MAMPILA (Roman Catholic Church), Republic of Zaire
Dr. Jaci MARASCHIN (Episcopal Church), Brazil
The Rev. Dorothea MARGENFELD (Evangelical Church in Germany: Lutheran), FRG
Dr. Gerhard M. MARTIN (Evangelical Church in Germany: United), FRG
The Rev. Martin MBWANA (Church of the Province of East Africa), Tanzania
Prof. Helen MILTON (Anglican Church of Canada), Canada
The Very Rev. Philip MOKUKU (Church of the Province of South Africa), South Africa
Dr. Masamba ma MPOLO (United Church of Christ), Zaire
Mr Jesse MUGAMBI (Church of the Province of Kenya), Kenya
Prof. Nikos NISSIOTIS (Church of Greece), Greece
The Rev. David NKWE (Church of the Province of South Africa), South Africa
Mrs Mercy ODUYOYE (Methodist Church), Nigeria
Prof. Keiji OGAWA (United Church of Christ in Japan), Japan
Metropolitan Geevarghese Mar OSTHATHIOS (Orthodox Syrian Church of the East), India
Prof. Wolfhart PANNENBERG (Evangelical Church in Germany: Lutheran), FRG
Dr. Jorge PANTELIS (Methodist Church), Brazil
Archimandrite Spyridon PAPAGEORGE (Ecumenical Patriarchate of Constantinople), Italy
Prof. Martti PARVIO (Church of Finland), Finland
Ms Carolina PATTIASINA (Maluku Protestant Church), Indonesia
Mrs Katakshamma PAUL RAY (South Andhra Lutheran Church), India
Prof. Per Erik PERSSON (Church of Sweden), Sweden
Prof. Ian PITT-WATSON (Church of Scotland), Scotland
Prof. Dumitru POPESCU (Rumanian Orthodox Church), Rumania
The Rev. Jeanne Audrey POWERS (United Methodist Church), USA
Dr. Karoly PROHLE (Lutheran Church in Hungary), Hungary
The Rev. Ursula RADKE (Federation of Evangelical Churches in the GDR: Lutheran), GDR
Prof. Samuel RAYAN (Roman Catholic Church), India
Dr. Paolo RICCA (Waldensian Church), Italy
The Rev. Hugh A. A. ROSE (United Church of Canada), Canada
Dr. Horace O. RUSSELL (Jamaica Baptist Union), Jamaica

Dr. Letty RUSSELL (United Presbyterian Church in the USA), USA
Prof. Luigi SARTORI (Roman Catholic Church), Italy
The Rev. Federico SCHÄFER (Evangelical Church of River Plata), Argentina
Dr. Gabriel SETILOANE (Methodist Church), Botswana
Prof Walter SIDJABAT (Lutheran Church in Indonesia), Indonesia
The Rev. Kelly Miller SMITH (American Baptist Convention), USA
Prof. Josef SMOLIK (Evangelical Church of Czech Brethren), CSSR
The Rev. Ardi SOEJATNO (Reformed Church in Indonesia), Indonesia
Dr. Juan STAM (Evangelical Church), Costa Rica
Ms Veronica SWAI (Evangelical Lutheran Church in Tanzania), Tanzania
Dr. Maurice TADROS (Coptic Orthodox Church), Egypt
Mrs Mary TANNER (Church of England), England
The Rev. Fr. Jean M. R. TILLARD (Roman Catholic Church), Canada
Fr. Philipos THOMAS (Orthodox Syrian Church of the East), India
The Rev. Ilda VENCE (Methodist Church), Uruguay
Dr. Günter WAGNER (Baptist Church, Germany), Switzerland
The Rev. Dr. Geoffrey WAINWRIGHT (Methodist Church of Great Britain), England
The Rev. Peggy WAY (United Church of Christ), USA
Dr. W.M.S. WEST (Baptist Union of Great Britian and Ireland), England
The Rev. Dr. H. D'Arcy WOOD (Uniting Church in Australia), Australia
Prof. J. Robert WRIGHT (Episcopal Church), USA
Prof. Urbano ZILLES (Roman Catholic Church), Brazil
Prof. John ZIZIOULAS (Ecumenical Patriarchate of Constantinople), Scotland

Liaison Officers

Dr. Claude BROACH (Baptist World Alliance), USA
Metropolitan DAMASKINOS (Ecumenical Patriarchate of Constantinople), Switzerland
The Rev. Fr. Pierre DUPREY (Roman Catholic Church), Vatican
Dr. H. Jackson FORSTMAN (Christian Church (Disciples of Christ), USA
Dr. Günther GASSMANN (Lutheran World Federation), FRG
The Rev. Joe HALE (World Methodist Council), USA
Prof. Christian OEYEN (Old Catholic Church), FRG
The Rev. Richmond SMITH (World Alliance of Reformed Churches), Switzerland

Consultants

Miss Helen ALEXANDER, England
Fr. René BEAUPERE, France
Mr. Marios BEGZOS. Greece
Dr. Emidio CAMPI, Switzerland
Mr. T.K. CHANDY, India
Dr. Chai-Yong CHOO, Korea
Mr. Martin CONWAY, England
Prof. Thomas DERR, USA
Dr. Karl-Christoph EPTING, FRG
Ms Nirmala FENN, India
Mr. Hugo GONNET, Uruguay
Dr. L.A. HOEDEMAKER, Holland
Dr. Anton HOUTEPEN, Holland
Mr. Elias JONES, USA
Dr. M.J. JOSEPH, India
Dr. George KONDOTHRA, India
Dr. Hanfried KRÜGER, FRG

Dr. Jorge LARA-BRAUD, USA
The Rev. Kenneth LEECH, England
Fr. Antonio MATABOSCH, Spain
Prof. Lucien MORREN, Belgium
Dr. Walter MÜLLER-RÖMHELD, FRG
Mr. Ajit MURRICKEN, India
Prof. Gyula NAGY, Switzerland
The Rev. Silas NCOZAMA, Malawi
Mr. Stylianos PAPALEXANDROPOULOS, Greece
Prof. Arthur PEACOCKE, England
Dr. Ingram SEAH, Republic of China
Ms P.C. SHANTAMMA, India
Dr. V. SIDDHARTHA, India
Fr. A. TANIELIAN, Lebanon
The Rev. M.A. THOMAS, India
Dr. M.M. THOMAS, India
Mr. T.K. THOMAS, Singapore
Frère Max THURIAN, France
Mr. Mathai ZACHARIAH, India

Guests

The Most Rev. Dr. Pakiam AVOKIASWAMY, Archbishop of Bangalore
Principal J.R. CHANDRAN, United Theological College, Bangalore
Rev. Fr. Matthew MARUVATHRAIL, Kristu Jyoti College, Bangalore

Staff

The Rev. Jean-Jacques BAUSWEIN, Communications
Dr. Ion BRIA, CWME
The Rev. Stephen CRANFORD
Mr. Peter MOSS, Youth
The Rev. Dr. Geiko MÜLLER-FAHRENHOLZ
The Rev. Dr. Constance PARVEY, CWMC
Mrs Renate SBEGHEN
Dr. Choan-Seng SONG
The Rev. Dr. Lukas VISCHER
Miss Anne WILLIAMSON

Interpreters

Mrs Donata COLEMAN
Mrs Tomoko EVDOKIMOV
Prof. Robert FAERBER
Mrs Ursula GASSMANN
Mrs Renate SBEGHEN (part-time)